# *Effective Writing*

Leeds Metropolitan University

17 0580556 7

# NINTH EDITION

# *Effective Writing*

# A Handbook for Accountants

## Claire B. May, Ph.D.

## Gordon S. May, Ph.D.

*University of Georgia, Emeritus*

DISCARDED

**PEARSON**

Prentice
Hall

## Pearson Education International

Boston   Columbus   Indianapolis   New York   San Francisco   Upper Saddle River   Amsterdam
Cape Town   Dubai   London   Madrid   Milan   Munich   Paris   Montreal   Toronto
Delhi   Mexico City   Sao Paulo   Sydney   Hong Kong   Seoul   Singapore   Taipei   Tokyo

If you purchased this book within the United States or Canada you should be aware that it has been imported without the approval of the Publisher or the Author.

**Editorial Director:** Sally Yagan
**Editor in Chief:** Donna Battista
**AVP Executive Editor:** Stephanie Wall
**Director of Editorial Services:**
  Ashley Santora
**Sr Project Manager Editorial:**
  Christina Rumbaugh
**Director of Marketing:** Patrice Jones
**VP Director of Marketing:**
  Kate Valentine
**Marketing Assistant:** Ian Gold
**Sr Managing Editor:** Cynthia Zonneveld
**Production Editor:** Carol O'Rourke

**Production Project Manager:**
  Clara Bartunek
**Creative Art Director:** Jayne Conte
**Cover Designer:** Bernadette Travis

**Permissions Manager:** Hessa Albader
**Full-Service Project Management:**
  Munesh Kumar/Aptara®, Inc.
**Composition:** Aptara®, Inc.
**Printer/Binder:** STP RRD/Harrisonburg

**Text Font:** Times Ten Roman, 10/12

Credits and acknowledgments borrowed from other sources and reproduced, with permission, in this textbook appear on appropriate page within text.

**Copyright © 2011, 2009, 2006, 2003, 1999 by Pearson Education, Inc., publishing as Prentice Hall, One Lake Street, Upper Saddle River, New Jersey 07458.** All rights reserved. Manufactured in the United States of America. This publication is protected by Copyright, and permission should be obtained from the publisher prior to any prohibited reproduction, storage in a retrieval system, or transmission in any form or by any means, electronic, mechanical, photocopying, recording, or likewise. To obtain permission(s) to use material from this work, please submit a written request to Pearson Education, Inc., Permissions Department, One Lake Street, Upper Saddle River, New Jersey 07458.

Many of the designations by manufacturers and seller to distinguish their products are claimed as trademarks. Where those designations appear in this book, and the publisher was aware of a trademark claim, the designations have been printed in initial caps or all caps.

LEEDS METROPOLITAN UNIVERSITY LIBRARY
DISCARDED
LEEDS BECKETT UNIVERSITY LIBRARY

10  9  8  7  6  5  4  3  2  1

**Prentice Hall**
is an imprint of

ISBN-13: 978-0-13-284299-0
ISBN-10:    0-13-284299-8

# Brief Contents

# Contents

Contents

# Preface

*Effective Writing: A Handbook for Accountants*, 9th edition, is designed
to help accounting students and practitioners improve their communication skills. It can be used as a supplementary text for regular
accounting courses, as a text in an accounting communications
course, or as a text in a business communications or technical writing
course when these courses include accounting students. The handbook is also a useful desk reference or self-study manual for accountants in practice.

*Effective Writing* guides the writer through all the stages of the
writing process: planning, including analysis of audience and purpose;
critical thinking about the problem to be solved or the job to be
accomplished; generating and organizing ideas; writing the draft;
revising for readable style and correct grammar; and designing the
document for effective presentation. In addition to these basic writing
principles, the book covers letters, memos, reports, and other formats
used by accountants in actual practice, including e-mail and other
forms of electronic communication. Throughout the text, *Effective
Writing* stresses coherence, conciseness, and clarity as the most important qualities of the writing done by accountants.

To supplement the instruction on writing effectively, we have
expanded Chapter 15 to include an extensive discussion of listening
skills. Chapter 15 also discusses the preparation of an oral presentation, including audience analysis and organization of materials, as well
as techniques of effective delivery and the use of visual aids.

In addition to its focus on effective writing and speaking, this edition of *Effective Writing* stresses other "soft skills" accountants need
to be successful practitioners, such as the ability to listen attentively,
read carefully, think critically, and interact with others in a respectful,
professional way.

Also in this edition of *Effective Writing* are sections on the ethics
of communication. Chapter 1 introduces students to ethical issues
related to accounting communication, and Chapter 7 shows them how
to use critical thinking skills to resolve ethical dilemmas.

Part III: Writing and Your Career includes a chapter on writing
essay examinations (including professional examinations), a chapter
on writing résumés and letters of application, and a chapter on writing
for publication.

The critical thinking focus of Chapter 7 introduces the principles of critical thinking and shows how careful reasoning can help students and professionals solve accounting problems. The chapter discusses inductive and deductive reasoning, the construction of an argument, and fallacies students will learn to recognize and eliminate.

Another special feature of this book is Chapter 8, which discusses accounting research. Here you will find valuable reference material on such topics as these:

- Where to find accounting information (including Internet sites)
- How critical thinking can help you solve problems and write persuasive documents
- How to write citations of accounting sources, including the new *FASB Accounting Standards Codification*™ and Internet sources

This edition of *Effective Writing* includes many new and revised assignments that reinforce the concepts covered in the text. Some exercises have answers within the text for independent review. The *Instructor's Manual* contains answers to many other exercises. Most chapters also include topics for writing or speaking assignments. The assignments, like the illustrations in the text, are concerned with accounting concepts and situations and thus will seem relevant and familiar to those studying and practicing accounting.

*Effective Writing* can be used in conjunction with traditional accounting courses. Instructors can assign cases and topics for research based on the accounting concepts being studied in class, or they can use the assignments provided in this handbook. Students then analyze the accounting problem, research the literature if necessary, and prepare answers according to an assigned format such as a letter, technical memo, formal report, or oral presentation. The handbook guides students toward principles of effective writing and speaking. Instructors can then evaluate students' performance based on the criteria discussed in the text and the *Instructor's Manual*.

The *Instructor's Manual* contains suggestions for everyone wishing to improve the communication skills of accounting students, whether in a regular accounting course or in a course devoted to communication. It includes topics such as motivating students to improve their communication skills, designing assignments, and evaluating performance as well as chapter commentaries and masters for transparencies and handouts.

## CourseSmart Textbooks Online

CourseSmart is an exciting new choice for students looking to save money. As an alternative to purchasing the printed textbook, students can purchase an electronic version of the same content. With a CourseSmart eTextbook, students can search the text, make notes online, print out reading assignments that incorporate lecture notes, and bookmark important passages for later review. For more information, or to purchase access to the CourseSmart eTextbook, visit www.coursesmart.com.

We hope that this book will help those preparing to enter the profession, as well as those already in practice, to achieve greater success through effective communication.

**Claire B. May**
**Gordon S. May**

# CHAPTER

# Accountants as Communicators

The ability to communicate effectively, whether through speaking or writing, is essential to success in the accounting profession and in the business world in general.[1] In a major report issued by the College Entrance Examination Board, the Board has stressed the importance of communication skills: "individual opportunity in the United States depends critically on the ability to present one's thoughts coherently, cogently, and persuasively on paper."[2]

In today's highly competitive business environment, "soft skills" such as written and oral communications, interpersonal skills, and leadership ability have become so important that companies hiring accounting students often place more importance on these skills than they do on technical accounting skills. Many people regard these soft skills as the key to business success and point out that the major differences among competitors may often be found in the degree their employees have mastered writing, speaking, and other non-technical skills.[3]

So to be successful as well as competent, accountants must be good communicators, showing that they can use words effectively. To help their employees improve these skills, multinational accounting firms offer special courses to help their accountants write and speak more effectively. Various accounting organizations—the American Institute of Certified Public Accountants (AICPA) and many state societies, for example—offer continuing education courses for writing. Many colleges and universities now stress effective writing for accounting coursework. The AICPA also evaluates candidates' writing skills in the computerized CPA Exam.[4]

As shown in the pie chart in Figure 1–1, the AICPA believes that communication skills are and will continue to be as important as professional knowledge, analysis and organization skills, technological skills, and research skills—all of which are essential for entry-level accountants. Among the personal attributes listed by the AICPA for competency in public accounting is "effective business writing." An AICPA report states that the writing of entry-level professionals should demonstrate standard grammar, appropriate style and tone, logical organization, clarity, and conciseness.[5]

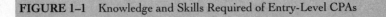

**FIGURE 1–1** Knowledge and Skills Required of Entry-Level CPAs

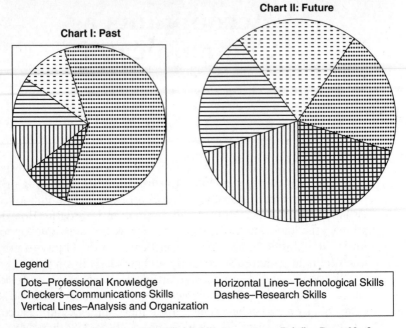

Legend

| | |
|---|---|
| Dots–Professional Knowledge | Horizontal Lines–Technological Skills |
| Checkers–Communications Skills | Dashes–Research Skills |
| Vertical Lines–Analysis and Organization | |

*Source:* American Institute of Certified Public Accountants, Briefing Paper No. 2, *Computerizing the Uniform CPA Examination—Issues, Strategies, and Policies: An Update*, March 5, 2001.

Unfortunately, some students and accountants lack the skills they need to be effective communicators. Accounting firms are on record as being dissatisfied with the communication skills of entry-level accountants,[6] and a high percentage of accounting firms have reported poor writing skills as one reason for job terminations.[7]

Accountants need communication skills to get a good job and to keep that job after they are hired. Of course, "communication skills" is a broad area that includes formal and informal oral presentations, interpersonal communication, reading, listening, and skills in other related areas, including the ability to think carefully and critically. Ethical issues can also affect communication, both what accountants say and how they say it. Because this book is primarily about writing, we will now look at some of the documents accountants write on the job.

# WHAT DO ACCOUNTANTS WRITE?

In every type of accounting practice, writing is an essential part of the job. Whether in public accounting, management accounting, not-for-profit accounting, or government accounting,[8] and whether specializing in tax, auditing, systems, or some other area, accountants write every day.

Examples in three specialized areas—tax, auditing, and systems—suggest a few of the many occasions that require accountants to write. Tax accountants in accounting firms often write memos to other members of the firm that describe the results of their research. These memos become part of the clients' files. A tax accountant might also write a letter advising the client about the best way to handle a tax problem. Tax accountants must also write letters to the Internal Revenue Service (IRS) on behalf of clients and occasionally may even have to write a judicial brief.

Auditors write memos to be filed with the audit working papers that describe the work done on an audit. They may also write memos to their colleagues to request advice or to report research results. After the audit engagement, auditors often write advisory letters to management that suggest ways to improve accounting and internal control procedures.

Systems specialists write documents for readers with varying degrees of computer expertise. They may write a beginners' guide on how to use a software package or a highly technical report on a complex accounting system application.

No matter what their specialty, all accountants write memos to their supervisors, subordinates, and co-workers to request or provide information. They also write letters to clients, agencies, and a variety of other readers. E-mail is also a common means of communication, especially within an organization.

Technical reports and memos, both formal and informal, are also important ways in which accountants communicate. For instance, an accountant working for a corporation might write a report for management on alternative accounting treatments for a particular kind of business transaction. An accountant working for an accounting or business services firm might write a technical memo on how best to handle a client's unusual accounting problem.

To be effective, letters, memos, e-mails, and reports must be well written. How will clients react if, after reading a letter from their CPA, they are still confused about their income tax problem? How will management or one's supervisors react to a report that is poorly organized and hard to follow?

Yet another kind of writing prepared by accountants is the narrative portion of financial statements. Footnote disclosures, for instance, communicate information that users may need to interpret the statements accurately. Unfortunately, the meaning of some footnote disclosures is not always clear to many financial statement readers. Several years ago, the Securities and Exchange Commission (SEC) issued a "plain English" disclosure rule requiring companies filing registration statements to write those statements in "plain English" so that readers would find them easier to understand. The rule enumerates several principles of "plain English," including the use of short sentences and clear, concise language.[9]

## HOW WELL DO ACCOUNTANTS WRITE?

Earlier we noted that many entry-level accountants lack adequate writing skills even though the ability to write well is essential for success in the business world. Some people believe the problem is getting worse in part because we have become a "dot-com" society in which a large part of everyday communications occurs via e-mail and other forms of electronic communications. Electronic communication usually emphasizes brevity over completeness, clarity, or attention to style. Therefore, we are being conditioned to use a type of writing that is not effective in many business situations. Yet even e-mail can be written effectively, as Chapter 10 of this book will show.

## WHAT MAKES WRITING WORK?

What is good writing? The list of tips for writers in Figure 1–2 summarizes many qualities of effective business writing, including writing by accountants. These qualities are stressed throughout this book. Let's examine these tips in a little more detail.

The first tip concerns the *content* of the document. You must know what you are talking about, and the information you give should be accurate and relevant. The second tip is *critical thinking*. You must analyze the issues with which you are dealing, including the questions and concerns of your readers. Can the issues be resolved in more than one way? If so, you will have to evaluate the alternatives carefully.

The third tip for effective writing is *to write appropriately for your readers*. Your writing should be suitable for readers in several ways: It should be written on a level they understand and find meaningful, and it should anticipate and answer their questions.

The fourth tip is *conciseness*. Say what needs to be said in as few words as possible. To keep your writing concise, avoid digressions, unnecessary repetition, and wordiness.

*Clarity* is the next tip. Write as simply as possible, using words and phrases with which the reader is familiar. To improve the clarity of your writing, choose words that mean precisely what you intend so that your sentences convey only one meaning: the meaning you want to convey. Well-structured sentences also contribute to clear writing.

*Coherence* is the logical, orderly relationship of ideas. Coherent writing is, simply, writing that is well organized. The flow of thought is easy to follow, and important ideas stand out. To write coherently, you

**FIGURE 1–2**   Tips for the Effective Writer

1. *Content:* Be sure that the accounting content is correct and complete. Have you addressed all relevant accounting issues?
2. *Critical Thinking:* Think carefully and critically about the issues with which you're dealing. Anticipate questions and objections your readers might raise.
3. *Appropriateness for Readers:* Write the document with a particular reader in mind. Check that issues are discussed on a level the reader can understand. For most documents, it is better to focus on practical, explicit information and advice related to the case you are discussing rather than on general accounting theory.
4. *Conciseness:* Write as concisely as possible, given the reader's needs and the issues to be addressed.
5. *Clarity:* Develop a style that is clear and readable. Choose words that convey your meaning with precision and clarity.
6. *Coherence:* Structure the document so that it is coherent. The organization should be logical and the train of thought easy to follow. Summarize main ideas near the beginning of the document, and begin each paragraph with a topic sentence.
7. *Revision:* Revise the document so that it is polished and professional. It should be free of all spelling errors and typos; grammatical errors should not detract from the message.

must carefully think through the ideas you want to convey. The ideas must be arranged logically and then written in a way readers can comprehend. Coherence is the sixth tip for effective writers.

The final tip is to *revise* your writing so that it is polished and professional. Documents should look attractive and be free of grammatical and mechanical errors.

## YOU CAN BECOME A GOOD WRITER

With all this talk about the importance of good writing to a successful career in accounting, you may feel overwhelmed or discouraged. Many people believe that they can never become good writers.

A word of encouragement is in order. Virtually anyone who succeeds in college work has the education and the skills to become at least an adequate writer, and probably even a good one. Problems with writing are often the result of two factors, both of which can be corrected: lack of adequate training in writing skills and lack of self-confidence.

Let's address the latter problem: the poor image some people have of themselves as writers. One reason to be optimistic about your writing ability is that you've already learned quite a bit about how to write from English courses and other writing classes as well as from your own experience. Most people are better writers than they realize. They have the potential to become even more effective after they've mastered a few strategies, such as the ones we'll cover in this book. As you read this book, note the techniques and principles you already use in your writing. Don't lose sight of your strengths while you work to improve the areas that could be better.

Another reason you should be able to write well as an accountant is that you will be writing about topics you understand and find interesting. If you have had unpleasant experiences with writing in courses other than accounting, the problem may have been that you were writing about topics you weren't particularly interested in or didn't feel qualified to discuss. When you write about subjects you like and understand, it's much easier to write clearly and persuasively.

Finally, you may find it much easier to do the kind of writing recommended in this book because it is simple, direct writing. Some people believe that they must write in long, complicated sentences filled with difficult, "impressive" vocabulary. In fact, just the opposite is true: Effective business writing is written as simply as possible. It is therefore easier to do.

## WRITING AND OTHER FORMS OF COMMUNICATION

Writing is only one of several forms of communication, along with such skills as reading, listening, speaking, and interpersonal communication. In fact, all these forms of communication work together to determine how well a person gives and receives information. Let's look at how reading, listening, and speaking skills can help you improve your writing.

### Reading

Reading affects writing in several ways. Often you will write a memo or letter in response to a written communication from someone else. In public practice, for example, you might write a letter to clients to answer questions they have posed in a letter to your firm. The ability to read the earlier correspondence carefully is essential to an effective response.

Careful reading is also important when you research accounting literature as background for the documents you write. The tax code, government regulations, Financial Accounting Standards Board (FASB) pronouncements, articles in professional journals, and *The Wall Street Journal* are examples of the material you must read to stay informed on accounting issues and procedures. You will need to understand this material and be able to apply it to particular situations.

You will also read information circulated and stored within your own firm or company, such as client files and memos or e-mails from colleagues. Reading this material carefully will provide many of the insights and facts you need to deal effectively with situations for which you are responsible.

Thus, careful reading, with an understanding of important ideas and key facts, can contribute to effective writing.

## Listening

Along with reading, the ability to listen carefully determines how well you receive information from others. On the job, you interact with colleagues, supervisors, subordinates, or clients; at school, you interact with professors and other students. Listening carefully to these people provides important information you can use as the basis of your writing. Listening gives you facts about projects you are working on, along with insights into other people's expectations and concerns.

In many situations, listening skills contribute to effective writing. Instructions given by the professor in class, interviews with clients, requests from supervisors, and phone conversations with colleagues are a few examples. In all these situations, attentive listening is necessary to hear what people are saying. It's often a good idea to take notes and, when necessary, ask questions for clarification or additional information.

Careful listening to what others say is often a key ingredient in effective writing. By listening carefully, you learn much about what others know about a situation, what their concerns are, and what they expect from you.

## Speaking

What you write also affects what you say to others. Informally, you may have meetings and conversations to discuss reports or memos you've written. What you write may also be the basis for formal oral presentations before a group. You might make a presentation to a board of directors, senior managers, or members of a professional organization.

## WRITING AND PROBLEM SOLVING

The nation's largest public accounting firms are unanimous in calling for improved communication skills for those entering the profession. These firms also identify problem-solving skills as essential to successful accounting practice:

> Individuals seeking to be successful in the diverse world of public accounting must be able to use creative problem-solving skills in a consultative process. They must be able to solve diverse and unstructured problems in unfamiliar settings. They must be able to comprehend an unfocused set of facts; identify and, if possible, anticipate problems; and find acceptable solutions.[10]

Problem solving requires many skills, such as identifying key issues, researching relevant literature, and thinking critically and analytically. At each step of the problem-solving process, writing can help you reach sound conclusions.

You can generate ideas on a topic by writing down what you know about that topic, as well as what you have yet to find out. The act of writing about a subject can actually help you clarify your thinking. As one wit put it, "How do I know what I think until I see what I say?" There's more truth in this quip than might at first be apparent. Research into how people think and learn has shown that writers often generate ideas and improve their insights into a subject as they write down their thoughts.

Writing can help you solve problems in other ways as well. For example, as you research accounting literature, you take notes. You might also write requests to other people for additional information you need to solve the problem.

Writing that you use to solve problems and make decisions is writing for yourself. After the problems have been solved, or at least clearly defined, you can put your insights and conclusions into writing that will help you and others make decisions. Writing, problem solving, and decision making are often inseparable, interactive processes that are essential to the practice of accounting.

## WRITING AND CRITICAL THINKING

We've seen that problem solving and decision making, like writing and other forms of communication, are significant parts of an accountant's job. But before you can solve a problem or make a decision, you need to think carefully and critically about the issues at hand.

What is *critical thinking*? It can be defined as fair, open-minded thinking that asks appropriate questions and considers all relevant information before reaching a conclusion. A critical thinker considers a situation from multiple points of view and evaluates the pros and cons of an argument before reaching a conclusion. Critical thinkers are careful to avoid errors, or fallacies, in their thinking and analyses. Chapter 7 discusses the critical thinking process in more detail.

Critical thinking and effective writing go hand in hand: As you take notes and write down your ideas about an accounting problem, the issues and alternative solutions will become clearer. This critical thinking becomes important as you prepare to write the final document.

## COMMUNICATIONS AND ETHICS

Accounting communication, including writing, may involve ethical considerations as well as critical thinking and problem solving. In fact, these three processes—analyzing ethical and other accounting issues, thinking critically, and solving problems—are often essential compo-nents of effective communication.

*Ethics* may be defined broadly as the standards we use to deter-mine what is right and what is wrong: a set of moral principles or values that govern how we act. We learn these ethical principles in a variety of ways, including from our families, religious communities, schools, or in general from the society of which we are a part. Professional people, including accountants, also acquire ethical standards as part of their professional training.

Accountants must adhere to very high ethical standards as they perform their professional responsibilities. CPAs must follow report-ing rules established by the SEC and other governmental agencies, and they must adhere to ethical standards established by nongovern-mental entities such as the FASB and the AICPA. In fact, the AICPA's Code of Professional Ethics is a major source of ethical standards for all accounting professionals, not just CPAs. Management accountants also adhere to ethical requirements established by the Institute of Management Accountants (IMA) as well as by federal, state, and local laws. Individual firms and corporations may also have ethical codes for their employees.

Legal requirements and codes of professional conduct provide standards of ethical behavior for accountants as they perform their professional responsibilities. Yet these laws and codes alone may not always provide enough guidance for specific ethical dilemmas. Accountants sometimes face situations for which ready-made answers are not available. When you are faced with these dilemmas and must make ethical decisions, you will need to think critically about the issues in light of your own personal ethical standards. Remember, too, that there may be a gap between what is legal and what is ethical. For many years, discrimination against ethnic minori-ties and women was legal in the United States, but such discrimina-tion was never ethical.

Ethical considerations often affect the way we communicate in a professional situation, whether orally or in writing. Remember that accounting is a process of measuring and *reporting* financial informa-tion. Ethical issues can relate to what we say, and how we say it.

The AICPA's Code of Professional Ethics requires that its mem-bers report all the information needed for a user of the information to make a reasonable decision; the Code also requires that financial data not be misrepresented. Thus, information must be reported in an honest, reasonably complete manner. Moreover, the information must be communicated clearly so that users can understand it. Accuracy, clarity, and completeness are all qualities of the ethical communication of accounting information.

Ethics also affects the attitude with which we regard other people, whether the public at large, our clients, or colleagues and co-workers.

An important principle here is that other people deserve to be treated with courtesy and respect. Later chapters discuss such ethical considerations as writing with a courteous tone, the respectful use of titles and pronouns, and the need to write clear and concise documents so that readers can find the information they need as quickly as possible. We will also discuss analyzing readers' interests and needs is an essential step in the writing process. Finally, sections of this book that discuss critical thinking and accounting research will show you how to analyze ethical dilemmas. You will learn how to decide what information to provide, and how to provide it in a way that not only adheres to professional and legal standards, but also shows respect for the people who will use the information.

## CONCLUSION

To be a successful accountant, you must master many skills. You must understand and be able to apply accounting principles, of course, but you must also be able to think critically and ethically, and to communicate effectively. A competent, ethical accountant who is also a critical thinker and an effective communicator usually is rewarded with professional success.

## EXERCISES

### Exercise 1–1 [General]

Look at some published corporate SEC Forms 10-K or annual reports for the most recent year and evaluate the financial statement disclosures they contain. Find examples of disclosures that are not written as clearly or concisely as they could be and rewrite them to be more clear and concise. Share your results with the class and discuss them. (Hint: You can access many 10-Ks and annual reports on the Internet by following the links to listed companies at the New York Stock Exchange (NYSE) Web site (**www.nyse.com**)

### Exercise 1–2 [General]

Prepare a written report on why the SEC is so concerned that corporations use "plain English" in their filings and what it is doing about the issue. Among the materials you consult, be sure to look at the following SEC publications, but do not limit your sources to just these:

- *A Plain English Handbook: How to Create Clear SEC Disclosure Documents* at **www.sec.gov/news/extra/handbook.htm**

- Updated Staff Legal Bulletin No. 7 at **www.sec.gov/interps/legal/cfslb7a.htm**
- Plain English Disclosure Final Rules at **www.sec.gov/rules/final/33-7497.txt**

## Exercise 1–3 [General]

Research the topic of "soft skills" and prepare a written report on their definition and importance in the accounting world.

## Exercise 1–4 [General/Ethics]

Do you believe ethical considerations are an important part of an accountant's professional responsibilities? Why or why not? Think about this question, and then write notes according to the following outline. Use only the sections of the outline that are relevant to your position on this issue.

1. Ethical considerations are important to accountants because: (list your reasons)
2. Ethical considerations are not very important to accountants because: (list your reasons)
3. Accountants find guidance in making ethical decisions from the following sources: (list the sources you find)

## Exercise 1–5

The chair of the accounting department at your school has asked you to address beginning accounting students at an orientation session. The topic of your presentation is to be "A Competitive Edge: The Importance of Writing Skills for Accountants." Your purpose is to convince the students to take the need for good writing skills seriously.

Write an outline you can use as a basis for your presentation. As steps in preparing your outline, follow these guidelines:

- Analyze your audience for this presentation. How will you present your topic so that attendees find it meaningful and interesting?
- Think critically about the objections your audience might raise to your arguments. How will you respond to their objections?
- What material will you include in your presentation? Remember to anticipate your audience's objections and the way you will respond. Also remember to arrange your ideas in a logical order.
- Using the guidelines found in Chapter 15, practice and present your talk. Your instructor may ask you to make your presentation in class. As an alternative, you may ask a few friends to listen to your presentation.

## Exercise 1–6

Assume that the talk you presented for Exercise 1–5 was very successful. In fact, the chair or your accounting department has asked you to write an article based on your talk for the departmental newsletter, which is distributed to all accounting majors.

Using the guidelines given in Chapter 14, write the article.

LEEDS METROPOLITAN UNIVERSITY LIBRARY

## NOTES

1. This is true not only in accounting, but also in almost any business occupation, including the areas of finance, marketing, and consulting. As pointed out in an article in *Business Week,* even new employees in these areas may have to prepare long reports or presentations as well as shorter forms of writing on the job. See Julie Gordon, "Memo to Students: Writing Skills Matter," *Business Week,* 26 April 2006. www.businessweek.com/bschools/content/apr2006/bs20060426_682947.htm (20 February 2010).

2. Report of the National Commission on Writing for America's Families, Schools, and Colleges, *"Writing: A Ticket to Work . . . Or a Ticket Out: A Survey of Business Leaders"* (New York: The College Board, 2004), 3.

3. For a good discussion of the importance of "soft skills," see Howard W. Wolosky, "Closing the Soft Skills Gap," *Web*CPA, 1 July 2008. www.accountingtoday.com/prc_issues/2008_7/28220-1.html (18 December 2010).

4. The Business Environment and Concepts (BEC) section of the exam contains 3 written communications tasks. See "New 2011 Uniform CPA Examination," at www.aicpa.org/BecomeACPA/CPAExam/ForCandidates/HowToPrepare/Downloadable Documents/New_2011_CPA_exam_guide_to_CBTe.pdf.

5. American Institute of Certified Public Accountants, Invitation to Comment, AICPA *Competency Model for the New Finance Professional* (New York: AICPA, 7 October 1997), 5.

6. *The Wall Street Journal,* 16 July 1986, "Words Count," 1.

7. Alan A. Cherry and Lucy A. Wilson, "A Study of the Writing Skills of Accounting Majors in California" (unpublished study, 1987).

8. In a 2006 survey of its members in government conducted by the AICPA, 80% of respondents indicated written and oral communication skills were essential. See "AICPA Survey—Phase II: Government Members Foresee 'Brain Drain' in the Government Workforce," Government E-News, American Institute of Certified Public Accountants (2006 May 17). fmcenter.aicpa.org/NR/rdonlyres/FA53AA12-25AF-4BCC-A25E-4281FCC56DBB/0/GPAC_NEWS_15.pdf (21 May 2007).

9. "Plain English Disclosure," Securities and Exchange Commission. *Staff Legal Bulletin No. 7(CF).* www.sec.gov/interps/legal/slbcf7.htm (19 July 2004): 1–2.

10. Duane R. Kullberg, William L. Gladstone, Peter R. Scanlon, J. Michael Cook, Ray J. Groves, Larry D. Horner, Shaun F. O'Malley, and Edward A. Kangas, *Perspectives on Education: Capabilities for Success in the Profession* (Arthur Andersen & Co., et al., 1989), 6.

# CHAPTER

# The Writing Process:
# An Overview

2

ffective writing, like accounting, is a process. One step in the accounting process is to analyze transactions to determine how to record them. Several questions basic to the accounting system underlie your analysis of financial transactions and their treatment. What is the purpose of the information recorded and ultimately reported? Who are the users of this information, and what are their needs? Do the readers expect this information to be presented in a certain form, such as the typical presentations found in annual reports? How can the information be most fairly and effectively presented?

These questions are as important to good writing as they are to good accounting. Planning, which emphasizes both the purpose of the writing and the needs and expectations of the readers, is the first step in the writing process.

In this chapter we discuss the writing process from beginning to end: planning for purpose and audience, including critical thinking about the issues; gathering information; generating and organizing ideas; drafting; revising; and proofreading. (Figure 2–1 summarizes the steps of the writing process.) You will learn how to apply this process to overcome much of the anxiety you may feel about writing, including the problem of writer's block. Throughout the chapter, we also discuss how computer technology can help you at every stage of the writing process.

In the previous chapter we identified seven tips for effective writing that focus on content, critical thinking, appropriateness for readers, conciseness, clarity, coherence, and revision (see Figure 1–2 in Chapter 1). In this and following chapters, we discuss specific guidelines and techniques that will help you achieve these goals.

## GETTING STARTED: IDENTIFYING PURPOSE

One of the first stages in the writing process—analyzing the purpose of the document—is easy to overlook. When you think about purpose, you decide what you want to accomplish with your letter, memo, or other document. Do you want to provide your readers with information

**FIGURE 2–1** The Writing Process

*Plan*
- Read the assignment or consider the task carefully.
- Analyze the purposes of the document.
- Identify the accounting issues, including different ways those issues might be addressed.
- Analyze the issues from the readers' point of view. What are their interests, needs, and expectations?
- Gather and organize material.

*Draft*
- Write down your ideas.
- Don't stop to edit.
- Write the parts of the paper in whatever order you want.
- Keep your readers in mind as you compose.

*Revise*
- Reread the document from the readers' point of view. Is your treatment of the accounting issues fair, thorough, and persuasive?
- Revise the document so that it is clear, coherent, and concise.
- Proofread for grammatical, mechanical, and typographical errors.

about some topic, answer their questions, recommend a course of action, persuade them to do something, or convince them to agree with you on some point?

These are just a few of the purposes a document can have. You should think carefully about the purpose *before* beginning to write. It might be helpful to think of your purpose in terms of three categories: to give information about something, to propose a course of action, or to solve a problem. The purpose of most writing tasks falls into one of these categories, or perhaps a combination of them.

A report on leases, for example, could have numerous purposes, but one of them will likely be its primary purpose. Should the report simply compare and contrast operating and capital leases? Should it recommend a particular kind of lease for a certain company in a given situation? Or is the purpose to analyze the income tax implications of a lease the company is evaluating?

As another example, assume you are the controller for Franklin Electrical Supplies. Franklin is considering purchasing stock in SolLite, Inc., one of Franklin's major suppliers of lighting fixtures. A report on this possible purchase could have any of the following purposes:

- To inform management of the advantages (or disadvantages) of the purchase
- To recommend that Franklin purchase (or not purchase) the stock
- To suggest a way to finance the purchase

The purpose of the report, or of any writing, determines what material it should contain. Consider another example. Your client, Coastal Development, is faced with a lawsuit that could result in a large loss. You might write a letter to Coastal's controller about the disclosure requirements for contingent loss liabilities as a result of pending litigation. In such a letter, you would not discuss gain contingencies or loss contingencies from bad debts. You would analyze the specific purpose of the letter to decide what information was relevant for this situation.

Another way to think about the purpose of a document is to identify the accounting issues it will address. Sometimes these issues are obvious, but at other times you must analyze the situation carefully before all the issues become apparent. For example, a client might seek your help on the best way to record a transaction to minimize income tax liability. As you analyze the transaction, you might become aware of accounting issues that would never occur to the client, such as the need to record the transaction consistently with generally accepted accounting principles. You might also become aware of ethical issues that the client had not considered.

Identifying the issues can help you define the purposes of the document you are writing, because one purpose might be to explain the accounting issues in a way your reader can understand.

After you have analyzed your purposes carefully, you should write them down. Be as specific as possible, and try to define the purposes in a sentence. This sentence might later become part of the introduction of the letter, memo, or report.

When you analyze your purpose, *be specific*. Remember that you are writing to particular individuals in a particular situation. Relate the purpose of your writing to these people and their concerns. That is, state the purpose in the context of this specific situation rather than in broad, general terms. In the Franklin Electrical Supplies example, suppose you were writing a report on how to finance the purchase of SolLite, Inc., stock. You would limit your discussion to the financing alternatives available to Franklin that are practical for the company to consider.

Sometimes, to determine the purpose of a document, you need to read previous correspondence on the subject, such as a letter or e-mail from a client. Be sure to read this correspondence carefully, noting important information and questions you've been asked to address. You may also receive an oral request to write something, perhaps by your supervisor. If you receive such a request to write, listen carefully to the directions. If the purpose of the document is not clear, ask questions until you're sure what the document should include.

# THINKING CRITICALLY ABOUT THE ISSUES

If the purpose for your writing involves analyzing complex accounting issues, think carefully about your topic as you plan your document, gather information, and write. Sometimes the issues are complex: a problem might have more than one reasonable solution, and some people might disagree with the course of action you recommend. As you plan your writing, keep alternative points of view in mind. Consider not only the reasons for your own opinion; but also the reasons other people might have a different view. How will you support your opinion, and how will you respond to the arguments of people who disagree with you? Critical thinking about the issues throughout the writing process helps ensure that the document you write is persuasive. Your readers will regard you as knowledgeable and fair, and they will take seriously what you write. (Chapter 7 discusses critical thinking in more detail.)

# ANALYZING THE READERS

Another important consideration when you are planning a writing task is who the readers will be. A memo on a highly technical accounting topic should be written one way for an accounting colleague, but another way for a client or manager with only limited knowledge of accounting procedures and terminology.

Effective writers analyze the needs and expectations of their readers before they begin to write. In writing a letter or memo, you will probably be writing to a limited number of people, perhaps to only one person. You also know, or can find out, important information about the reader or readers. Again, you must ask certain questions: How much do the readers know about the subject being discussed? What else do they need to know? Have they already formed opinions on the accounting issues? The answers to these questions suggest the level at which you will write, including the terms and procedures you will explain, the background you will provide, and the arguments you will make.

Accountants who deal with the public should be particularly careful in analyzing the needs of their readers. A tax specialist, for example, might have clients with widely varying experience and knowledge of tax terminology. A corporate executive would probably understand such concepts as depreciation and accruals, but a small shopkeeper might not be familiar with them. Business letters to these two clients, even on the same topic, should be written differently.

Consider the readers' attitudes and biases. Are they likely to be neutral to your recommendations, or will they need to be convinced? The critical thinking about the issues you have already done will help you write to your readers in a convincing way. Remember your readers' interests and concerns as you write. How will they benefit, directly or indirectly, from what you propose? How can you present your arguments to overcome their objections and biases? To answer this last question, you must anticipate readers' questions, research the issues, and then organize your arguments into a convincing sequence.

Other important considerations when analyzing readers' needs and expectations are tone and style. What are readers' attitudes and biases? Some readers react well to an informal, friendly style of writing, but other readers believe that professional writing should be more formal. Whoever your readers are, remember always to be courteous. Whether you write in a technical or conversational style, all readers appreciate (and deserve) consideration, tact, and respect. Treating your readers with courtesy and respect will help ensure that your writing is ethical, as well as effective.

Word choices also contribute to an effective and responsible writing style. Many readers might find the following sentence troubling:

A successful *CEO* will treat *his* subordinates with respect.

Some readers might argue that the choice of pronouns (*CEO/his*) implies a gender bias. Use plural nouns and pronouns to avoid this bias:

Successful *CEOs* will treat *their* subordinates with respect.

Sometimes your readers will have additional expectations about your documents. In a classroom situation, the instructor usually gives directions about different aspects of your papers, such as style, format, and due date. The instructor expects you to follow these directions. How well you do so usually affects your grade.

Readers' expectations are also important when you write on the job. Managers in some firms expect in-house memos and reports to follow certain conventions of format, organization, and style. If you work for such a firm, your memos and reports will seem more professional—and be more effective—if they are consistent with these expectations.

In fact, meeting readers' expectations might actually be a matter of company policy. Policies often govern how certain documents are written and what procedures they must go through for approval. Many professional services firms do not let new staff members send letters to clients unless a manager or partner first approves them. If you were a new staff member in such a firm, you might draft the client letter, but a manager or partner would review it and possibly ask you to make revisions. Moreover, for certain documents, such as some engagement letters and auditing reports, the actual language used in the letter might be determined by company policy. The partner will expect you to follow these policies with great care.

In the example of the client letter just discussed, there are actually two or three readers: the manager and/or partner who reviews and approves the letter, and the client who receives it. This letter should be

**FIGURE 2–2** Planning a Paper

*Consider these questions as you plan the documents you write.*

1. Answer after you read and analyze the assignment or consider the task:
   - What are the accounting issues in this case?
   - Are there ethical issues I should consider?
   - What literature will I research to resolve these issues?
   - Who will read this document?
   - What different opinions might readers have about the issues?
   - What are the readers' concerns?
   - What are the purposes of this document?

2. Answer after you research and analyze the case:
   - What are the main points (conclusions) I need to make in this document?
   - What material should I include to make these conclusions clear and meaningful to the reader(s)?
   - How will I support my conclusions and respond to readers' objections?

written on a technical level that is appropriate for the client, and it should address the client's concerns, but it should also meet the expectations of the manager and partner. Analyzing readers' needs, interests, and expectations is obviously more complex when there are several readers. Think carefully about the different readers and use your best judgment to meet the expectations of them all.

Analyzing readers' needs, expectations, and opinions is an important part of the preparation for writing. Planning, during which you think carefully about both your audience and your purpose, is the first guideline for effective writing. We'll add more to this list throughout the chapter.

1. **Analyze the purpose of the writing, the accounting issues involved, and the needs and expectations of the readers.**

Figure 2–2 summarizes questions you can ask yourself to help plan your writing.

## GETTING YOUR IDEAS TOGETHER

After you have evaluated the purpose of the writing and the needs of the readers, you are ready for the second stage in the writing process: gathering information and organizing the ideas you want to present. This step might be quick and simple. For a short letter, you may not need to do further research; organizing your ideas may involve only a short list of the main topics you want to include in the letter—perhaps one topic for each paragraph.

For much of the writing you do, gathering information and organizing might be a more complicated process that involves much thought and perhaps some research as well. Let's look at some techniques you can use.

## Gathering Information

Before you begin to write the document, be sure you have complete, accurate information. You can check the work that has already been done, and then locate new information you'll need.

For many projects, some information might already be available. If you're working on an audit, for example, information might be available from other members of the audit team as well as from the files from the previous years' audits. Explore these sources of information fully. Review the files carefully, and, when necessary, talk with the people who have already worked on the project.

Sometimes you might need to do additional research. This task can involve background reading on a technical topic or a careful review of professional standards or law, such as FASB publications, the tax code, IRS publications, or SEC publications. As you read this material, take notes carefully, and be alert for information that might be helpful when you write. Remember also that accounting issues often have more than one possible solution. As you research, look for material that supports more than one point of view.

This research may require you to interview people who will be affected by the project that you are working on. Suppose you intend to propose in a report a new accounting information system for your company. You can gain important insights into topics your report should cover by talking with the people who would be affected by the proposed system. You can learn what they want the system to accomplish, what they might need to know about it, and whether they have already formed opinions that should be considered when you write your report.

## Generating Ideas

After you have gathered the information you need, you are ready to begin the next phase of the writing process: deciding exactly what to say.

If you have not already written your statement of purpose, now is the time to do so. Try to break up the purpose into several subtopics. Suppose the purpose of a client letter is to recommend that the client company update its computerized accounting system. The statement of purpose for this letter could specify the different accounting jobs for which the expanded system would be useful, outline its major advantages, and respond to questions and objections the client might have.

Another useful technique for generating ideas is brainstorming. With this technique, you think about your topic, and write down all your ideas, in whatever order they come to you. Don't worry about organizing the ideas or evaluating them; later, you can consider how these ideas fit into the outline you developed when you analyzed the purposes of the document.

You may find brainstorming easier to do at the computer. As you type in the keywords and phrases that occur to you, the phrases might start to become sentences and the sentences might flow together to become paragraphs. Most people can type faster than they can write with a pencil or pen. You may find that the faster you record your ideas, the more freely the ideas flow. Thus, using a computer can be valuable when you need to generate ideas quickly.

## Arranging Ideas: Organization

After you've decided what you want to say, it's important to consider how best to arrange these ideas so that the readers will find them easy to follow. In other words, it's time to think about how the document will be organized.

Much of the work you've already done will help you decide on the best pattern of organization. You may be able to use your statement of purpose as the basis of your organization, or your paper may be structured so that the readers' major concerns are your principle of organization—that is, each concern might be a major division of your paper. Some documents can be organized according to the accounting issues they address.

When considering all these approaches to organization, and possibly deciding among them, remember this principle: The needs and interests *of your readers* should determine the document's organization. Arrange your ideas in the order that readers will find most helpful and easiest to follow. Anticipate when your readers are likely to raise objections or ask questions, and respond to those needs when they are likely to occur.

A few other points of organization are important to consider. First, most writing has the same basic structure: an introduction, a concise summary of important ideas, development of the main ideas, and a conclusion. This structure is shown in Figure 2–3. In later chapters of this handbook, we will discuss more fully this basic structure as it is used for particular kinds of writing.

Another point is that ideas should be arranged in a logical order. To describe how to reconcile a bank statement, for instance, you would discuss each step of the procedure in the order in which it is performed.

Finally, you can often organize ideas according to their importance. In business writing, always arrange ideas from the most to the least important. Note that this principle means you start with the ideas that are most important *to the reader*.

> **FIGURE 2–3**  Basic Writing Structure
>
> - *Introduction:* identifies the subject of the document and tells why it was written. Sometimes the introduction also provides background information about the topic or stresses its importance. You may also use the introduction to build rapport with your reader, perhaps by mentioning a common interest or concern or referring to previous communication on the topic.
> - *Concise statement of the main ideas:* summarizes explicitly main ideas, conclusions, or recommendations. This part of a document may be part of the introduction or a separate section. It can be as short as a one-sentence purpose statement or as long as a three-page executive summary.
> - *Development of the main ideas:* includes explanations, examples, analyses, steps, reasons, arguments, and factual details. This part of an outline or paper is often called the body.
> - *Conclusion:* brings the paper to an effective close. The conclusion may restate the main idea in a fresh way, suggest further work, or summarize recommendations, but an effective conclusion avoids unnecessary repetition.

Suppose you are writing a report to recommend that your firm purchase new software for maintaining its accounting records. Naturally, you will want to emphasize the advantages of this purchase, describing them in the order that is likely to be most convincing to the readers. However, this investment might also have drawbacks, such as the problems involved in converting from the old system to the new one. For your report to appear well researched and unbiased, you need to include these disadvantages in your discussion. You might use the following structure:

**I.** Introduction, including your recommendation

**II.** Body

    **A.** Advantages, beginning with those most appealing to the readers

    **B.** Disadvantages, including, when possible, ways to minimize or overcome any drawbacks

**III.** Conclusion

One final word about organization: After you've decided how to arrange your ideas, it's a good idea to write an outline if you haven't already done so. Having an outline in hand as you draft your paper will help you keep the paper on track. You'll be sure to include all the information you had planned and avoid getting off the subject.

The guidelines for effective writing can now be expanded:

1. **Analyze the purpose of the writing, the accounting issues involved, and the needs and expectations of the readers.**
2. **Organize your ideas so that readers will find them easy to follow.**

## WRITING THE DRAFT

The next major step in the writing process is writing the draft. The purpose of this step is to put your ideas in writing. Most writers find that they can write a first draft more easily if they don't try to edit at this stage. Spelling, punctuation, and style are thus not important in the draft. What is important is to write the ideas so that you can later polish and correct what you have written.

If you did your brainstorming at the computer, you may already have parts of your draft if the list of ideas you began with evolved into sentences or paragraphs as you typed.

As pointed out previously, you'll probably be able to type the draft faster than you can write it by hand. Using a computer may also be easier because your ideas will flow more quickly, and your stream of thought won't be impeded by the mechanics of writing.

The outline you have prepared will guide you as you write. However, you may decide to change the outline as you go, omitting some parts that no longer seem to fit or adding other ideas that seem necessary. Changing the outline is fine; when you revise the draft later, you can make sure your thoughts are still well organized.

Although you will use your outline as a guide to the ideas you want to include in your draft, you might find it easier to write the various parts of the document in an order different from the one used in the outline. Some people find introductions hard to write, so they leave them until last. You may also choose to write the easiest sections of your draft first, or you may start writing some parts of the draft while you are still getting the material together for other parts. Word processing programs allow you to rearrange the parts of your paper by moving entire blocks of text.

One final word of advice on the draft stage: Don't allow yourself to get stuck while you search for the perfect word, phrase, or sentence. Leave a blank space, or write something that is more or less what you mean. You'll probably find the right words later.

## REVISING THE DRAFT

The next stage in the writing process is the revision of the draft. In this step, you check your spelling and grammar, polish your style, and make a final check to see that the ideas are effectively and completely presented. As you revise, read the document *from the reader's point of view*.

You'll need to revise most of your writing more than once—perhaps three or four times. The key to revising is to let the writing get cold between revisions; a time lapse between readings enables you to read the draft more objectively and see what you have actually said, instead of what you meant to say. Ideally, revisions should be made at least a day apart.

Another technique is to have a colleague review the draft for both the content and the effectiveness of the writing. Choose a reviewer who is a good writer, and evaluate the reviewer's suggestions with an open mind.

You can also check your text with software that edits or checks for grammar problems. These programs identify certain errors in style, such as sentences that are too long and paragraphs that use the same word too often. The software may also identify some mistakes in punctuation and grammar as well as most misspelled words.

A word of caution about these style analyzers, spelling checkers, and grammar checkers—they're not infallible. They can't catch all the weaknesses in your text, and sometimes they flag problems that aren't really there. If you use a computer to analyze your writing, you still must use your own judgment about what changes to make. The poem shown in Figure 2–4 illustrates these points!

Another revision technique that works with a computer is to print the document and edit the hard copy by hand. You can then make the revisions later in your computer file. Some writers find that they revise more effectively if they work with a hard copy rather than text on a screen.

The next four chapters of this handbook discuss what to look for when putting your writing in final form.

---

**FIGURE 2–4**    Spelling Checkers Don't Catch Everything!

---

Candidate for a Pullet Surprise

I have a spelling checker, it came with my PC
It plane lee marks four my revue miss steaks aye can knot sea.
Eye ran this poem threw it. Your sure reel glad two no
Its vary polished in it's weigh. My checker tolled me sew.
A checker is a bless sing. It freeze yew lodes of thyme.
It helps me right awl stiles two reed, and aides me when aye rime.
Each frays come posed up on my screen eye trussed too bee a joule.
The checker pours o'er every word, to cheque sum spelling rule.
Be fore a veiling checkers, hour spelling mite decline.
And if were lacks or have a laps, we wood be maid to wine.
Butt now bee cause my spelling is checked with such grate flare
Their are know faults with in my cite. Of non eye am a wear.
Now spelling does not phase me. It does not bring a tier.
My pay purrs awl due glad den with wrapped words fare as hear.
To rite with care is quite a feet of witch won should be proud.
And wee mussed dew the best wee can sew flaws are knot aloud.
Sow eye can sea why aye dew prays such soft ware four pea seas
And why I brake in two averse by righting want too pleas.

---

*Source: The Journal of Irreproducible Results,* the science humor magazine. Reprinted with permission.

We now have three guidelines for effective writing:

1. **Analyze the purpose of the writing, the accounting issues involved, and the needs and expectations of the readers.**
2. **Organize your ideas so that readers will find them easy to follow.**
3. **Write the draft and then revise it to make the writing polished and correct.**

## THE FINAL DRAFT

After you have polished the style and organization of the paper, you will be ready to put it in final form. Consider questions of document design, such as the use of headings, white space, and other elements of the paper's appearance.

Proofreading is also an important step. Here are some suggestions for effective proofreading:

1. Proofreading is usually more effective if you leave time between typing and looking for errors. You will be able to critique the paper more clearly if you have been away from it for a while.
2. Use your computer's spell-check program to eliminate spelling and typographical errors. Remember that the computer program may not distinguish between homonyms such as *their* and *there* or *affect* and *effect*.
3. In addition to your computer's spelling checker, you may also need to use a dictionary to look up any word that could possibly be misspelled, such as words the computer doesn't recognize or homonyms it may not have flagged. Check also that you've spelled people's names correctly. If you are a poor speller, have someone else read the paper for spelling errors.
4. If you know that you tend to make a certain type of error, read through your paper at least once to check for that error. For example, if you have problems with subject–verb agreement, check every sentence in your paper to be sure the verbs are correct.
5. Read your paper *backward*, sentence by sentence, as a final proofreading step. This technique isolates each sentence and makes it easier to spot errors you may have overlooked in previous readings.

## DEALING WITH WRITER'S BLOCK

Writer's block is a problem everyone faces at some time or another. We stare at blank paper or at a blank screen with no idea of how to get started. The ideas and the words just don't come.

Many of the techniques already discussed in this chapter will help you overcome writer's block. Thinking of writing as a process, rather than a completed product that appears suddenly in its final form, should help make the job less formidable. Any difficult task seems easier if you break it down into manageable steps.

The discussions of the steps in the writing process, especially the section on writing the draft, included suggestions that will help you overcome writer's block. Here is a summary of these techniques:

1. Plan before you write so that you know what you need to say.
2. Write with an outline in view, but write the paper in any order you want. You can rearrange it later.
3. Don't strive for perfection in the draft stage. Leave problems of grammar, spelling, style, and so forth to the revision stage.
4. Begin with the easiest sections to write.
5. Don't get stuck on difficult places. Skip over them and go on to something else. You may find that when you come back to the rough spots later, they are not as hard to write as you thought.

## WRITING UNDER PRESSURE

Throughout this chapter, you've seen how writing is easier if you break down the project into steps. It's easy to manage these steps when you have plenty of time to plan, research, draft, revise, and polish.

What about situations in which you don't have the luxury of time? What about writing essay questions on an exam, or on-the-job writing tasks where you have only a little while to produce a letter or memo?

The truth is that any writing project, no matter how hurriedly it must be done, will go more smoothly if you stick with the three basic steps of the writing process: plan, draft, and revise. Even if you have only a few minutes to work on a document, allow yourself some of that time to think about who you're writing to, what you need to say, and the best way to organize that material. Then draft the paper.

Allow yourself some time to revise as well. Use a spell-check program to help locate embarrassing spelling and typographical errors.

## HELP FROM COLLEAGUES: CRITIQUING

Once you have improved your document as much as you can, you may have another source of help: constructive feedback from one or more colleagues. If you are preparing an assignment for a course, this help may come from other students in the class. In a job situation, you might ask a colleague to review your writing. You will, of course, be willing to return the favor to your colleagues if they ask you to critique their writing.

Here are some tips for giving helpful critiques:

• Reviews of the writing should be both tactful and honest.
• Always point out strengths of the writing, and then make a few suggestions if you see ways the writing could be improved.

- Make suggestions in positive ways, and be as specific as possible. For example, you wouldn't say, "I can't make any sense of this, and your grammar is deplorable!" Rather, you might say, "Can you explain this concept more clearly? Perhaps shorter sentences would help. Also, you might want to check your verbs."
- Ask the writer if you can write your feedback on the paper itself. Then be prepared to discuss what you liked about the paper, as well as ways it could be improved.
- For specific guidelines on what to look for in the papers you critique, use Tips for The Effective Writer found in Figure 1–2.

If a colleague critiques your writing, here are some things to keep in mind:

- Whenever possible, ask people to critique your writing who are themselves good writers.
- Keep an open mind, and resist the natural temptation to be defensive. On the other hand, remember that final responsibility for the document is yours; you'll decide which suggestions to use. Not all advice, however well intended, is helpful.
- Thank the reviewers for their help.

# EXERCISES

## Exercise 2–1 [General]

Analyze the letter in Figure 2–5. How would you react if you received this letter?

1. Think about these questions, and then discuss them with your classmates:
   - What are the strengths of this letter? (It does have some strengths!)
   - What are the weaknesses of the letter? (Hint: Can you find all the typos and spelling errors? In addition to these problems, the letter has a number of less obvious weaknesses. What are they?)
2. Revise the letter so that it is more effective. Invent any details you may need.

   Chapter 9 provides information on letter writing.

## Exercise 2–2 [General]

You are a member of Beta Alpha Psi (the accounting honorary society) at a major university. A large local high school has contacted your chapter of the honorary society and asked it to prepare a two-page flyer about opportunities provided by an accounting career and the skills (hard and soft) required to succeed both as an accounting student and as an accounting professional. You have been asked by the president of the honorary society, Sandy West, to write the flyer. She has asked that you prepare it in the form of a memo written to her. Chapter 10 provides information on writing memos. Write a memo to Sandy West responding to her request.

**FIGURE 2–5**   Letter for Exercise 2–1: What Is Wrong with This Letter?

Wright and Wrongh, CPAs
123 Anystreet
Anytown, US 12345

Corner Dress Shop
123 Anyother Street
Anytown, US 12345

Gentleman
We are in receipt of your correspondence and beg to thank you.
After extensive research we have found what we hope will be a satisfactory responce to your questions, we hope you will find our work satisfactory. It is the goal of our firm to alway offer the best, most expert and reliable service possible to all our clients, all of whom are value and with whom we hope to have a lont-term working relationship to our mutual advantage.
There were two possibilities for the resolution of this issue that we considered after a careful analyses of the applicable IRC sections to your situation. If the first possibility proved relevant, then you would be subject to a fine of $5500, plus penalties and interest. If athe other possibility was the best solution, then you would receive a $4400 credit because of a loss carryforard to your current year returns. As you no doubt know, IRC Sec.341(6)a [paras. 5-9] stipulate that the regulations we must follow. Thus, to be in compliance with the rules and regs. you must follow the provisions of the pertinent sections.
As your CPAs, we are most concerned that we be in complianse with all standards of professional ethics, and we always keep this in mind when we advise you on your tax and accounting questions. We don't want to go to jail, and we're sure you don't either!
After extensive research, we advise you to file an amended return immediately because the first possibility enumerated in the above paragraph proves to be the correct solution to your problem.
Thanking you in advance, we remain

Yours with highest regards,

*M. Ostley Wrongh*

M. Ostley Wrongh
Wright and Wrongh, CPAs

## Exercise 2–3  [Managerial]

Jim Kakes, CEO of Kakes Manufacturing Company, needs to hire a new controller as the current controller is retiring. Several other CEOs he knows have suggested he look for someone who is a Certified Management Accountant (CMA). Mr. Kakes is not familiar with this designation and has asked you what it is and whether you believe, given the extra amount he will have to pay in salary, hiring a CMA would be a good idea.

Write a memo to Mr. Kakes responding to his request. You may wish to consult Chapter 10 for suggestions on memo organization and format.

### Exercise 2–4 [Systems]

You are employed by the consulting division of a large professional services firm. One of your clients, Chattahooche Canoe Manufacturers, has been struggling with inefficiencies but has been reluctant to introduce many controls ensuring the safety of assets for fear of "inhibiting operations" too much. Write a letter to the firm's president, George Chiefton, that explains how controls can improve efficiency and effectiveness.

Chapter 9 provides advice on how to write a letter.

### Exercise 2–5 [Managerial]

Duncan Clarke is controller of Clarke Manufacturing Company, one of your clients. Clarke Manufacturing makes molded plastic containers for beverage producers such as dairies. Mr. Clarke has implemented a new strategic plan, which he hopes will help his company become more competitive. He has recently heard of something called a "balanced scorecard" technique that might be of use in the plan's implementation. He has asked you to prepare a memo explaining what this management tool is, and how it might be of use. Write the memo. You may wish to consult Chapter 10 for suggestions on memo organization and format.

### Exercise 2–6 [Auditing]

You are a partner in a medium-size CPA firm and want to convince your partners that the firm should expand the services provided to clients. Specifically, you believe the firm should begin offering *WebTrust* and *SysTrust* services.

Write a memo to your partners to explain what the concepts of *WebTrust* and *SysTrust* services are, and why your firm should begin to offer such services. Chapter 10 contains suggestions on memo organization and format.

### Exercise 2–7 [Tax]

Your accounting honorary society maintains a Web site on which it includes short articles on various accounting topics. The readers of this Web site are primarily other accounting students. The Web master has asked you to write a short article explaining the differences among progressive, proportional, and regressive tax systems, including their relative advantages and disadvantages. Give examples.

## Exercise 2–8 [Financial]

Many financial experts believe that one of the most important issues facing capital markets both in the European Union and in the United States is the convergence of accounting standards.

Prepare a written report to be used as a basis for a speech to your accounting club on the desirability and the problems of achieving such convergence, as well as on the consequences of not achieving it.

# CHAPTER

# The Flow of Thought: Organizing for Coherence

**3**

Coherence is one of the seven tips for effective business writing discussed in Chapter 1 (see Figure 1–2 in Chapter 1). Coherent writing is organized so that important ideas stand out. The flow of thought is logical and easy to follow.

Chapter 2 introduced several techniques to help you make your writing more coherent: analyzing purpose and the reader's needs, then outlining before you begin to write. This chapter discusses additional ways to ensure that your writing is coherent. You'll learn how to write with unity, use summary sentences and transitions, and structure effective paragraphs and essays.

## WRITING WITH UNITY

The key to unified writing is to establish the main idea of each document. An office memo may contain only one paragraph, but that paragraph has a central idea. A report might be many pages long, but it still has a central idea or purpose, and probably secondary purposes as well. It's important to determine your purpose and main ideas before you begin writing, as discussed in Chapter 2.

You should be able to summarize a main idea in one sentence. Within a paragraph, this sentence is called the topic sentence. In longer documents involving more than two or three paragraphs, this sentence is called the thesis statement or statement of purpose.

The main idea is the key to the entire document. Any sentences or details that are unrelated to the main idea, either directly or indirectly, are irrelevant and should be omitted. In longer documents, entire paragraphs may be irrelevant to the main purpose. These irrelevant paragraphs are called digressions.

When you remove digressions and irrelevant sentences, your writing becomes unified; every sentence is related to the main idea.

The following paragraph is not unified. Which sentences are irrelevant to the topic sentence?

(1) Incorporation offers many advantages for a business and its owners. (2) For example, the owners are not responsible for the business's debts. (3) Investors hope to make money when they buy stock in a corporation. (4) Incorporation also enables a business to obtain professional management skills. (5) Corporations are subject to more government regulation than are other forms of organization.

Sentence 1, the topic sentence, identifies the main idea of the paragraph: the advantages of incorporation. Sentences 3 and 5 are off the subject.

Writing with unity is an important way to make your writing coherent.

## USING SUMMARY SENTENCES

In coherent writing, the main ideas stand out. You can emphasize your main ideas by placing them in the document where they will get the reader's attention.

First, as suggested in Chapter 2, it's usually a good idea to summarize your main ideas at the beginning of the document. A long document, especially a report, should have a separate summary section at or near the beginning of the paper. This formal summary may be called an abstract, an executive summary, or simply a summary.

When writing these summary sections, be specific and remember the reader's interests and needs. Let's say you are writing a memo to the management of Turnipseed Importers to explain the advantages of an accounting software package that it will use to manage its inventory. You'll need to summarize those advantages specifically and relate them to Turnipseed. One of these advantages might be stated this way: "This software is particularly easy to use because it provides online help for the type of inventory control issues we often encounter with our seed stores. Competing software companies do not offer this type of online support."

The summary at the beginning of a document can consist of several sentences or even several pages, depending on the length of the document and the complexity of the main ideas or recommendations. Here is an example:

The following procedures will ensure a smooth transition to the new software:

• Management should designate a representative from each department to attend the training workshop provided by the vendor. This workshop will be offered on October 15. (Details will be provided later.)

- Each department should plan a training session for its employees to emphasize the department's use of the system.
- A two-week transition period should be allowed for converting from the old system.
- Troubleshooters should be available to all departments to solve any problems that occur.

Summary sentences are important in other places in a document, especially at the beginning of each section and in the conclusion.

Any paper that is longer than three or four paragraphs probably has more than one main idea or recommendation; each of these ideas is suggested in the introduction or in a separate summary section. Often, the logical way to organize the remainder of the document is to use a separate section of the paper to discuss each idea further. Each section begins with a summary statement to identify the main idea, or the topic, of that section. The reader will then have a clear idea of what that section is about. It's a good idea to use somewhat different wording from that used in the beginning of the paper.

The principle we've been discussing sounds simple: Begin with your conclusion, and then give your support. This arrangement of ideas is called a deductive structure. However, many writers have trouble putting this advice into practice. The difficulty may occur because this order of ideas is the reverse of the process writers go through to reach their conclusions. Most research is done inductively, rather than deductively. That is, the typical research process is to gather information first and then to arrive at the conclusions. A writer might try to take the reader through the same investigative steps as those he or she used to solve the problem or answer the question.

Think about your readers' needs. They're mainly interested in the findings of your research, not in the process you went through to get there. They might want to read about the facts you considered as well as your analytical reasoning; in fact, some readers will carefully evaluate the soundness of your data and methodology. However, their first concern is with the conclusions.

Conclusions can be presented again in a concluding section, especially if the document is very long. Once again, you may need to remind the reader of your main ideas, but be careful not to sound repetitive. The length and complexity of the document determine how much detail to include in your conclusion.

## RESPONDING TO READERS' QUESTIONS AND CONCERNS

Earlier chapters of this text discussed planning a document so that it responds to your readers' concerns. That is, you anticipate questions readers might have as well as objections they might raise to your recommendations. As you plan the organization of your document, consider the best places to address these concerns. Questions are simple to handle: Anticipate where the readers are likely to have questions, and answer them at that part of your paper.

For responses to objections, again, consider where in the document your readers are likely to raise objections, and respond at that part of your paper if at all possible. Where you place your responses also depends on how many objections there are and how complicated your responses are. Sometimes responses to readers' concerns are better in a separate section of the paper. For example, suppose you are recommending a certain accounting treatment for a transaction, but you realize that your readers might disagree with you. The first part of the document might explain the reasons for your recommendation, and the final part of the document might explain the disadvantages of other treatments.

## TRANSITIONS

Transitions, which are another element of coherent writing, link ideas. They can be used between sentences, paragraphs, and major divisions of the document. Transitions show the relationship between two ideas: how the second idea flows logically from the first, and how both are related to the main idea of the entire document.

As an example of how transitions work, consider the following paragraph. The topic sentence (main idea) is the first sentence; the transitional expressions are in italics:

> (1) Financial statements are important to a variety of users. (2) *First*, investors and potential investors use the statements to determine whether a company is a good investment risk. (3) These users look at such factors as net income, the debt-to-equity ratio, retained earnings, and economic value added (EVA). (4) *Second*, creditors use financial statements to determine whether a firm is a good credit risk. (5) Creditors want to know whether a firm has a cash flow large enough to pay its debts. (6) *Third*, government agencies analyze financial statements for a variety of purposes. (7) *For example*, the Internal Revenue Service wants to know whether the company has paid the required amount of taxes on its income. (8) These examples of financial statement users show how diverse their interests can be.

The sentences beginning *first* (2), *second* (4), and *third* (6) give three examples of the paragraph's main idea: the variety of financial statement users. These three sentences relate to one another in a logical, sequential way, which the transitions make clear. These sentences also relate directly to the topic sentence; they illustrate it with specific examples. Sentence 7, which begins with *for example*, relates only indirectly to the main idea of the paragraph, but it relates directly to sentence 6. Sentence 7 identifies one reason why government agencies need access to financial statements.

Transitions can express a number of relationships between ideas. In the sample paragraph, the transitions indicate an enumerated list (2, 4, and 6) and a specific illustration of a general statement (7). Transitions can also imply other relationships between ideas—conclusions, additional information, or contrasts, for example.

To see the importance of transitions within a paragraph, look at the following example, which lacks transitions:

> Incorporation offers several advantages to businesses and their owners. Ownership is easy to transfer. The business is able to maintain a continuous existence even when the original owners are no longer involved. The stockholders of a corporation are not held responsible for the business's debts. If the Dallas Corporation defaults on a $1,000,000 loan, its investors will not be held responsible for paying that liability. Incorporation enables a business to obtain professional managers with centralized authority and responsibility. The business can be run more efficiently. Incorporation gives a business certain legal rights. It can enter into contracts, own property, and borrow money.

Now see how much easier it is to read the paragraph when it has appropriate transitions:

> Incorporation offers several advantages to businesses and their owners. *For one thing*, ownership is easy to transfer, and the business is able to maintain a continuous existence even when the original owners are no longer involved. *In addition*, the stockholders of a corporation are not held responsible for the business's bad debts. If the Dallas Corporation defaults on a $1,000,000 loan, *for example*, its investors will not be held responsible for paying that liability. Incorporation *also* enables a business to obtain professional managers with centralized authority and responsibility; *therefore*, the business can be run more efficiently. *Finally*, incorporation gives a business certain legal rights. *For example*, it can enter into contracts, own property, and borrow money.

## Transitional Words and Phrases

Following is a list of commonly used transitional expressions, their meanings, and example sentences showing how some of them work.

- **Adding a point or piece of information:** *and, also, in addition, moreover, furthermore, first/second/third, finally*

  Example: We appreciate the opportunity to conduct your audit this year and will send you a detailed schedule of our work next week.

- **Making an exception or contrasting point:** *but, however, nevertheless, on the other hand, yet, still, on the contrary, in spite of . . . , nonetheless*

  Example: Most of our divisions showed a profit this quarter. However, the Houston division was not so successful.

- **Giving specific examples or illustrations:** *for example, for instance, as an illustration, in particular, to illustrate*

  Example:   Financial statements serve a variety of users. For example, investors use them to evaluate potential investments. Other users include . . . .

- **Clarifying a point:** *that is, in other words, in effect, put simply, stated briefly*

  Example:   The basic accounting equation is *assets equal liabilities plus owners' equity*. That is, $A = L + OE$.

- **Conceding a point to the opposite side:** *granted that, it may be true that, even though, although*

  Example:   Although upgrading our equipment will require a large capital outlay, increased efficiency will more than justify the use of funds.

- **Indicating place, time, or importance:**

  | | |
  |---|---|
  | **Place:** | *above, beside, beyond, to the right, below, around* |
  | **Time:** | *formerly, hitherto, earlier, in the past, before, at present, now, today, these days, tomorrow, in the future, next, later on, later* |
  | **Importance:** | *foremost, most important, especially, of less importance, of least importance* |

  Example:   In earlier centuries there was no need for elaborate accounting systems. However, the size and complexities of today's businesses make modern accounting a complicated process indeed.

- **Indicating the stages in an argument or process, or the items in a series:** *initially, at the outset, to begin with, first, first of all, up to now, so far, second, thus far, next, after, finally, last*

  Example:   The accounting process works in stages. First, transactions must be analyzed.

- **Giving a result:** *as a result, consequently, accordingly, as a consequence, therefore, thus, hence, then, for that reason*

  Example:   Generally accepted accounting principles allow flexibility in their application. Therefore, accountants are able to meet the changing needs of the business world.

- **Summing up or restating the central point:** *in sum, to sum up, to summarize, in summary, to conclude, in brief, in short, as one can see, in conclusion*

  Example:   In conclusion, transitions often make writing much easier to read.

## Repetition of Key Words and Phrases

Another way to add coherence to your writing is to repeat key words and phrases. Such repetitions are particularly useful for connecting paragraphs and major divisions of documents. These repetitions are typically located at the beginning of a new paragraph or section.

The following outline of a student's essay shows the structure of a discussion on alternatives to the historical cost basis of accounting. Notice how the combination of transitional expressions and repeated key phrases holds the report together. These techniques also tie the parts of the report to the main idea of the paper, which is summarized in the thesis statement. Notice how summary sentences appear throughout the outline.

## THE MONETARY UNIT ASSUMPTION

**I.** Introductory paragraph

    **A.** Introductory sentences

        One of the basic assumptions made by accountants is that money is an effective common denominator by which the operations of business enterprises can be measured and analyzed. Implicit in this assumption is the acceptance of the stable and unchanging nature of the monetary unit. However, the validity of this assumption has been questioned, not only by academicians and theorists but by practitioners as well.

    **B.** Thesis statement (main idea of entire paper)

        Several solutions have been proposed by accountants to correct for the changing value of the monetary unit.

**II.** Body

    **A.** Nature of the problem

        The unadjusted monetary unit system has been criticized because it distorts financial statements during periods of inflation.

    **B.** First solution to the problem

        **1.** One solution to overstating profits solely because of inflation is to adjust figures for changes in the general purchasing power of the monetary unit. (This paragraph describes the solution and its advantages.)

        **2.** However, the general purchasing power approach has been criticized for several reasons. (This paragraph describes the disadvantages of this approach.)

    **C.** Second solution to the problem

        **1.** Instead of the general purchasing power procedure, some favor adjusting for changes in replacement cost. (This paragraph describes this solution.)

        **2.** One of the major advantages of the replacement cost approach .... (This paragraph discusses several advantages.)

        **3.** One authority has summarized the criticisms of replacement cost accounting: "Most of the criticisms . . . ." (This paragraph discusses the disadvantages of this approach.)

    **D.** Third solution to the problem

        **1.** Still others favor a mark-to-market approach in which current exit values are used to value assets when possible.

        **2.** For certain assets, the FASB now requires the use of this approach. In general the advantages are . . . .

        **3.** Critics of widespread use of this approach argue that . . . .

**III.** Concluding paragraph

    Adjusting for changes in the general purchasing power, adjusting for changes in replacement cost, and the use of the mark-to-market approach represent attempts to correct the problems of the stable monetary unit assumption in times of inflation.

## Pronouns Used to Achieve Coherence

Another tool you can use to achieve coherent writing is the pronoun. A pronoun stands for a noun or a noun phrase that has previously been identified. The noun that the pronoun refers to is called its *antecedent*. Consider this sentence:

Investors expect that, over time, their portfolios will increase in value.

In this sentence, the pronoun *their* refers to the noun *investors*. Put another way, *investors* is the antecedent of *their*.

Because pronouns refer to nouns that the writer has already used, pronouns help connect the thoughts of a paragraph. Look at how the pronouns work in this paragraph:

The audit staff reviewed the financial statements of Western Manufacturing to determine whether the statements had been prepared in accordance with generally accepted accounting principles. *We* found two problems that may require *us* to issue a qualified opinion. First, Western has not been consistent in *its* treatment of accounts receivable. Second, *we* identified several transactions that may violate the matching principle. *We* suggest a meeting with Western's management to discuss these issues.

Using pronouns requires a word of warning, however. Unless a writer is careful, the reader may not be sure to what noun the pronoun refers. Look at the problem in this sentence:

The managers told the accountants that they did not understand company policy.

Who didn't understand company policy—the managers or the accountants? This sentence illustrates the problem of ambiguous pronoun reference. Chapter 5 discusses this problem further.

## Problems with Transitions

A few problems can occur with transitions other than the failure to use them when they are needed. One problem occurs when a writer uses transitional expressions too often. These expressions are necessary to make the relationship of ideas clear when there might be some confusion. Often this logical relationship is clear without the use of transitional expressions. Consider this paragraph:

Accountants never finish their education. They work hard for their college degrees; after college they must continue studying to stay current on the latest developments in the profession. They must be thoroughly familiar with changing government regulations and new pronouncements by professional organizations such as the FASB. To improve their professional competence, they participate in a variety of continuing education programs sponsored by such organizations as the AICPA and state accounting societies. Indeed, well-qualified accountants are lifetime students, always seeking better ways to serve their clients and the public.

Notice how easy this paragraph is to follow, even though it doesn't use a single transitional expression.

Another problem with transitions occurs when the writer uses the wrong expression, suggesting an illogical connection of ideas. Consider these examples:

FAULTY TRANSITION:   GAAP are not established by federal law. For instance, organizations such as the FASB issue these standards, and the FASB is not part of the federal government.

REVISED:   GAAP are not established by federal law. Rather, organizations that are not part of the federal government, such as the FASB, issue these standards.

FAULTY TRANSITION:   If accountants do not follow GAAP, they may lose their CPA licenses. Therefore, they must follow GAAP to conform to their code of professional ethics.

REVISED:   If accountants do not follow GAAP, they may lose their CPA licenses. They must also follow GAAP to conform to their code of professional ethics.

Transitions, when used correctly, are valuable tools for clarifying the relationship between ideas. If you use transitions carefully, along with summary sentences and a logical organization, your writing will be easy to follow.

The next sections of this chapter show how to use these techniques to write coherent paragraphs, discussion questions, essays, and other longer forms of writing.

# PARAGRAPHS

This section of the chapter is devoted to techniques of paragraphing: how to plan length, structure, and development so that your paragraphs are coherent.

## Length

You might not be sure how long paragraphs should be. Are one-sentence paragraphs acceptable? What about paragraphs that run on for nearly an entire typed page?

One rule is that a paragraph should be limited to the development of one idea. Thus, the length of most paragraphs is somewhere between one sentence and an entire page. However, an occasional short paragraph, even of only one sentence, can be effective to emphasize an idea or to provide a transition between two major divisions of the writing.

Be wary of long paragraphs, which look intimidating and are often hard to follow. You may need to divide a long paragraph into two or more shorter ones. Appropriate transitions can tie the new paragraphs together and maintain a smooth flow of thought.

> ***A good rule is to limit most of your paragraphs to four or five sentences.***

## Structure

Another feature of well-written paragraphs is an appropriate structure. We have already suggested that a strong topic sentence can contribute to a unified, coherent paragraph. A topic sentence states the main idea of the paragraph. It is usually the first sentence in the paragraph, and sometimes it contains a transition tying the new paragraph to the previous one. All other sentences in the paragraph should develop the idea expressed in the topic sentence.

Two patterns of paragraph organization are useful for most writing tasks that accountants will tackle: the simple deductive paragraph and the complex deductive paragraph. The simple deductive arrangement states the main idea in the first sentence (topic sentence); all other sentences *directly* develop that idea by adding details. A concluding sentence is sometimes helpful. Look again at this paragraph, which illustrates a simple deductive organization:

> (1) Accountants never finish their education. (2) They work hard for their college degrees, but after college they must continue studying to stay current on the latest developments in the profession. (3) They must be thoroughly familiar with changing government regulations and new pronouncements by professional organizations such as the FASB. (4) To improve their professional competence, they participate in a variety of continuing education programs sponsored by such organizations as the AICPA and state accounting societies. (5) Indeed, well-qualified accountants are lifetime students, always seeking better ways to serve their clients and the public.

In this paragraph, sentence 1 is the topic sentence, sentences 2 through 4 develop the main idea, and sentence 5 is the conclusion. A simple deductive paragraph has a simple structural diagram, such as this one:

> (1) Topic sentence—main idea
>    (2) Supporting sentence
>    (3) Supporting sentence
>    (4) Supporting sentence
> (5)   Concluding sentence (optional)

A complex deductive paragraph has a more elaborate structure. This paragraph is complex deductive:

> (1) Financial statements are important to a variety of users. (2) First, investors and potential investors use the statements to determine whether a company is a good investment risk. (3) These users look at

such factors as net income, the debt-to-equity ratio, retained earnings, and economic value added (EVA). (4) Second, creditors use financial statements to determine whether a firm is a good credit risk. (5) Creditors want to know whether a firm has a large enough cash flow to pay its debts. (6) Third, government agencies analyze financial statements for a variety of purposes. (7) For example, the Internal Revenue Service wants to know whether the company has paid the required amount of taxes on its income. (8) These examples of financial statement users show how diverse their interests can be.

In this paragraph, sentence 1 (the topic sentence) states the main idea. Sentence 2 directly supports the main idea by giving an example, but sentence 3 explains sentence 2. Thus, sentence 3 directly supports sentence 2, but it only indirectly supports sentence 1. Complex deductive paragraphs have a structural diagram similar to this one:

(1) Topic sentence—main idea
   (2) Direct support
      (3) Indirect support
   (4) Direct support
      (5) Indirect support
   (6) Direct support
      (7) Indirect support
(8) Conclusion (optional)

Complex deductive paragraphs can have numerous variations. The number of direct supporting sentences can vary, as can the number of indirect supports. Sometime direct supports do not require any indirect supports.

Consider another example of a complex deductive paragraph:

(1) Two of the most popular inventory flow assumptions used by businesses today are FIFO (first-in, first-out) and LIFO (last-in, first-out). (2) FIFO assumes that the first goods purchased for inventory are the first goods sold. (3) Therefore, ending inventory under FIFO consists of the most recent purchases. (4) Because older, usually lower, costs are matched with sales revenues, FIFO results in a higher net income and thus higher income tax liabilities. (5) The LIFO flow assumption, on the other hand, assumes that the most recent purchases are the first goods sold. (6) Cost of goods sold, however, is based on more recent and higher prices. (7) Thus, LIFO usually results in lower net income and lower income tax liabilities. (8) This advantage makes LIFO very popular with many businesses.

This paragraph can be outlined to reveal the following structure:

**I.** Topic sentence (1): Two popular inventory flow assumptions
  **A.** FIFO (2–4)
    **1.** Description (2)
    **2.** Effect on inventory (3)
    **3.** Effect on net income and taxes (4)

**B.** LIFO (5–8)
       **1.** Description (5)
       **2.** Effect on inventory (6)
       **3.** Effect on net income and taxes (7)
       **4.** Popularity (8)

The descriptions of FIFO and LIFO in this paragraph are very condensed, probably too condensed for most purposes. Moreover, the paragraph is really too long. It would probably be better to divide it between sentences 4 and 5, resulting in two shorter but closely related paragraphs:

> (1) Two of the most popular inventory flow assumptions used by businesses today are FIFO (first-in, first-out) and LIFO (last-in, first-out). (2) FIFO assumes that the first goods purchased for inventory are the first goods sold. (3) Therefore, ending inventory under FIFO consists of the most recent purchases. (4) Because older, usually lower, costs are matched with sales revenues, FIFO results in a higher net income and thus higher income tax liabilities.

> (5) The LIFO flow assumption, on the other hand, assumes that the most recent purchases are the first goods sold. (6) Cost of goods sold, however, is based on more recent and higher prices. (7) Thus, LIFO usually results in lower net income and lower income tax liabilities. (8) This advantage makes LIFO very popular with many businesses.

Both paragraphs now have simple deductive structures. However, the first paragraph is a modified version of a simple deductive structure because the main idea of this paragraph is in the second sentence.

The important idea about both simple and complex deductive paragraphs is their unity: All sentences, either directly or indirectly, develop the main idea of the paragraph as expressed in the topic sentence.

One advantage of deductive paragraphs is that they enable a reader to skim the document quickly and locate main ideas. A busy CEO, for example, may scan a document, reading only the first sentence of each paragraph.

Some writers might wonder about a third type of paragraph organization: paragraphs with an inductive structure. Inductive paragraphs put the main idea last. Supporting sentences lead up to the topic sentence, which is the last sentence in the paragraph. For most business writing, inductive paragraphs are not as effective as simple or complex deductive paragraphs. Business readers like to identify main ideas from the start. They don't like to be kept in suspense, wondering, "What's all this leading up to? What's the point?" Thus, it's a good idea to stick with deductive organization for most, if not all, of your paragraphs.

## Paragraph Development

An effective paragraph is not only well organized, but it is also well developed. That is, the idea expressed in the topic sentence is adequately explained and illustrated so that the reader has a clear understanding of what the writer is saying.

Several techniques are useful for paragraph development: descriptive and factual details, illustrations or examples, definitions, and appeals to authority.

Descriptive and factual details give a more thorough, concrete explanation of the idea that is expressed in a general way in the topic sentence. Factual details give measurable, observable, or historical information that can be objectively verified. Descriptive details are similar to factual details. They give specific characteristics of the subject being discussed.

When you use details with which your readers are familiar, they can better understand your observations and conclusions. In the following paragraph, the main idea is stated in the first sentence. The paragraph is then developed with factual details:

> Our net income for next year should increase because we've signed a contract with an important new customer. Flip's Frog Ponds, Inc., which last year had more than $4 billion in revenue, has ordered a million lily pads from our horticultural division. This new business should increase our revenues by at least 15%.

Another useful paragraph development technique is using illustrations or examples—typical cases or specific instances of the idea being discussed. Illustrations can take a variety of forms. A paragraph might combine several brief examples, or use one long, extended illustration. The examples can be factually true, or they may be hypothetical, invented for the purpose of illustration.

Definitions are useful to explain concepts or terms that might be unfamiliar to the reader. A definition can be formal, such as the meaning given in a dictionary or an accounting standard, or it can be a more informal explanation of a term. Often a definition is more effective when combined with an illustration.

The following paragraph is developed by definition and illustration:

> *Assets* can be defined as things of value (economic resources) owned by a business. For example, cash is an asset; so are the land, buildings, and equipment owned by a business. Sometimes assets are resources owned by a business, though not tangible. An example of this kind of asset is an account receivable.

Finally, some paragraphs are developed by appeals to authority— facts, illustrations, or ideas obtained from a reputable source such as a book, article, interview, or official pronouncement. Appeals to authority can be paraphrases—someone else's idea expressed in your own words—or direct quotations from the source being used. Chapter 8 gives more information on the correct use of quotations and paraphrases.

By using a variety of techniques, you can fully develop the ideas expressed in the topic sentences of your paragraphs. Factual and descriptive detail, illustration, definition, and authority all give the reader a clear understanding of what you want to explain.

However, if you decide to develop your paragraphs, remember the importance of your reader's interests and needs. It's better to select supporting details and examples with which the reader is already familiar.

## DISCUSSION QUESTIONS AND ESSAYS

A section about discussion questions and essays might seem too academic for a writing handbook for accountants, but many accounting students take exams with discussion questions. In addition, many of the principles of organizing and developing an essay are applicable to memos, reports, and other types of writing used by accountants in practice.

### Discussion Questions

The key to answering a short discussion question (one to three paragraphs) is to write well-organized deductive paragraphs with strong topic sentences. Usually, the question suggests the first sentence of the answer. Consider this example:

> Discuss the sources of authoritative accounting principles.

The answer to this discussion question might begin with the following sentence, which gives the main idea of the answer:

> Authoritative accounting principles derive from many sources.

The answer might then go on to discuss accounting principles promulgated by the FASB and its predecessor organizations. A second paragraph might then discuss accounting principles promulgated by the SEC and other governmental agencies. Finally, a third paragraph might discuss other less authoritative sources such as textbooks and articles in professional accounting publications. The third paragraph might begin with this topic sentence:

> Although less authoritative, textbooks and articles in professional accounting publications can also be important.

Short paragraphs with strong topic sentences, as in the answer outlined in the preceding paragraphs, will help the exam grader identify your main ideas and give you credit for what you know.

### Essays

Before you read this section, review the discussion of paragraph development on pages 41–42. Pay particular attention to the complex deductive pattern of organization.

Complex deductive paragraphs have a main idea (topic sentence) supported by major and minor supports.

Essays—discussions of four or more paragraphs—are similar to answers to discussion questions in their use of a deductive structure, with a few modifications. One difference is that the organization of an essay is complex deductive, in that it uses both major and minor supports of the essay's main idea (thesis statement). That is, the essay's paragraphs offer direct support of the thesis. The sentences within each paragraph develop the topic sentence of the paragraph, and thereby they indirectly support the thesis.

Another difference between an essay and a response to a discussion question is that the thesis statement (main idea of the essay) may come at the end of the first paragraph in which case it may be preceded by sentences that give background on the topic or otherwise interest the reader in what is being discussed. Finally, the conclusion of an essay may be longer and more complex than the conclusion of a discussion question response.

Below is the outline of a six-paragraph essay.

**I.** Introduction—first paragraph
  **A.** Attention-getting sentences (optional)
  **B.** Thesis statement—main idea of the essay, usually expressed in one sentence
**II.** Body of the essay—develops the thesis through analysis, explanation, examples, proofs, or steps
  **A.** Major support—second paragraph
    1.
    2. } Minor supports—sentences that develop the paragraph
    3.   in a simple or complex deductive organization
  **B.** Major support—third paragraph
    1.
    2. } Minor supports
    3.
  **C.** Major support—fourth paragraph
    1.
    2. } Minor supports
    3.
  **D.** Major support—fifth paragraph
    1.
    2. } Minor supports
    3.
**III.** Conclusion—sixth paragraph
  **A.** Repeats the essay's main idea (a variation of the thesis statement) or otherwise provides closure
  **B.** Forceful ending (optional)

Some of the parts of this outline need more discussion.

### Attention-Getting Sentences

Some essays begin with attention-getting sentences, which are intended to get the reader interested in the subject. Several techniques can be used:

- Give background information about the topic. Why is the topic of current interest?
- Pose a problem or raise a question (to be answered in the essay).
- Define key terms, perhaps the topic itself.
- Show the relevance of the topic to the reader.
- Begin with an interesting direct quotation.
- Relate a brief anecdote relevant to the topic.
- Relate the specific topic to a wider area of interest.

The following essay introduction uses two of these techniques. It poses a question and then suggests the relevance of the topic to the reader, assuming that the essay was written for accountants. The final sentence of the paragraph is the thesis statement.

> Do accountants need to be good writers? Some people would answer "No" to this question. They believe an accountant's job is limited to arithmetical calculations with very little need to use words or sentences. But this picture of an accountant's responsibilities is a misconception. In fact, good writing skills are essential to the successful practice of accounting.

Sometimes you might choose not to use attention-getting sentences but instead to begin your essay with the thesis statement. This is a particularly good strategy to use for exam questions.

### Thesis Statement

The thesis statement summarizes the main idea of the essay, usually in one sentence. It can be a *simple* thesis statement, such as the following:

> Good writing skills are essential to the successful practice of accounting.

Alternatively, the thesis statement can be *expanded*. That is, it can summarize the main supports of the discussion. Here is an example of an expanded thesis statement:

> In fact, successful accountants must have good writing skills to communicate with clients, managers, agencies, and colleagues.

Sometimes, to avoid a long or awkward sentence, you might want to use two sentences for the thesis statement:

> In fact, good writing skills are essential to the successful practice of accounting. For example, during a typical business day, an accountant may write to clients, managers, agencies, or colleagues.

### Conclusion

The conclusion should provide the reader with a sense of closure—a feeling that the essay is complete and that the train of thought has come to a logical end. You can give your essays closure by repeating the main idea, usually in some variation of the thesis statement. You may also want to end with a forceful statement that will stay in the reader's mind, thus giving the discussion a more lasting impact. For a strong ending, you can use several techniques, many of which resemble those used in the introduction:

- Show a broad application of the ideas suggested in the discussion.
- End with an authoritative direct quotation that reinforces your position.
- Challenge the reader.
- Echo the attention-getting sentences. For example, if you began by posing a question in the introduction, you can answer it explicitly in the conclusion.

If you're writing an essay on an exam, a concluding paragraph might not be necessary, but it's important that the essay seem finished. The essay will seem complete if you've developed your thesis statement fully.

## Applying Essay Techniques to Other Kinds of Writing

If you are answering an essay question on an exam, you can use the techniques just discussed to organize and develop an effective discussion. Chapter 12, which discusses essay exams more fully, provides additional suggestions. But how do the techniques you use for essays work with the writing formats more typically used by accountants (letters, memos, and reports)?

Everything you write should have a main idea. In an essay, this idea is called the thesis statement; in a memo or report, the main idea might be included in the statement of purpose or recommendations. Whatever you're writing, you should identify the main idea before you even begin your outline. Unless this idea is clear in your mind—or clearly written in your notes—your writing may be rambling and confusing. Your reader might then wonder, "What's this person trying to say? What's the point?"

Whatever you write should be organized around a central idea, just as an essay is organized. Letters, reports, and memos share other features of an essay as well: a basic three-part structure (introduction, body, conclusion), complex deductive organization, and the need for adequate transitions and concrete support.

If you understand the principles discussed in this chapter, you will find it easier to plan and organize the writing tasks that are part of your professional responsibilities.

## Sample Essay

The following is an assignment for an essay given in an accounting class. The answer in Figure 3–1 illustrates some of the principles of good organization and development.

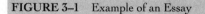

FIGURE 3–1     Example of an Essay

### The Importance of International Accounting Standards

The need for international accounting standards has received great attention since the late 1980s. Increasing globalization of business and capital markets has been the major reasons for this attention. When different countries have different business regulations and use different accounting methods, the increased complexity of conducting business and raising capital across national borders presents major challenges. By analogy, consider how difficult the reporting process in our own country would be if each of the 50 states employed different business regulations and a different set of accounting standards. Clearly, in such a case our capital markets as reflected by the activities of the New York Stock Exchange and the NASDAQ could not operate as efficiently or robustly as they now do.

If investors in international capital markets must make investment choices among corporations that use different accounting standards, competing investment opportunities become less comparable and much more risky. The result is likely to be that fewer investors will undertake the effort or assume the risk of investing in foreign corporations or in corporations that have a lot of foreign holdings. Consequently, fewer corporations may list their securities on a foreign exchange. Ultimately, such difficulties could seriously impede the expansion of international capital markets and the development of more healthy international economies.

The International Accounting Standards Board (IASB) has been responsible for setting international standards since 2001. Together with its predecessor, the International Accounting Standards Committee (IASC), these two organizations have issued numerous International Accounting Standards (IASs) and International Financial Reporting Standards (IFRSs). Through its efforts the IASB hopes to achieve convergence of international financial reporting standards.

Most international accounting organizations, securities exchanges, and governments support the basic concept of harmonization of standards. Several of the world's securities exchanges either permit or require compliance with IASs and IFRSs by their registrants. The International Organization of Securities Commissions (IOSCO) and the Organization for Economic Cooperation and Development (OECD) cooperate with the IASB in its development of international financial reporting standards. The European Union has accepted the international standards issued by the IASC and the IASB for its member countries.

Although the prospect for uniform financial reporting standards among all countries is not realistic, reducing differences through the concept of harmonization is clearly a worthwhile goal.

*Assignment.* The International Accounting Standards Board (IASB) is responsible for the development of a set of international accounting standards. Explain in 300 to 500 words why the development of international accounting standards may be important.

This chapter has added four guidelines to our list of ways to make your writing more effective. We now have seven guidelines:

1. Analyze the purpose of the writing, the accounting issues involved, and the needs and expectations of the readers.
2. Organize your ideas so that readers will find them easy to follow.
3. Write the draft and then revise it to make the writing polished and correct.
4. Make the writing unified. All sentences should relate to the main idea, either directly or indirectly. Eliminate digressions and irrelevant detail.
5. Use summary sentences and transitions to make your writing coherent.
6. Write in short paragraphs that begin with clear topic sentences.
7. Develop paragraphs by illustration, definition, detail, and appeals to authority.

## TEST YOURSELF

Is the following paragraph coherent? If not, revise it to improve its organization, using some of these techniques:

- Write a strong topic sentence stating the paragraph's main idea.
- Use transitional devices to show the relation between sentences.
- Eliminate sentences that don't fit.
- Divide long, disunified paragraphs into shorter, unified ones.
- Rearrange sentences by grouping together ideas (add sentences if necessary).

Accountants used to enter data into spreadsheets by hand. Accountants performed calculations by hand, and they had adding machines. Much of the work accountants did in the past was tedious and time consuming. Computers have drastically changed the practice of accounting. If accountants made errors, accountants would have to erase the mistakes with chemicals that would dissolve the ink. These chemicals could stain their clothes and sometimes irritate their skin and make their desks messy.

## TEST YOURSELF: ANSWER

This paragraph needs revision. Here is one possibility:

Computers have drastically changed the practice of accounting in the past few decades. In the past, accountants performed calculations by hand, or perhaps with the help of adding machines. They entered data into spreadsheets by hand; if they made errors in their entries, they would have to erase the mistakes with chemicals that dissolved the ink, or they would have to enter the data again from the beginning. These examples suggest that much of the work accountants did in the past was tedious and time consuming.

# EXERCISES

## Exercise 3–1 [Financial]

Write about the following topics using the techniques covered in this and earlier chapters. Your answers might range from one to six paragraphs or more, depending on the topic.

1. Discuss the role of *relevance* in accounting theory.
2. Discuss the role of the Conceptual Framework in the setting of accounting standards by the FASB.
3. Explain the difference between revenues and gains.
4. Explain the differences among depreciation, amortization, and depletion.
5. Discuss three different valuation bases used in generally accepted accounting principles.
6. Discuss the importance of convergence in the context of setting international accounting standards.

## Exercise 3–2 [Systems]

Write about the following topics using the techniques covered in this and earlier chapters. Your answers may range from one to six paragraphs or more, depending on the topic.

1. Define internal control, and discuss its importance.
2. Explain the role of a controller in a medium-size business.
3. Explain what an REA data model is and how it is used.
4. Discuss the fundamentals of data storage.
5. What are some reasons for computer fraud? How can businesses protect themselves from this danger?

## Exercise 3–3 [Systems]

Write about the following topics using the techniques covered in this and earlier chapters. Your answers might range from one to six paragraphs or more, depending on the topic.

1. Explain the two approaches to database design, normalization, and semantic data modeling.
2. A database can view data in either a physical view or a logical view. Explain each of these views and when each may be useful.
3. Explain what COBIT is and the benefits of its use.
4. Explain the Systems Development Life Cycle, which describes the design and implementation of an information system. What role do accountants play in this cycle?

## Exercise 3–4 [Managerial]

Write about the following topics using the techniques covered in this and earlier chapters. Your answers might range from one to six paragraphs or more, depending on the topic.

1. Discuss the pros and cons of centralized and decentralized managerial decision making.
2. Discuss what the phrase "different costs for different purposes" means in managerial accounting.
3. Discuss the why ethics is important in managerial accounting.
4. Discuss what is meant by the concept of *relevant range* and why it is important.
5. Discuss what cost pools are and how they may be used to allocate costs.

## Exercise 3–5 [Auditing]

Write about the following topics using the techniques covered in this and earlier chapters. Your answers might range from one to six paragraphs or more, depending on the topic.

1. Discuss the purpose and requirements of a review of public company interim financial information.
2. Discuss the role of the National Peer Review Committee (NPRC), which was formally known as the Center for Public Company Audit Firms Peer Review Program (CPCAFPRP).
3. Discuss what the consequences may be if the Public Company Accounting Oversight Board (PCAOB) finds significant performance deficiencies during its inspection of an audit firm.
4. Discuss why it is so important to gain an understanding of a client's business and industry before planning an audit.

## Exercise 3–6 [Tax]

Write about the following topics using the techniques covered in this and earlier chapters. Your purpose is to provide a very general explanation to readers who have never heard of these terms or topics. Your answers might range from one to six paragraphs or more, depending on the topic.

1. Discuss the concepts of *dependency exemption* and *personal exemption* as they apply to the income tax of individuals.
2. Discuss the concept of *constructive receipt* as it applies to the income tax of individuals.
3. Discuss the American Opportunity Tax Credit and the Lifetime Learning Credit, including the requirements of these credits.
4. For individual tax purposes, why is the distinction between deductions *for* adjusted gross income and deductions *from* adjusted gross income important?
5. Discuss the distinction between Treasury Regulations and Revenue Rulings and the role each plays.

# CHAPTER

# A Sense of Style: Writing with Conciseness and Clarity

So far we've looked at writing mainly as an organizational task: planning the structure and contents of the paper so that it achieves its purpose in a way readers will find meaningful. We have stressed the quality of coherence: writing that is easy to follow, with main ideas that stand out. Chapters 2 and 3 looked at writing in terms of large units. They discussed the structure of the paper as a whole and the organization of sections and paragraphs.

We turn now to a more detailed level of effective writing. This chapter looks at word choices and sentence structures that contribute to a vigorous and readable writing style. In this discussion of style, we emphasize two other important qualities of effective writing: conciseness and clarity (two of the writing tips listed in Figure 1–2 in Chapter 1).

## CONCISENESS

Readers prefer concise writing so they can find the information they need quickly and easily. Chapter 3 suggested several ways to make your writing more concise by eliminating digressions and irrelevant detail. In general, concise writing contains no unnecessary elements_no extra words, phrases, sentences, or paragraphs. This makes up the eighth rule of effective writing:

*Be concise—make every word count.*

### Unnecessary Words

The easiest way to make every word count is to see how many words you can cross out of your writing, often with only a simple revision of the sentence. These examples show how sentences can be revised by eliminating unnecessary words:

WORDY: We are hopeful that all the clients we serve will avail themselves of these additional services that we will offer to them. [22 words]

CONCISE: We hope all our clients will use these additional services that we will soon offer. [15 words]

WORDY: Profits forecast for the coming year range all the way from $300,000 to upward of $500,000. [16 words]

CONCISE: Forecast profits for next year range from $300,000 to $500,000. [10 words]

WORDY: There is one organization that has been very influential in improving the profession of accounting: the AICPA. [17 words]

CONCISE: The AICPA has improved the accounting profession significantly. [8 words]

WORDY: To stay informed on the latest information, accountants must read a great number of published materials about accounting. [18 words]

CONCISE: To stay current, accountants must read many accounting publications. [9 words]

WORDY: In order to reach our tax liability reduction goals, we changed the way we accounted for the purchase. [18 words]

CONCISE: To reduce our tax liability, we changed the way we accounted for the purchase. [14 words]

Watch out for *there is* and *there are*. They can usually be eliminated. *The fact that, which is*, *who is*, and *which are* can sometimes be left out as well:

WORDY: There are several planning strategies that we can use to reduce our income taxes. [14 words]

CONCISE: We can reduce our income taxes through strategic planning. [9 words]

WORDY: I would like to call your attention to the fact that we have a staff meeting scheduled for next Wednesday. [20 words]

CONCISE: Remember our staff meeting scheduled for next Wednesday. [8 words]

*or (even better)*

We have a staff meeting next Wednesday. [7 words]

WORDY: In spite of the fact that our costs rose by 10%, we still were able to keep our prices stable. [21 words]

CONCISE: Although costs rose by 10%, our prices remained stable. [10 words]

## Simplicity

Another way to make your writing concise is to write as simply as possible. Sometimes writers get into the habit of using big words and long, complicated sentences. Such writing is hard to read.

CHAPTER 4     A Sense of Style: Writing with Conciseness and Clarity     53

SEC Commissioner, Cynthia A. Glassman, offered this example of a footnote disclosure that is almost impossible to understand:[1]

> Any interest collections on the loans remaining after payments of interest on the notes and the company's expenses will be available to cover any losses on the loans that are not covered by the insurance policies.

Glassman suggests this translation into plain English:

> After we pay our expenses and interest on the notes, we will use any remaining funds to cover uninsured losses.

The ninth technique for effective writing style is simplicity.

### *Keep it simple—simple vocabulary and short sentences.*

Good writers use short, everyday words as much as possible. For example, they usually write *use* instead of *utilize* and *help* instead of *assistance*. Shorter, familiar words are easier to read and make writing more forceful.

Table 4–1 shows two columns of words. Column B lists short, familiar words; Column A lists longer, more difficult words that are often substituted for the everyday words in Column B. The table also shows how single words (*because*) can often replace phrases (*for the reason that*). As a general rule, use the words and phrases in Column B rather than those in Column A. Some of the terms in Column A can be omitted (such as *it should be noted that*).

Another way to achieve a simple, readable style is to use short sentences. Short sentences are particularly important when you are explaining complicated ideas.

### *The average sentence should be about 15 words long.*

Note that 15 words is an *average*. Some sentences are longer, some shorter. In fact, it's a good idea to vary sentence lengths so that the writing doesn't become monotonous. Sentence variation will be discussed again later in this chapter.

## Verbs and Nouns

Another technique to make writing more concise is to use active verbs and descriptive nouns, rather than lots of adverbs and adjectives. The tenth rule of effective writing is:

### *Write with active verbs and descriptive nouns.*

See how this sentence can be improved:

WORDY:   There are many positive advantages to making investments in the latest state-of-the-art technology [16 words]
CONCISE: State-of-the-art technology offers many advantages. [8 words]

**TABLE 4–1** Simplifying Word Choices

As a rule, use the words and phrases in Column B rather than those in Column A.

| Column A | Column B |
| --- | --- |
| above-mentioned firms | these firms |
| absolutely essential | essential |
| activate | begin |
| advise | tell |
| aggregate | total |
| along the lines of | like |
| anticipate | expect |
| as per your request | as you requested |
| assist | help |
| at all times | always |
| at this point in time | now |
| at this time | now |
| attempt | try |
| commence | begin |
| communicate | write, tell |
| completely eliminated | eliminated |
| comprise | include |
| consider | think |
| constitute | are, is |
| discontinue | stop |
| disutility | uselessness |
| due to the fact that | because |
| during the time that | while |
| earliest convenience | promptly, soon |
| effort | work |
| enclosed herewith | enclosed |
| enclosed please find | enclosed is |
| endeavor | try |
| exercise care | be careful |
| facilitate | ease, simplify |
| failed to | didn't |
| few in number | few |
| for the purpose of | for |
| for the reason that | since, because |
| from the point of view that | for |
| furnish | send, give |
| i.e. | that is |
| implement | carry out |
| in advance of | before |
| in all cases | always |
| in many cases | often |
| in most cases | usually |
| on behalf of | for |
| in connection with | about |
| in terms of | in |
| in the amount of | of, for |
| in the case of | if |
| in the event that (of) | if |

(cont.)

**TABLE 4–1**    *(cont.)*

| Column A | Column B |
| --- | --- |
| in the nature of | like |
| in the neighborhood of | about |
| in this case | here |
| indicate | show, point out |
| initiate | begin |
| in view of the fact that | because |
| inasmuch as | since |
| investigate | study |
| it has come to my attention | Ms. Jones has just told me; I have just learned |
| it is felt | I feel; we feel |
| it is our understanding that | we understand that |
| it should be noted that | (omit) |
| maintain | keep |
| maintain cost control | control cost |
| make a purchase | buy |
| make application to | apply |
| make contact with | see, meet |
| maximum | most, largest |
| minimum | least, smallest |
| modification | change |
| obtain | get |
| on the order of | about |
| on the part of | by |
| optimum | best |
| past history | history |
| per annum | annually, per year |
| period of time | time, period |
| pertaining to | about, for |
| philosophy | plan, idea |
| please be advised that | (omit) |
| prepare an analysis | analyze |
| presently | now |
| prior to | before |
| procure | get, buy |
| provide | give |
| provide continuous indication | indicate continuously |
| pursuant to your inquiry | as you requested |
| range all the way from | range from |
| regarding | about |
| relative to | about |
| represent | be, is, are |
| require | need |
| so as to | to |
| subsequent to | after, later |
| substantial | large, big |
| sufficient | enough |
| terminate | end, stop |
| the major part of | most of |
| the manner in which | how |

*(cont.)*

**TABLE 4–1**   *(cont.)*

| Column A | Column B |
| --- | --- |
| the undersigned; the writer | I, me |
| thereon, thereof, thereto, therefrom | (omit) |
| this is to acknowledge | thank you for; I have received |
| this is to inform you that we shall send | we'll send |
| through the use of | by, with |
| transpire | happen |
| true facts | facts |
| under separate cover | by June 1, tomorrow, separately, by parcel post |
| until such time as | until |
| utilize | use |
| vital | important |
| with a view to | to |
| with reference to | about |
| with regard to | about |
| with respect to | on, for, of, about |
| with the object to | to |
| with the result that | so that |

One common cause of wordy writing is hidden verbs. For example,

> **came to a conclusion** instead of **concluded**
> **causes a misstatement of** instead of **misstates**
> **makes an analysis of** instead of **analyzes**
> **will serve as an explanation of** instead of **will explain**

What are the hidden verbs in the following sentences?

> Maria Ortega made reference to recent research in her report.
> The company's history of marginal performance over the past several years may be an indication of future solvency problems.

In the first sentence, the hidden verb is *refer*; in the second sentence, it is *indicate*. The revised sentences are a little less wordy, a little more forceful:

> Maria Ortega referred to recent research in her report.
> The company's history of marginal performance over the past several years may indicate future solvency problems.

Here are some other sentences with hidden verbs, followed by revisions to make them more concise:

HIDDEN VERB:   The IT specialist made an analysis of the department's computer problems. [11 words]

    REVISED:   The IT specialist analyzed the department's computer problems. [8 words]

HIDDEN VERB:  The manager will make a recommendation concerning the best way to record this transaction. [14 words]

REVISED:  The manager will recommend the best way to record this transaction. [11 words]

HIDDEN VERB:  I have come to the conclusion that we should update our equipment. [12 words]

REVISED:  I have concluded that we should update our equipment. [9 words]

HIDDEN VERB:  This method will result in a distribution of the costs between the balance sheet and the income statement. [18 words]

REVISED:  This method will distribute the costs between the balance sheet and the income statement. [14 words]

HIDDEN VERB:  We are able to make the determination of the historical cost of an asset due to the fact that we have records of its purchase. [25 words]

Revised:  We can determine an asset's historical cost because we have records of its purchase. [14 words]

Finally, avoid sentence introductions that weaken the sentence idea. Don't apologize for or hedge about what you're saying:

WORDY:  Enclosed please find our invoice for $400. [7 words]
CONCISE:  Our invoice for $400 is enclosed. [6 words]

WORDY:  It has come to my attention that this software is obsolete. [11 words]
CONCISE:  This software is obsolete. [4 words]

WORDY:  This memo is an attempt to explain how we should account for the investment in new computers. [17 words]
CONCISE:  This memo explains how we should account for the new computers. [11 words]

WORDY:  This is to acknowledge receipt of your letter of June 1. [11 words]
CONCISE:  Thank you for your letter of June 1. [8 words]

WORDY:  This is to inform you that we are sending a check in the amount of $798.14. [16 words]
CONCISE:  We're sending a check for $798.14. [6 words]

In summary, clear, readable writing contains no unnecessary or dead words. Be concise_your writing will be more forceful.

# CLARITY

Clarity is important; unless the writing is clear, the reader may find it difficult to understand. One way to write clearly is to be concise so that important ideas are not buried in unnecessary words and details. Writing as simply as possible will also help you achieve clarity because you'll be using words the reader knows and feels comfortable using.

Other techniques for improving the clarity of your writing include the careful use of jargon and precise, concrete word choices.

## Jargon

Jargon is the "technical terminology . . . of a special activity."[2] We all know what accounting jargon is. It's words and phrases such as *amortization, accrual, debit, GAAP,* and *deferred income taxes*.

One kind of jargon is acronyms: words composed of the first letter of a group of words, such as *FASB, GAAP,* and *LIFO*. To introduce an acronym, write out the words of the acronym, with the acronym in parentheses:

> One of the earliest groups to set accounting standards was the Committee on Accounting Procedure (CAP).

After you have identified the acronym, you can use the acronym alone throughout the rest of the document. If you're sure that the readers will be familiar with an acronym, and if you're writing an informal document, it's usually acceptable to use the acronym without writing it out.

Unless you use acronyms and other forms of jargon carefully, they will detract from the clarity of your writing. Two guidelines can help you decide when to use jargon and when to look for other words. The first is to remember the readers' needs and to use language they will understand. Another accountant will probably understand what you mean by *straight-line depreciation*, but managers or clients who have not studied accounting may not. Be careful when using jargon even with your accounting colleagues. Would everyone with a degree in accounting know what you mean by *back-flush costing*?

The second guideline for the use of jargon is to keep your word choices as simple as possible. Avoid jargon when ordinary language will say what you mean. For example, why say "the bottom line" if you mean net income or loss?

Of course, jargon is often unavoidable when you need to communicate technical information as efficiently as possible, but remember the needs of your readers. Define or explain any technical terminology with which they may not be familiar, as stated in the next rule of effective writing:

> *Use jargon only when your readers understand it.*
> *Define technical terms when necessary.*

## Precise Meaning

Precision is one of the most important elements of clear writing. Word choices must be accurate, and sentences must be constructed so that their meaning is clear. Precision is particularly important in accountants' writing because accountants are often legally responsible for the accuracy of what they write. Moreover, the technical nature of accounting makes precise writing a necessity. Thus, the next rule for an effective writing style is precision.

### Be precise—avoid ambiguous and unclear writing.

*Word Choices*

Imprecise writing has several causes. One culprit is poor diction, or the inaccurate use of words:

> The major *setback* of the current method is that it is inefficient. [Poor diction. The writer meant *drawback*.]

> The advantage of measurements in terms of market values is that the values reflect *what the item is worth*. [What is the precise meaning of the italicized phrase? *Worth* is vague.]

In these examples, the diction problems are italicized:

POOR DICTION:  Our advertising expense, which is 1 percent of total sales, is a *negligent* amount.

REVISED:  Our advertising expense, which is 1 percent of total sales, is a negligible amount.

POOR DICTION:  The reason for this purchase was to *help from* liquidating LIFO layers.

REVISED:  The reason for this purchase was to prevent the liquidation of LIFO layers.

POOR DICTION:  This memo will discuss how to account for the *theft of* the convenience store. [This sentence says that the convenience store itself was carried off.]

REVISED:  This memo will discuss how to account for the robbery at the convenience store.

Unclear, awkward writing can also result from the misuse of words ending in *-ing*:

AWKWARD AND UNCLEAR:  The lease does not meet the 90 percent test, therefore classifying the lease as an operating lease.

REVISED:  The lease does not meet the 90 percent test, so it must be classified as an operating lease.

AWKWARD AND UNCLEAR:  In finding out this information, we will have to be thorough in our asking of questions of the concerned parties.

REVISED:  To find out this information, we must thoroughly question the concerned parties.

*Faulty Modifiers*

Another type of imprecise writing is misplaced and dangling modifiers. With a misplaced modifier, the modifying word or phrase is not placed next to the sentence element it modifies. The result is a confusing sentence:

> Process cost systems are often used by businesses that manufacture products for general distribution *such as oil refineries and dairies*. [The italicized phrase appears to modify *products*, but it really modifies *businesses*.]

> Process cost systems are often used by businesses such as oil refineries and dairies, which manufacture products for general distribution.

Consider another sentence with a misplaced modifier:

> This technique identifies tax returns for audits with a high probability of error.

Revised:

> To identify tax returns for audit, this technique flags returns that have a high probability of error.

Dangling modifiers, which usually come at the beginning of a sentence, do not actually modify any word in the sentence. Usually the word modified is implied rather than stated directly. Look at this sentence:

> After buying the bonds, the market price will fluctuate.

The writer probably meant something like this:

> After we buy the bonds, the market price will fluctuate.

Here's another example:

> As a successful company, disclosure of quarterly profits will attract investors.

One possible revision:

> Because we are a successful company, disclosure of our quarterly profits will attract investors.

### Pronoun Reference

Faulty pronoun reference can also cause writing to be ambiguous and confusing:

> Capitalization of interest is adding interest to the cost of an asset under construction which increases its book value.

The meaning of this sentence is unclear. What increases book value? *Which* and *its* are confusing; their references are vague. Here is one possible revision:

> Capitalization of interest is adding interest to the cost of an asset under construction. The added interest increases the asset's book value.

CHAPTER 4    A Sense of Style: Writing with Conciseness and Clarity    **61**

Faulty pronoun reference can be labeled *vague*, *ambiguous*, or *broad*. These terms all mean that the writer doesn't make clear what the pronoun refers to. The pronoun *this* is particularly troublesome:

FAULTY REFERENCE:   The regulations affecting our industry have changed substantially since we issued statements last year. Because of *this*, we plan a seminar to explain the new regulations.

REVISED:   The regulations affecting our industry have changed substantially since we issued statements last year. Because of these changes, we plan a seminar to explain the new regulations.

FAULTY REFERENCE:   The use of generally accepted accounting principles does not always produce the true financial position of a company. *This* is a problem for the FASB.

REVISED:   The use of generally accepted accounting principles does not always produce the true financial position of a company. This weakness in the principles is a problem for the FASB.

A good rule is to never use *this* by itself. Add a noun or phrase to define what *this* is.

Another pronoun that can cause reference problems is *it*:

FAULTY REFERENCE:   Many people prefer to itemize deductions for their income tax to decrease their tax liability, but *it* is not always done.

REVISED:   Many people prefer to itemize deductions for their income tax, but not everyone chooses to itemize.

Misplaced and dangling modifiers and faulty pronoun reference are grammatical errors, which are discussed further in Chapter 5. However, writing can be grammatically correct and still be imprecise. Consider this sentence:

The major drawback of the current value method is verifiability.

Revised:

The major drawback of the current value method is the lack of verifiability.

The revision makes quite a difference in meaning!

Often, the ability to write precisely is a function of careful reading and critical thinking. For example, an accounting professor assigned his Accounting Theory students two papers for the quarter. He then wrote the following statement on the board:

An Accounting Theory student who completes the course requirements for this class will write a total of two papers this semester. True or false?

The careful thinkers in the class realized that the statement might not be true. The students could write papers for other classes as well. Therefore, some students could write more than two papers for the semester.

Learn to analyze carefully what you read and then you'll be able to perfect your own writing so that your meanings are clear and precise.

Here are some other examples of sentences revised to improve their clarity:

UNCLEAR: This bond is not considered risky because it sells at only 70 percent of its maturity.

REVISED: The selling price of this bond, which is 70 percent of its maturity value, does not necessarily indicate that the bond is risky.

UNCLEAR: When purchasing bonds at a discount, the investment cost is less than the face value of the investment.

REVISED: When bonds sell at a discount, the investment cost is less than the face value of the investment.

## Concrete, Specific Wording

Chapter 3 discussed using concrete facts, details, and examples to develop paragraphs. Concrete, specific writing adds clarity to your documents and makes them much more interesting.

Concrete writing can be best explained by defining its opposite: abstract writing. Abstract writing is vague, general, or theoretical. Abstract writing is hard to understand because it's not illustrated by particular, material objects. Concrete writing, on the other hand, is vivid and specific; it brings a picture into the reader's mind. Concrete writing is next on the list of effective writing techniques.

Illustrations of abstract and concrete writing styles make them easier to understand:

ABSTRACT: Historical cost is important in accounting. It is easy for accountants to use, and it is often seen in the financial statements. Historical cost has some disadvantages, but it has its good points, too.

CONCRETE: Historical cost is the amount of money paid for an object when it was purchased. For example, if a truck was purchased in 2011 for $60,000, then $60,000 is the truck's historical cost. Many accountants favor historical cost accounting because the values of assets are easy to determine from invoices and other records of the original purchase.

However, in times of inflation the historical cost of an asset may not indicate its true value. For example, an acre of land bought in 1980 for $20,000 might be worth several times that amount today, but it would still be recorded in the owner's books and on the balance sheet at its historical cost. Thus, one disadvantage of historical cost accounting is that it often undervalues assets.

By giving more detailed information and specific, concrete examples of historical cost, the second example makes this concept easier to understand and more interesting to read.

In the following examples, vague, abstract sentences are replaced by more concrete writing:

VAGUE:    Accountants should write well.
REVISED:  Accountants need to write clear, concise letters to their clients and other business associates. [This sentence replaces the vague *well* with two characteristics of effective writing: *clear* and *concise*. The revision also gives an example of one type of accountants' writing: letters to clients and associates.]

VAGUE:    Action on today's stock market was interesting.
REVISED:  The Dow Jones Industrial Average dropped 223 points today.

The example just given illustrates a particularly effective technique you can use to make your writing concrete: Illustrate your ideas with specific details about the situation you're discussing. That is, if you're writing about action on the stock market, as in the example above, add relevant details about what happened to clarify what you mean.

By adding specific, concrete details, you will avoid vague sentences like this one:

We should disclose this expense because of comparability.

If we revise the sentence to be more specific and concrete, the meaning becomes much clearer:

We should disclose the advertising expense so that this year's statements will be comparable to those of prior years.

See how specific wording improves the clarity of this sentence:

VAGUE:  This liability should appear on the income statement because of materiality.
CLEAR:  This liability should appear on the income statement because the amount is material.

Finally, remember the readers' interests when you select the details to include in your writing; choose the details they will find meaningful and relevant. Which of the following two sentences would you prefer to read in a letter from your tax accountant?

Your tax situation this year poses some interesting possibilities.

If you can document your business expenses this year with the necessary receipts, you may be eligible for a refund of at least $5,500.

*Be concrete and specific—use facts, details, and examples.*

## READABLE WRITING

If your writing is interesting to read, it will almost always be clear. Lively, natural sentences hold readers' attention and keep them involved in what you are saying, so they have an easier time understanding your ideas.

This section of the chapter is devoted to several techniques that will make your sentences readable and clear: using active voice, writing with variety and rhythm, and using the appropriate tone.

## Passive and Active Voice

This technique for achieving a good writing style might seem technical, but it will become clear after a few definitions and examples.

### *Use active voice for most sentences.*

In the active voice, the subject of the sentence performs the action described by the verb.

ACTIVE: Most corporations issue financial statements at least once a year.

Passive voice, on the other hand, describes an action done to somebody or something by another agent. The agent is not always named in the sentence.

PASSIVE: Financial statements are issued (by most corporations) at least once a year.

This formula will help you identify passive voice verbs:

| Passive voice | = | a form of the verb *to be* | + | the past participle of another verb (usually ending in *-ed*) |
|---|---|---|---|---|

| **Forms of the verb to be:** | **Typical past participles:** |
|---|---|
| is, are, were, was, been, being, be, am | accrued, received, used, computed, given, kept |

Sometimes passive verb phrases also contain a form of *to have* (*has, have, had, having*) or an auxiliary (*will, should, would, must*, and so on), but passive voice always contains a *to be* form plus a past participle.

Active voice sentences are often clearer than passive voice sentences. Consider these examples:

PASSIVE: It is predicted that the stock's price will double. [In this example, most readers would want to know who made the prediction.]
ACTIVE: The controller predicted that the stock's price will double.

PASSIVE: It was decided that employees would be required to work on Saturday.
ACTIVE: The company president decided to require employees to work on Saturday.

PASSIVE: Deliberate understatement of assets and stockholders' equity with the intention of misleading interested parties is prohibited.
ACTIVE: SEC regulations prohibit deliberate misstatement of assets and stockholders' equity if the intention is to mislead interested parties.

Unfortunately, writers of "officialese," especially in government, business, and research, have so badly overused passive voice that we tend to accept it as standard style. Passive voice is seldom effective—it lacks the forcefulness and clarity of active voice. Compare the following pairs of sentences:

PASSIVE:  The correct procedures for inventory control weren't followed.
ACTIVE:   The manager didn't follow the correct procedures for inventory control.

PASSIVE:  A determination has been made that the statements are in violation of GAAP.
ACTIVE:   The auditors have determined that the statements are in violation of GAAP.

PASSIVE:  Further research should be conducted before an opinion can be issued.
ACTIVE:   The auditors should conduct further research before they issue an opinion.

PASSIVE:  In SAS No. 1, it is required that items such as these be disclosed in the financial statements.
ACTIVE:   SAS No. 1 requires that the financial statements disclose items such as these.

Good writers avoid using passive voice in most situations. They ask themselves two questions: What is the action (verb)? Who or what is doing it (subject)?

One word of warning: Avoid substituting a weak active verb for passive voice. Be particularly careful of colorless verbs such as *to exist* and *to occur*. The following sentences are written in active voice, but the sentences are weak:

Capitalization of option costs on land subsequently purchased should occur.

FIFO bases itself on the assumption that the first inventory acquired is the first inventory sold.

Use descriptive, vigorous verbs to substitute for weak verbs:

We must capitalize option costs on land subsequently purchased.

The assumption that underlies FIFO is that the first inventory acquired is the first inventory sold.

*When to Use Passive Voice*

Although it's usually better to write in active voice, passive voice is sometimes preferable. For example, the two sentences in the preceding example could be effectively written in passive voice:

Option costs on land subsequently purchased should be capitalized.

FIFO is based on the assumption that the first inventory acquired is the first inventory sold.

Passive voice may also be necessary to avoid an awkward repetition of sentence subjects, especially in paragraphs where the same agent is performing all the action or the agent is obvious or irrelevant:

> The property was appraised in 2011 at $400,000.

In this sentence, it would probably not be necessary to identify who did the appraisal.

Another consideration about active and passive voice is that sometimes you may want to emphasize the passive subject. For example, you would say:

> The Corner Grocery Store was robbed.

rather than:

> Some person or persons unknown robbed the Corner Grocery Store.

Finally, passive voice may enable you to be tactful when you must write bad news or some sort of criticism:

> These figures were not calculated correctly.

This sentence doesn't say who is at fault for the erroneous calculation; here, passive voice may be the most diplomatic way to identify the problem without assigning blame.

We talk more about writing tactfully later in this chapter.

## Variety and Rhythm

Another way to make your writing natural and more readable is to add variety, which is the next technique on the list.

> ***Vary vocabulary, sentence lengths, and sentence structures.***
> ***Read the writing aloud to hear how it sounds.***

The purpose of sentence variety is to avoid monotony—a singsong, awkward repetition of the same sentence rhythms or overuse of a word or phrase. Read the following paragraph aloud:

> Financial analysts use ratios to analyze financial statements. Ratios show a company's liquidity. The current ratio shows the ratio of current assets to current liabilities. Ratios also show a company's solvency. The equity ratio is an example of a solvency ratio. It shows the ratio of owners' equity to total assets. Ratios also show profitability. The return-on-investment ratio is an example. It shows the ratio of net earnings to owners' equity.

This paragraph does not sound pleasing. In fact, it could easily lull the reader to sleep. The sentences are too similar in length and structure, and the word *ratio* is repeated too often. Let's try again:

> Ratios based on financial statements can reveal valuable information about a company to investors, creditors, and other interested parties.

Liquidity ratios show whether a company can pay its debts; the quick ratio, for example, is a good indication of debt-paying ability for companies with slow inventory turnover. Ratios can also indicate a company's solvency; the equity ratio, for instance, shows the percentage of owners' equity to total assets. Investors in bonds use this figure to evaluate the safety of a potential investment. Finally, ratios can give a measure of a company's profitability, which is of special interest to potential investors. The earnings-per-share ratio is probably the most popular of the profitability ratios.

Another cause of monotonous sentences is too many prepositional phrases, particularly when several are linked together. In the following sentence, prepositions are in bold type; the rest of the phrase is underlined:

The communication **of** information **about** the income **of** a corporation will provide **to** potential investors **in** the corporation help **in** the making **of** their investment decision.

This sentence contains seven prepositional phrases, several of which are linked together. A good rule is to avoid more than two or three prepositional phrases in a sentence. The sentence can be revised as follows:

Information about a corporation's income will help investors make sound decisions.

Here is a partial list of prepositions:

| | | | |
|---|---|---|---|
| about | by | like | together with |
| after | during | near | under |
| as | for | of | until |
| at | from | on | up |
| because of | in | over | with |
| before | in front of | through | |
| between | in regard to | to | |

Variety is an important element of readable writing because it gives sentences and paragraphs a pleasing rhythm. Read your paragraphs aloud. If you notice a word or phrase repeated too often, look for a synonym. If the sentences sound choppy and monotonous, vary their structures and lengths. Often a change in the way sentences begin improves the rhythm of the paragraph. Add an occasional short sentence and an occasional longer one (but be sure longer sentences are still easy to understand). Avoid using too many prepositional phrases. You don't want to bore your readers, and varied sentences are one way to keep your writing lively.

## Tone

The tone of a document reflects the writer's attitude toward the topic or the readers. Tone might also be described as the effect the writing has on the reader or the impression the document makes. A letter can have a formal or informal tone, and be personal or impersonal. It also can be apologetic, cold, humorous, threatening, arrogant, respectful, or friendly.

Choosing the best tone for a document depends, in part, on who the reader will be. If you are writing to a colleague who is also a good friend, you can be much more informal than if you are writing to someone you don't know well. Be particularly careful to show respect to those who are much older than you are or those in higher positions of authority.

One way to decide on the proper tone for a document you are writing is to imagine that you are in a conversation with your reader. How formal would you be? How would you show that you were interested in your reader's point of view and concerns? No matter how formal (or casual) you decide to make your tone, always be courteous. Treat your correspondent with tact, politeness, and respect. Avoid abruptness, arrogance, condescension, or any other form of rudeness. Remember that the choice of tone may involve ethical considerations: Treat others as you wish to be treated.

Here are some examples of poor tone:

Tax planning is a complicated subject, so I have tried to simplify it for you. [This sentence is condescending; it implies that the reader is not very bright.]

I acknowledge receipt of your letter and beg to thank you. [Too formal and artificial.]

Send me that report immediately. I can't understand why it has taken you so long to prepare it. [In certain situations you might *think* this way, but it's better to write with tact and courtesy.]

For all but the most formal documents, such as some contracts, the use of personal pronouns (*you, I, we*) contributes to a warm, personal tone. Keep the first person singular pronouns (*I, me, my, mine*) to a minimum; focus instead on the reader with second person (*you, your, yours*) or, in some cases, first person plural (*we, us, our, ours*).

A personal tone, including personal pronouns, is especially effective when the message you are conveying is good news or neutral information. When you must write bad news or criticize someone, it's better to be impersonal in order to be tactful. Passive voice can also make a sentence more tactful:

TACTLESS:  You failed to sign your income tax return.
  BETTER:  Your return wasn't signed.

Another guideline for an effective tone is to stress the positive. Emphasize what can be done rather than what cannot:

NEGATIVE:  Because you were late in sending us your tax information, we cannot complete your tax return by April 15.

POSITIVE:   Now that we have the information on your taxes, we can complete your tax return. We will request an extension of the dead-
line so that you will not be fined for a late filing.

Finally, be honest and sincere; avoid exaggeration and flattery.

In the final analysis, the guidelines for an effective writing tone
are the same as those for good relationships. Learn to view a situation
from the other person's point of view and communicate in a way that
shows empathy and respect.

Here, then, is another guideline for an effective writing style.

*Write from the reader's point of view.*
*Use tone to show courtesy and respect.*

This chapter on style has added nine guidelines for effective writing, making a total of sixteen.

1. Analyze the purpose of the writing, the accounting issues involved, and
   the needs and expectations of the readers.
2. Organize your ideas so that readers will find them easy to follow.
3. Write the draft and then revise it to make the writing polished and
   correct.
4. Make the writing unified. All sentences should relate to the main idea,
   either directly or indirectly. Eliminate digressions and irrelevant detail.
5. Use summary sentences and transitions to make your writing coherent.
6. Write in short paragraphs that begin with clear topic sentences.
7. Develop paragraphs by illustration, definition, detail, and appeals to
   authority.
8. Be concise—make every word count.
9. Keep it simple—simple vocabulary and short sentences.
10. Write with active verbs and descriptive nouns.
11. Use jargon only when your readers understand it. Define technical terms
    when necessary.
12. Be precise—avoid ambiguous and unclear writing.
13. Be concrete and specific. Use facts, details, and examples.
14. Use active voice for most sentences.
15. Vary vocabulary, sentence lengths, and sentence structures. Read the
    writing aloud to hear how it sounds.
16. Write from the reader's point of view. Use tone to show courtesy and
    respect.

## TEST YOURSELF

Revise the following sentences so that they are written in a more
effective style, using the techniques covered in this chapter. Answers
are provided on page 70.

1. After reading the following paragraphs, a recommendation will suggest
   a way we can reduce the cost of the purchase.

2. Complete information was wanted by management on the new project that had been proposed by the engineers.
3. The important issue to address in this company's situation is that of the expression of an opinion of the going concern.
4. To determine what information to include in our report for 2011, we will make an analysis of the users' needs.
5. I have attempted to explain the three proposed alternatives for recording the cost of the machinery.
6. This recommendation can easily be implemented by our clients.
7. The main problem of this company is to minimize the amount of taxes for 2011.
8. It is our recommendation that Byron Corporation choose to value the property at $95,000.
9. The letter discussed the alternative ways to finance the purchase of the new equipment. Its purpose was. . . .
10. This information was prepared by our research department.

## TEST YOURSELF: ANSWERS

(Note: Some of the errors in the previous sentences can be corrected in more than one way; this key shows only one possible correction. If you recognize the error, you probably understand how to correct it.)

1. The following paragraphs will explain how we can reduce the cost of the purchase.
2. Management wanted complete information on the new project that the engineers had proposed.
3. We must determine whether this company is a going concern.
4. To determine what to include in our 2011 report, we will analyze users' needs.
5. I have explained the three proposals for recording the cost of the machinery.
6. Our clients can easily implement this recommendation.
7. This company's main problem is to minimize taxes for 2011.
8. We recommend that Byron Corporation value the property at $95,000.
9. The letter discussed the alternative ways to finance the purchase of the new equipment. The purpose of the letter was. . . .
10. Our research department prepared this information.

## EXERCISES

### Exercise 4–1  [General]

Revise the following sentences so that they are written as simply and concisely as possible. Be alert for hidden verbs.

1. The history of Elliot Industry's performance, which is marginal at best, may be an indication of solvency problems that will occur in the future.

2. A number of problems have come to light that may make it necessary for us to issue an opinion that is other than unqualified.
3. We should not make reference to prior years' financial statements in our report.
4. I am in need of improved writing skills.
5. In conclusion, I would like to state that I feel this seminar is an excellent opportunity.
6. There are several benefits that can come from attending the seminar.
7. Per the discussion held with you during our recent visit, there are several control objectives within the above-mentioned cycles that need to have techniques established or refined to assure that these objectives are met.
8. These techniques will provide for an increased understanding of the problem.
9. Utilization of linear models alone may lead to unnecessary limitations as to the inferences that one may be able to draw from the data.
10. This method provides proper matching of expenses to revenues.

## Exercise 4–2 [General]

Review the lists of simplified word choices in Table 4–1. Then, without looking at the list again, write a shorter and/or simpler version of the following words and phrases.

### Example

Simplify to:
      in all cases     always

1. i.e.
2. enclosed please find
3. facilitate
4. initiate
5. prior to
6. so as to
7. the major part of
8. make a purchase
9. make an analysis of
10. for the purpose of
11. in the amount of
12. optimum
13. maintain cost control
14. the writer
15. this is to acknowledge

## Exercise 4–3 [General]

Identify the jargon in the following sentences.

1. SOX requirements have created additional work for our department.
2. The CPA's recommendation is based on thorough research into the regs and the rules.

3. The FASB and the SEC, as well as the AICPA, are organizations that concern the profession of accounting.
4. GAAP requires a different treatment of inventory costs.
5. The project's NPV was negative, so it was rejected.
6. We must file a qualified opinion on this audit.
7. My CPA advised me to file a Schedule C with my return.
8. Because of her income this year, she will be able to recapture.
9. Our auditors must follow all requirements of the PCAOB.
10. Credit Cash for $200.

## Exercise 4–4 [General]

The meaning of the following sentences is not clear. Revise the sentences so that they are unambiguous and precise.

1. The stock's price dropped by a negligent amount.
2. Because our business has grown, we need a larger cite for the warehouse.
3. This product is unique. Only two manufacturers produce it.
4. The HB Transportation Company's improved position is due to decreasing fuel prices and the company's response in increasing prices.
5. The riskiness of these bonds alone does not determine their selling price.
6. Expense recognition states that once a cost expires, we should recognize expense.
7. After calculating the tax effects, the selling price of the property seemed more reasonable.
8. This policy is based on a logical rational.
9. The FASB has not officially written a pronouncement on the handling of requisition costs.
10. These financial statements upset two accounting standards.

## Exercise 4–5 [General]

The following sentences are abstract or vague. Revise them, using facts, details, or examples to make them more concrete. You may need to replace one vague sentence with several concrete sentences, or even a short paragraph. Alternatively, you could introduce a short paragraph with an abstraction and then develop the idea with more concrete, specific sentences. Feel free to invent details that make the ideas more specific.

1. This is an unwise course of action.
2. The new legal action is encouraging.
3. Accounting for leases is tricky.
4. Investors were interested in the president's report.
5. The firm sold the asset for its cost. [Hint: What cost?]
6. Morale is a problem.
7. The audit did not satisfy me.
8. I've discovered a shocking thing about our pension plan.
9. These mutual funds look like a good buy.
10. Communication is important.

## Exercise 4–6 [General]

Identify the passive voice constructions in the following sentences and revise them to active voice. Be careful not to substitute weak active verbs for passive voice. For some sentences you may need to invent a subject for the active verb.

### Example

PASSIVE:  That alternative could have been followed.
ACTIVE:   We (or the firm, our client, McDonough Corporation, etc.) could have followed that alternative.

1. I have explained the three proposed alternatives for recording the cost of the equipment that has been purchased.
2. The option kept the land available until a decision was reached.
3. These disclosures are required for external reporting.
4. This procedure can easily be implemented.
5. It is recommended that finished parts inventories be physically controlled.
6. Although our computer was purchased last year, it is already obsolete.
7. At the seminar guidelines will be provided for lease accounting.
8. In many college accounting courses effective writing skills are emphasized.
9. The prior years' working papers were reviewed.
10. No audit work was performed on internal control by our firm.

## Exercise 4–7 [General]

Identify the prepositional phrases in the following sentences. Where too many phrases are linked together, revise the sentence.

### Example

The problem of Breland Company is solved through the selection of one of the accounting methods presented.

**Prepositional phrases identified:**

The problem **of** Breland Company is solved **through** the selection **of** one **of** the accounting methods presented.

**Revised:**

One of the accounting methods should solve Breland Company's problem.

1. Now that the choice of sites has been made and the expiration of options is occurring, this transaction must be recorded in the books of our firm correctly.
2. We have designed an audit program for use in future audits of the accounts receivable of ABC Company.
3. An accrual of expenses reports a more accurate picture of the operations of the current business period of the company.

4. Improvements of the efficiency of production will change the forecast for income in the year to come.

5. The main problem of the staff is the determination of the cost at which to record the purchase.

6. The effect on our audit report of the sale of the bonds is twofold.

7. The return on an investment in bonds is based on the number of years to maturity and the current rate of interest in the market.

8. The calculation of the present values of the principal of the bonds and their cash flows will reveal our risk.

9. The amortization of the discount of the bond will allow us to realize the cash flows of the bond at an even rate throughout the life of the bond.

10. The determination of the net income of the company will pose no problems for the accountants in our department.

## Exercise 4–8 [General]

Read this paragraph aloud and notice how monotonous it sounds. Then revise it so that sentence lengths and structures are more varied. Note also when a word or phrase is repeated too often.

> Regional Coach Lines (RCL) runs bus service between several cities in three states. RCL also carries freight for several regional businesses. RCL's financial statements have reported poor profits for several years. Poor profits were caused by increased costs of operations including fuel costs, labor costs, and other costs. Increased costs caused RCL to increase passenger fares and freight prices. These increases caused passenger and freight volume to decrease drastically. Therefore, 2011 was a disastrous year for RCL. Preliminary information shows RCL is on the verge of bankruptcy.

## Exercise 4–9 [General]

Revise the following sentences so that they are more effective, based on the guidelines discussed in this chapter.

1. The managers should make reference to requirements of the Sarbanes-Oxley Act.

2. A qualified opinion was issued on the 2011 financial statements.

3. Two weeks of vacation will be taken by new employees.

4. The completion of the project by the due date of next week will challenge the accountants in the department.

5. Wordiness is the problem that makes my writing ineffective.

6. This memo provides an explanation of our policies on the use of company e-mail.

7. The auditors came to the conclusion that additional procedures should be performed by them on inventory.

8. There are several benefits that can come from investing in new equipment.

9. Expense recognition states that once a cost expires, we should recognize expense.

10. The option kept the land available until a decision was reached about whether to buy it.

## Exercise 4–10 [General]

Revise the following paragraph, using the techniques covered in the chapter, as necessary.

Per the discussion that was held with you by our audit staff during their recent communication with you at your Denver office, there are several objectives for control within several accounting cycles that need to have control techniques and procedures established or refined to ensure that these objectives are met by your company. It is vital that all the objectives of control within each of these cycles have control objectives established or improved to provide assurance that the objective is achieved by the company in order to provide data that is accurate and timely, to preserve the integrity of the financial records of the company, and to maintain an adequate system of internal control, especially over the company's accounts receivable. In addition to the specific control techniques discussed in the following report, written procedures should be established so that data will be recorded in the way that management of the company intends.

## NOTES

1. Cynthia A. Glassman, "Speech by SEC Commissioner: Remarks at the Plain Language Association International's Fifth International Conference," Securities and Exchange Commission, 2005. www.sec.gov/news/speech/ spch110405cag.htm (3 December 2010).

2. By permission. From MERRIAM-WEBSTER'S COLLEGIATE® DICTIONARY, 11TH EDITION © 2010 by Merriam-Webster, Incorporated (www.Merriam-Webster.com).

# CHAPTER

## Standard English: Grammar, Punctuation, and Spelling

O ne way to improve the clarity of your writing is to use standard English, the language used by business, government, and professionals for daily business purposes. Standard English is defined as language that is "well established by usage in the formal and informal speech and writing of the educated and is widely recognized as acceptable."[1]

In addition to improving the clarity of what you write, using standard English will help you produce professional, polished documents, which is the final tip for writers given in Figure 1–2 in Chapter 1. A mastery of standard English tells the reader much about you as a person and as a professional. Your use of correct grammar says that you are an educated person who understands and appreciates the proper use of language.

A grammatically correct document, free of mechanical and typographical errors, also shows that you know the importance of detail and are willing to spend the time necessary to prepare an accurate, precise document. Careful attention to detail is an important quality of an accountant, whether the detail is verbal or quantitative.

This chapter presents some of the most common errors in grammar, punctuation, and spelling. Because only a few principles can be covered in this limited space, you should consult an English handbook for more complete coverage. This discussion focuses on areas that give accountants the most trouble.

## MAJOR SENTENCE ERRORS

Major sentence errors include three kinds of problems: fragments, comma splices, and fused sentences. These errors are very distracting to readers and often seriously interfere with their ability to understand the meaning of a sentence.

## Fragments

A sentence fragment is just what its name suggests: part of a sentence. Recall that every sentence needs two essential elements: a subject (a noun or pronoun) and a verb. In sentence fragments, at least one of these elements may be missing. A sentence fragment may also be recognized because it expresses an incomplete thought. Here are some examples:

> To increase our market share.

> For example, all the employees who are eligible for retirement. [The subject is *employees*. In the phrase that modifies the subject, the verb *are* is related to the pronoun *who*, but the predicate for the sentence is missing.

> The reason being that we must find ways to cut overhead. [*Being* is a present participle;* it cannot be substituted for a complete verb such as *is* or *was*.]

> Although our new system makes billing much faster. [This dependent clause has a subject and verb, but it cannot stand alone as a sentence because it is introduced by a subordinate conjunction, *although*.]

## Comma Splices

The second major sentence error is comma splices, which occur when independent clauses are linked by a comma alone. An independent clause is a group of words with a subject and a verb; it can stand alone as a sentence. These two independent clauses are punctuated as separate sentences:

> Accounting is a demanding profession. It can also be very rewarding.

Sometimes writers want to combine two independent clauses into one sentence. This can be done correctly in several ways:

1. Put a semicolon (;) between the clauses.

   > Accounting is a demanding profession; it can also be very rewarding.

2. Combine the clauses with a coordinating conjunction (*and, but, for, or, nor, yet, so*).

   > Accounting is a demanding profession, but it can also be very rewarding.

3. Combine the clauses with a semicolon, a conjunctive adverb, and a comma. (Conjunctive adverbs include *however, therefore, thus, consequently, that is, for example, nevertheless, also, furthermore, indeed, instead, still*.)

   > Accounting is a demanding profession; however, it can also be very rewarding

---

*Consult a grammar handbook for explanations of technical grammatical terms such as this.

Study the following comma splices. The independent clauses are joined by a comma alone:

COMMA SPLICE: Accountants write many letters as part of their professional responsibilities, for example, they may write letters to the IRS.

REVISED: Accountants write many letters as part of their professional responsibilities. For example, they may write letters to the IRS.

COMMA SPLICE: We have expanded the service offered to our clients, we need to hire additional staff accountants.

REVISED: Because we have expanded the service offered to our clients, we need to hire additional staff accountants. [This revision changes the first independent clause into a dependent clause.]

COMMA SPLICE: These transactions were not recorded correctly, they were not recorded in the proper accounts.

REVISED: These transactions were not recorded correctly; they were not recorded in the proper accounts.

*or*

*(to make the sentence more concise)*
These transactions were not recorded in the proper accounts.

## Fused Sentences

Fused sentences, which are also called run-on sentences, occur when two independent clauses are joined without any punctuation at all:

FUSED SENTENCE: Generally accepted accounting principles are not laws passed by Congress; however, the AICPA's code of professional ethics requires accountants to follow GAAP.

REVISED: Generally accepted accounting principles are not laws passed by Congress. However, the AICPA's code of professional ethics requires accountants to follow GAAP.

FUSED SENTENCE: The Director of Human Resources e-mailed all employees about the new vacation policy he wanted them to have time to plan their vacations.

REVISED: The Director of Human Resources e-mailed all employees about the new vacation policy so they would have time to plan their vacations.

# PROBLEMS WITH VERBS

The correct use of verbs is a complicated matter in any language, as you will appreciate if you have ever studied a language other than English. For writers whose first language is English, the correct use of verbs usually presents few problems.

A few kinds of verb problems do occur, however, even in the writing of educated, native speakers of English. We will now look briefly at some of those problems.

## Tense and Mood

The *tense* of a verb reflects the time of the action described by the verb:

PAST TENSE:   The auditors *met* with the client last week.
PRESENT TENSE:   The auditors *are meeting* with the client now.
*or*
*Are* the auditors *meeting* with the client now?
*or*
Auditors meet with clients regularly.
FUTURE TENSE:   The auditors *will meet* with the client next week.

Usually the choice of tense is logical and gives writers few problems.

The *mood* of a verb, however, is a little more confusing than its tense. Three moods are possible: indicative (states a fact or asks a question), imperative (a command or request), and subjunctive (a condition contrary to fact). The subjunctive mood causes the most trouble although we often use it without realizing it:

If I *were* you, I would double-check those vouchers. [condition contrary to fact]

The most common use of the subjunctive is to follow certain verbs such as *recommend*, *suggest*, and *require*:

I recommend that our firm *issue* a qualified opinion.

I suggest that he *contact* the sales representative immediately to discuss the lost orders.

The IRS requires that our client *include* that income in this year's return.

One common problem is an unnecessary shift in tense or mood:

TENSE SHIFT:   The president approached the podium and then announces the good news.
REVISED:   The president approached the podium and then announced the good news.

MOOD SHIFT:   We *must credit* Cash to account for the purchase of the computer paper. Then *debit* Office Supplies. [Shift from indicative to imperative mood.]
REVISED:   We must credit Cash to account for the computer paper purchase and then debit Office Supplies. [This sentence has a single subject, *we*, and compound indicative verb, *must credit . . . and . . . debit.*]

MOOD SHIFT:   If we *increase* inventory, we *would service* orders more quickly. [Shift from indicative to subjunctive.]

REVISED: If we increase inventory, we will service orders more quickly.

*or*

If we increased inventory, we would service orders more quickly.

MOOD SHIFT: If we *changed* our credit policy, we *will attract* more customers. (Shift from subjunctive to indicative.)

REVISED: If we changed our credit policy, we would attract more customers.

*or*

If we change our credit policy, we will attract more customers.

## Subject-Verb Agreement

Another major problem with verbs is subject-verb agreement. A verb should agree with its subject in number. That is, singular subjects take singular verbs; plural subjects take plural verbs. Note that singular verbs in the present tense usually end in *s*:

The [one] *manager* checks the work of new employees.

The [two or more] *managers* check the work of new employees.

Some irregular verbs (*to be*, *to have*, etc.) look different, but you will probably recognize the singular and plural forms:

Rogelio's *investment is* profitable.

Rogelio's *investments are* profitable.

The Drastic Measures *Corporation has* five frantic accountants on its staff.

Some *corporations have* enough accountants to handle the workload efficiently.

This rule presents a few difficulties. First, some singular subjects are often thought of as plural. For example, *each*, *every*, *either*, *neither*, *one*, *everybody*, and *anyone* take singular verbs:

*Each* of the auditors *is* an experienced accountant.

Second, sometimes phrases coming between the subject and the verb make agreement tricky:

The *procedure* used today by most large companies governed by SEC regulations *is explained* in this article.

Finally, two or more subjects joined by *and* take a plural verb. When subjects are joined by *or*, the verb agrees with the subject closest to it:

Either Ellen Atkins or John Simmons is the partner-in-charge.

Either the *controller or the managers have called* this meeting.

## PROBLEMS WITH PRONOUNS

Two common problems with pronouns are agreement and reference. Understanding *agreement* is easy: A pronoun must agree with its antecedent (the word it stands for). Thus, singular antecedents take singular pronouns and plural antecedents take plural pronouns:

*Eric* dropped *his* cell phone on the floor.

Each *department* is responsible for servicing *its* own equipment.

This rule usually gives trouble only with particular words. Note that *company*, *corporation*, *firm*, *management*, and *board* are singular; therefore, they take singular pronouns:

The *corporation* hired two new accountants to supervise *its* internal control procedures. [Not *corporation* . . . *their*.]

The Board of Directors discussed earnings projections in its quarterly meeting. [Not *Board* . . . *their*.]

*Management* issued *its* quarterly report. [But: The *managers* issued *their* report.]

The second problem with pronouns is vague, ambiguous, or broad *reference*. The pronouns that give the most trouble are *this*, *that*, *which*, and *it*. This problem was discussed in Chapter 4, but here are some additional examples for you to consider:

FAULTY REFERENCE: Although our bottling machines were purchased last year, this year's revenue depends on them. *This* associates the true cost with this year's revenues.

REVISED (ONE POSSIBILITY): Although our bottling machines were purchased last year, this year's revenue depends on them. To associate the true cost with this year's revenue, we must apply the matching principle.

FAULTY REFERENCE: Adjusting entries are needed to show that expenses have been incurred but not paid. *This* is a very important step.

REVISED: Adjusting entries are needed to show that expenses have been incurred but have not been paid. Making these adjusting entries is a very important step.

Although agreement and reference cause writers the most problems with pronouns, occasionally other questions arise.

One question is the use of first and second person, which some people have been taught to avoid. In the discussion of tone in Chapter 4, you saw how using these personal pronouns can often contribute to an effective writing style for many informal documents. Personal pronouns are not usually appropriate in formal documents, such as some reports and contracts.

A few other cautions apply in the use of personal pronouns. First, use first person singular pronouns (*I*, *me*, *my*, and *mine*) sparingly to avoid writing that sounds self centered. The second problem to avoid is using *you* as a substitute for another pronoun or in a broad sense to mean people in general:

> INCORRECT: I don't want to file my income tax return late because the IRS will fine *you*.
>
> REVISED: I don't want to file my income tax return late because the IRS will fine me.

## Pronouns and Gender

English has no singular personal pronouns that refer to an antecedent that could be either masculine or feminine. Until about a generation ago, the masculine pronouns (*he, him, his*) were understood to stand for either gender:

> Every investor is concerned that his stocks perform well.

Sentences like this one were common even though the pronoun's antecedent (in this case, *investor*) could be either male or female.

Today most people believe that this older pronoun usage is no longer appropriate. They prefer to use pronouns that are gender neutral, unless, of course, the antecedent is clearly male or female:

> The *controller* of Marvelous Corporation was pleased with *his* company's financial statements. [The controller is a man.]
>
> *or*
>
> The *controller* of Marvelous Corporation was pleased with *her* company's financial statements. [The controller is a woman.]

When the pronoun's antecedent is not clearly male or female, many people write sentences like these:

> Every *investor* is concerned that *his or her* stocks perform well.
>
> Every *investor* is concerned that *his/her* stocks perform well.

Unfortunately, the *he or she* and *he/she* constructions can be awkward, especially if several occur in the same sentence:

> Every investor is concerned that *his or her* stocks perform well so that *his or her* portfolio will increase in value.

What's the solution? The best approach for most sentences is to use plural nouns and pronouns:

> Investors are concerned that *their* stocks perform well so that *their* portfolios will increase in value.

For some sentences, however, you can't use plurals. In these situations, some writers use gendered pronouns arbitrarily and switch often;

sometimes they use a feminine pronoun and sometimes a masculine one. Whatever approach you use to avoid gender bias in your use of pronouns, keep these guidelines in mind:

- Most of today's business publications use language that avoids a gender bias, including a careful use of pronouns. If you use the older style, your writing will seem outdated.
- Some of your readers will be annoyed by a choice of pronouns that seems to be gender biased.

## PROBLEMS WITH MODIFIERS

Chapter 4 discussed the two main problems that can occur with modifiers: misplaced modifiers, which occur when the modifier is not placed next to the word it describes, and dangling modifiers, which do not modify any word in the sentence:

MISPLACED MODIFIER: We only shipped five orders last week. [*Only* is misplaced. It should be next to the word or phrase it modifies.]

REVISED: We shipped only five orders last week.

DANGLING MODIFIER: When preparing financial statements, GAAP must be adhered to.

REVISED: When preparing financial statements, we must adhere to GAAP.

The best guideline for using modifiers correctly is to place them next to the word or phrase they describe. For a further discussion of problems with modifiers and additional examples, see Chapter 4.

## PARALLEL STRUCTURE

Parallel sentence elements are those that are grammatically equal (such as nouns, phrases, clauses, and so on). When these items appear in a list or a compound structure, they should be balanced, or parallel. Nouns should not be matched with clauses, for example, nor should sentences be matched with phrases:

STRUCTURE NOT PARALLEL: During the meeting management will explain the purpose of the new policy, when it will go into effect, and its advantages. [This sentence combines a noun phrase, a dependent clause, and another noun phrase.]

REVISED: During he meeting management will explain the purpose of the new policy, its implementation date, and its advantages.

STRUCTURE NOT PARALLEL: We recommend the following procedures:
- Hire a consultant to help us determine our needs. [verb phrase]

- Investigate alternative makes and models of equipment. [verb phrase]
- We should then set up a pilot program to assess retraining needs for employees who will use the new equipment. [sentence]

REVISED:  We recommend the following procedures:
- Hire a consultant to help us determine our needs. [verb phrase]
- Investigate alternative makes and models of equipment. [verb phrase]
- Set up a pilot program to assess retraining needs for employees who will use the new equipment. [verb phrase]

## APOSTROPHES AND PLURALS

The rules for apostrophes and plurals are quite simple, but many people get them confused. Most plurals are formed by adding either *s* or *es* to the end of a word. If you are unsure of a plural spelling, consult a dictionary.

With one exception, apostrophes are never used to form plurals. Apostrophes are used to show possession. For singular words, the apostrophe precedes the s (*'s*). For plural words the apostrophe follows the *s* (*s'*):

| **Singular** | **Plural** |
|---|---|
| client's file | clients' files |
| statement's format | users' needs |
| business's budget | businesses' budgets |

A common mistake occurs with the term *stockholder's equity*. When stockholder(s) is plural (it usually is), the apostrophe comes after the *s*: *stockholders' equity*.

The plural-apostrophe rule has one exception: The plurals of letters or acronyms can be formed with *'s*. Either choice in the following sentences is correct:

Most CPA's [or CPAs] are familiar with these regulations.

Cross your *t*'s and dot your *i*'s. [Or: Cross your *t*s and dot your *i*s.]

Often a phrase requiring an apostrophe can be rewritten using *of* or its equivalent:

the company's statements [the statements of the company]
June's income [the income for June]
a week's work [the work of a week]
the year's total [the total for the year]

Although either of the preceding possessive forms is correct, remember the caution given in Chapter 4 about using too many prepositional phrases in a sentence. The result can be awkward or wordy.

And note these possessive plurals:

two companies' statements
five months' income
three weeks' work
prior years' statements
ten years' total

*Ten years' total* might also be written *ten-year total*, but analyze the difference in meaning between *ten-year total* and *ten years' totals*.

Finally, some writers confuse *it's* with *its*. *It's* is a contraction of *it is*; *its* is the possessive pronoun:

It's important to file complete returns on time.

The corporation increased its profits by 10%.

## COMMAS

Commas are important because they can make sentences easier to understand. Lack of a comma makes the meaning of this sentence ambiguous:

I wouldn't worry because you appear to have a thriving business.

Adding a comma clears up the confusion:

I wouldn't worry, because you appear to have a thriving business.

### Comma Guidesheet

This guidesheet will help you determine when to use (or not use) commas.

*Use Commas:*
1. Before *and*, *but*, *or*, *not*, *for*, *so*, and *yet* when these words come between independent clauses:

We sent Mr. Alvarado an invoice for our services, and he mailed a check the next day.

Our competitors increased their advertising, but our customers remained loyal.

2. Following an introductory adverbial clause:

If we purchase this program, we will be able to generate our reports more quickly.

Although we worked all night, we didn't finish the report.

**3.** Following transitional expressions and long introductory phrases:

In a letter addressed to its corporate clients, the firm explained the changes in the services it would offer.

To improve the service to our Atlanta customers, we are adding three new sales representatives. However, we still need four more representatives.

**4.** To separate items in a series (including coordinate adjectives):

Accounting students must be intelligent, dedicated, and conscientious.

Jenny Tran, Sam Clark, and Raul Ramirez announced they would retire next year.

**5.** To set off nonrestrictive clauses and phrases (compare to rule 4 under the heading *DO NOT USE COMMAS*):

The SEC, which is an agency of the federal government, is concerned with the independence of auditors.

The annual report, which was issued in March, contained shocking news for investors.

The main office, located in Boston, employs 350 people.

**6.** To set off contrasted elements:

Treasury stock is a capital account, not an asset.

We want to lower our prices, not raise them.

**7.** To set off parenthetical elements:

Changes in accounting methods, however, must be disclosed in financial statements.

"Our goal," he said, "is to dominate the market."

*Do Not Use Commas:*
**1.** To separate the subject from the verb or the verb from its complement:

***Incorrect:***
Some international mutual funds, have shown high returns.

***Correct:***
Some international mutual funds have shown high returns.

***Incorrect:***
We must correctly record, these entries.

***Correct:***
We must correctly record these entries.

**2.** To separate compound verbs or objects:

***Incorrect:***
She wrote angry letters to her CPA, and to her attorney.

*Correct:*
She wrote angry letters to her CPA and to her attorney.

*But note this usage:*
She wrote angry letters to her CPA, her attorney, and the Chamber of Commerce. [Commas are correct in this sentence because they separate the items in a series. See rule 4 under *USE COMMAS*.]

**3.** To set off words and short phrases that are not parenthetical:

*Incorrect:*
Financial transactions are recorded, in journals, in chronological order.

*Correct:*
Financial transactions are recorded in journals in chronological order.

**4.** To set off restrictive clauses, phrases, or appositives (compare to rule 5 under *USE COMMAS*):

*Incorrect:*
An advantage, of computerized tax programs, is the accuracy of the returns.

*Correct:*
An advantage of computerized tax programs is the accuracy of the returns.

*Incorrect:*
The person, who discovered this error, deserves a promotion.

*Correct:*
The person who discovered this error deserves a promotion.

**5.** Before the first item or after the last item of a series (including coordinate adjectives):

*Incorrect:*
Some asset accounts are noncurrent, such as, land, buildings, and equipment.
[The faulty comma is the one before *land*.]

*Correct:*
Some asset accounts are noncurrent, such as land, buildings, and equipment.

## COLONS AND SEMICOLONS

The rules for colons (:) are few and easy to master although sometimes writers use them incorrectly. Used correctly—and sparingly—colons can be effective because they draw the readers' attention to the material that follows the colon.

Colons can be used in the following situations:

**1.** To introduce a series:

Three new CPA firms have located in this area recently: Smith and Harrison, CPAs; Thomas R. Becker and Associates; and Johnson & Baker, CPAs.

**2.** To introduce a direct quotation, especially a long quotation that is set off from the main body of the text:

The senior partner issued the following instruction: "All audit workpapers should include concise, well-organized memos summarizing any problem revealed by the audit."

**3.** To emphasize a summary or explanation:

Our study of Sebastian Enterprises has revealed one primary problem: unless management hires new researchers to develop technical innovations, Sebastian will lose its position of market dominance.

**4.** Following the salutation in a business letter:

Dear Ms. Wade:

When a colon introduces a series, an explanation, or a summary, the clause that precedes the colon should be a complete statement:

We have sent engagement letters to the following clients: B and B Conglomerates, Abigail's Catnip Boutique, and Sharkey's Aquarium Supplies.

*not*

We have sent engagement letters to: B and B Conglomerates, Abigail's Catnip Boutique, and Sharkey's Aquarium Supplies.

Semicolons (;) are used for only two situations: between independent clauses (see page 71) and between items in a series if the items themselves have internal commas:

Promotions were announced for Ann Moore, regional vice president; Larry Yeo, sales manager; and John Green, internal control manager.

## DIRECT QUOTATIONS

The punctuation of direct quotations depends on their length. Short quotations (fewer than five typed lines) are usually run in with the text and enclosed with quotation marks. Longer quotations are set off from the text with no quotation marks and indented 1 inch from the left margin. Direct quotations should be formally introduced; a colon may separate the introduction from the quoted material. Study the following examples:

According to a recent publication of the FASB, *"Accounting Standards Codification*™ is the source of authoritative generally accepted accounting principles (GAAP) recognized by the FASB to be applied to nongovernmental entities."[2]

The FASB has issued the following statement about codification:

The FASB *Accounting Standards Codification*™ is the source of authoritative generally accepted accounting principles (GAAP) recognized by the FASB to be applied to nongovernmental entities. The Codification is effective for interim and annual periods ending after September 15, 2009. All previous level (a)-(d) US GAAP standards issued by a standard setter are superseded. Level (a)-(d) US GAAP refers to the previous accounting hierarchy. All other accounting literature not included in the Codification will be considered nonauthoritative.[3]

A direct quotation requires a citation identifying its source. It's also better to identify briefly the source of a quotation within the text itself, as the preceding examples illustrate. If a quotation comes from an individual, use his or her complete name the first time you quote from this person. You may also need to give the title or position of the person you are quoting or to otherwise explain that person's credentials. Study the following examples:

According to Richard Smith, an executive officer of the Fairways Corporation, "The industry faces an exciting challenge in meeting foreign competition."

Elaine Howard, who supervised the market research for the new product, provided this assessment of its sales potential: "Within five months from the product's introduction into the market, we expect sales to approach 500,000 units."

Notice the placement of punctuation in relation to quotation marks:

- Inside quotation marks:
  period            *quotation."*
  comma           *quotation,"*

- Outside quotation marks:
  colon             *quotation":*
  semicolon        *quotation";*

- Inside or outside quotation marks:
  question mark        ?" or "? —depending on whether the question mark is part of the original quotation:

Mr. Shipley asked, "When will the report be ready?"

Did Mr. Shipley say, "The report is overdue"?

A final remark: Sometimes writers depend too heavily on direct quotation. It's usually better to paraphrase—to express someone else's ideas in your own words—unless precise quotation would be an advantage. As a rule, no more than 10% of a paper should be direct quotation. To be most effective, quotations should be used sparingly, and then only for authoritative support or dramatic effect.

Chapter 8, which discusses research papers, gives more information on the use of sources, including direct quotations and paraphrases.

## SPELLING

Finished, revised writing should be entirely free of misspelled words. When you work at a word processor, use a spell-checker to catch misspelled words and typographical errors. Note that a spell-checker will not distinguish between homonyms such as *affect* and *effect* or *their* and *there*; nor will it check the spelling of most proper nouns, such as names. You may find it helpful to keep a dictionary on your desk for use when you aren't sure about a word's spelling.

### *Spelling: Always check every word!*

The following short list contains words commonly misspelled or misused by accountants:

accrual, accrued
advise/advice
affect/effect
cost/costs, consist/consists, risk/risks
led, misled
occurred, occurring, occurrence
principal/principle
receivable, receive
separate, separately

The italicized words in the following sentences are often confused:

Please *advise* the customers to put the invoice number on their checks. [*Advise* is a verb.]
The *advice* we received was quite helpful. [*Advice* is a noun.]

This change in accounting policy will not *affect* the financial statements. [*Affect* is usually a verb; in the social and cognitive sciences, it can be used as a noun meaning *emotion* or *mood*.]
This change in accounting policy will have no *effect* on the financial statements. [*Effect* is usually a noun. Rarely, *effect* is a verb meaning to cause to happen.]

The replacement *cost* for the equipment is more than we had estimated. [*Cost* is singular.]
The *costs* to repair the equipment will affect the budget. [*Costs* is plural, but when you say the word aloud, you can't hear the final *s*.]

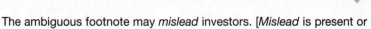

The ambiguous footnote may *mislead* investors. [*Mislead* is present or future tense.]

This ambiguous footnote *misled* investors. [*Misled* is past tense.]

How should we record the *principal* of this loan? [The *principal* is the face amount of the loan.]

This procedure does not follow generally accepted accounting *principles*. [*Principles* are rules.]

The *principal* reason for the investment is to generate income. [*Principal* means most important.]

## HELP FROM THE COMPUTER

Some writers check their text for grammatical errors by using grammar-check software. These programs can help you identify some problems with grammar, including errors with verbs, pronouns, and punctuation. Like programs that analyze writing style, these computer aids may not catch all your grammatical errors, and they may flag as an error a usage that is actually correct. Thus, the decision to use grammar-checkers to review your text is a matter of personal experience and preference: Some excellent writers praise such software highly, but others find its usefulness limited.

Using a spell-checker is another matter. As we've pointed out many times, a spell-checker is also a tremendous help in correcting spelling and typographical errors.

A final word: Be sure to proofread the final hard copy of your document for errors you may have missed earlier. Computers aren't foolproof; sometimes what appears on the screen doesn't look the same on a printed page. Any errors, including those caused by the computer or printer, make work look sloppy and the writer seem careless. Effective writing should look professional: correct, neat, and polished.

In summary, standard English—including correct grammar, punctuation, and spelling—is essential for polished, professional writing. Don't just guess about the correct usage. Resolve your uncertainties with a grammar handbook, dictionary, spell-checker, or grammar-checker. Remember the needs of your readers. Using standard English is necessary for smooth, clear reading.

This chapter has provided another guideline for effective writing; we now have 17.

1. **Analyze the purpose of the writing, the accounting issues involved, and the needs and expectations of the readers.**
2. **Organize your ideas so that readers will find them easy to follow.**
3. **Write the draft and then revise it to make the writing polished and correct.**
4. **Make the writing unified. All sentences should relate to the main idea, either directly or indirectly. Eliminate digressions and irrelevant detail.**
5. **Use summary sentences and transitions to make your writing coherent.**

6. Write in short paragraphs that begin with clear topic sentences.
7. Develop paragraphs by illustration, definition, detail, and appeals to authority.
8. Be concise — make every word count.
9. Keep it simple — use simple vocabulary and short sentences.
10. Write with active verbs and descriptive nouns.
11. Use jargon only when your readers understand it. Define technical terms when necessary.
12. Be precise — avoid ambiguous and unclear writing.
13. Be concrete and specific. Use facts, details, and examples.
14. Use active voice for most sentences.
15. Vary vocabulary, sentence lengths, and sentence structures. Read the writing aloud to hear how it sounds.
16. Write from the reader's point of view. Use tone to show courtesy and respect.
17. Proofread for grammar, punctuation, spelling, and typographical errors.

## TEST YOURSELF

Identify and correct the errors in the following exercises, using the guidelines discussed in this chapter. Answers are provided on pages 96.

1. Honeybees Honey Supplies Corporation must not only improve its internal control system it must also review its procedures for accounts receivable.
2. One provision of the new policies are causing confusion for the auditors.
3. New SEC requirements for handling this kind of transaction forces accountants to change the way they perform some procedures.
4. Each auditor is required to keep detailed records of their work on the audit.
5. We currently value our inventories according to LIFO not FIFO.
6. Many types of users rely on financial statement information, for example, investors may use the information to decide whether to purchase stock in the company.
7. If we change our marketing strategy, we would attract more customers.
8. We might suggest to the controller that he consider the FASB's Statement No. 141, which deals with business combinations.
9. A statement with supplementary disclosures provide additional information to investors.
10. In spite of the uncertain outlook for the housing industry, however, we project that our sales will increase this year by at least 10%.

## TEST YOURSELF: ANSWERS

(Note: Some of the errors can be corrected in more than one way. For most sentences, this key shows only one possible correction. If you recognize the error, you probably understand how to correct it.)

1. Fused sentence. Correction:
   Honeybees Honey Supplies Corporation must not only improve its internal control system; it must also review its procedures for accounts receivable.

2. Subject-verb agreement. Correction:
   One provision of the new policies is causing confusion for the auditors. (The verb should agree with *provision*.)

3. Subject-verb agreement. Correction:
   New SEC requirements for handling this kind of transaction force accountants to change the way they perform some procedures. [The verb should agree with the subject *requirements*.]

4. Pronoun agreement. Correction:
   The auditors are required to keep detailed records of their work on the audit. [Alternative: *each auditor/his or her*. With this wording, the sentence should be as follows: Each auditor is required to keep detailed records of his or her work on the audit.]

5. Comma error. Correction:
   We currently value our inventories according to LIFO, not FIFO.

6. Comma splice. Correction:
   Many types of users rely on financial statement information. For example, investors may use the information to decide whether to purchase stock in the company. [Alternative: Many . . . information; for example, . . .]

7. Mood shift. Correction:
   If we changed our marketing strategy, we would attract more customers.
   *or*
   If we change our marketing strategy, we will attract more customers. [The original sentence contained a shift in mood from indicative to subjunctive. Either mood is correct here; the key is to be consistent.]

8. Comma error. Correction:
   We might suggest to the controller that he consider the FASB's Statement No. 141, which deals with business combinations. [In this example, we assume we know the controller, who is a man.]

9. Subject-verb agreement. Correction:
   A statement with supplementary disclosures provides additional information to investors. [The verb should agree with *statement*.]

10. Correct. [*However* doesn't come between two independent clauses in this sentence.]

---

# EXERCISES

## Exercise 5–1  [General]

Join together these independent clauses in three ways.

under variable costing a company's sales will influence income

under absorption costing both sales and production will affect income

## Exercise 5–2 [General]

Identify and correct fragments, comma splices, or fused sentences. Some sentences are correct.

1. Glenn Manufacturing may argue that these costs do not provide future benefits, thus Glenn may choose to expense them.
2. To improve our profits; therefore, we reduced expenses.
3. Therefore, the Board requested additional information.
4. Tax season is our busiest time of the year everyone works long hours.
5. After the president announced the new policy, employees became worried.
6. Although, the new equipment has improved our rate of production.
7. The reason for our poor profit performance being that the market is saturated.
8. Our new computer system is much faster than the old one, therefore, we will complete the year-end work on time.
9. Two managers postponed their vacations and thus we were able to handle the emergency.
10. Although we increased our advertising, sales did not improve.

## Exercise 5–3 [General]

Some of these sentences have errors in subject-verb agreement. Identify these errors and correct the sentences.

1. Changes in the general purchasing power of the dollar forces accountants to deal with an unstable monetary unit.
2. Neither the president nor the supervisors understand the new policy.
3. One problem we found in our reviews of the records were that revenues were not always recorded in the proper period.
4. A statement with supplementary disclosures provide additional information to investors.
5. The physical flow of goods generally follow the FIFO pattern.
6. Each of these statements is prepared according to GAAP.
7. Neither the president not the controller understand the new policy.
8. The future benefits provided by the bond is partly due to its high interest rate.
9. Restating asset values to current costs results in realized and unrealized holding gains and losses.
10. Due to the changing value of the dollar, meaningful interpretation of historical cost statements and comparisons among firms has become nearly impossible.

## Exercise 5–4 [General]

Correct any pronoun errors you find in the following sentences.

1. When an investor or creditor wishes to compare two companies, they cannot always rely on the historical cost statements for the comparison.
2. Ace Manufacturing should remember that they are allowed to expense the cost of certain property.

3. The FASB deals with research and development costs in their pronouncements.
4. Management is interested in improving the revenue figures for their report to the stockholders.
5. Each accountant is required to complete his report on time.
6. The Smallwood Corporation has greatly increased it's advertising expense.
7. A switch to LIFO usually results in a lower income tax liability and a lower inventory figure on the balance sheet; this would be important to our company.
8. The Board of Directors will hold its next meeting in July.
9. Every corporation coming under SEC regulations must follow certain procedures in preparing their financial statements.
10. Everyone registering for the convention will receive a package of information when they arrive.

## Exercise 5–5 [General]

Revise the following sentence for parallel grammatical structure:

We recommend the following improvements in your system of internal controls:

- The controls over cash should be strengthened.
- an accounting manual to ensure that transactions are handled uniformly
- improved documentation of accounting procedures.

## Exercise 5–6 [General]

**a.** Complete the following chart.

| Singular | Singular Possessive | Plural Possessive |
|---|---|---|
| statement | | |
| company | | |
| business | | |
| cost | | |
| risk | | |
| CPA | | |
| year | | |
| industry | | |

**b.** Use the words from the preceding chart to fill in the following sentences. The singular form of the correct word is given in the parentheses.

1. (CPA) _____ from all over the country will be at the convention.
2. (business) Investors examine a _____ statements to determine its financial condition.
3. (cost) Record all these _____ in the proper accounts.
4. (statement) Which of the _____ is in error?
5. (cost) What is the replacement _____ of this machine?
6. (risk) Investors in these bonds must accept certain _____.
7. (industry) Research and development are crucial in many _____.
8. (year) We should see a profit in two _____ time.

9. (company) The Board of Directors considered the _____ pension plan.
10. (statement) We are making changes in the two _____ totals.

## Exercise 5–7 [General]

Punctuate the following sentences correctly.

1. When the Board of Directors met in December the company showed a net loss of $5,000,000.
2. To increase the revenues from its new product the company introduced an advertising campaign in New York Chicago and Los Angeles.
3. The biggest problem in our firm, however, is obsolete inventories.
4. The firm hired two new auditors thus the work will be finished on time.
5. For example Elixir Products should consider FASB Statement No. 13 which deals with leases.
6. The auditors revealed several problems in Thompson Company's financial records such as its depreciation policy its handling of bad debts and its inventory accounting.
7. The presidents letter contained the following warning "If our revenues don't increase soon the plant may be forced to close"
8. "We're planning a new sales strategy" the manager wrote in reply.
9. We have decided not to invest in the Allied bonds at this time instead we are considering Blackstone's common stocks.
10. Although our revenues increased during June expenses rose at an alarming rate.

## Exercise 5–8 [General]

Identify and correct any misspelled words in the following list. Look up any words you are unsure of; not all these words were included in the chapter.

1. its (the possessive pronoun)
2. recieve
3. occured
4. seperate
5. accural
6. benefitted
7. existance
8. principle (the rule)
9. cost (plural)
10. mislead (past tense)
11. advise (the noun)
12. effect (the noun)
13. thier
14. intrest
15. trail balance

## Exercise 5–9 [General]

Revise the following sentences, using the guidelines covered in this chapter.

1. If we upgraded our software, we will prepare reports more quickly.
2. The guidelines will explain who is eligible for the benefits, costs, and how to apply.
3. We have increased our advertising thus we hope to sell more of our product.
4. The report was signed by the controller the internal auditor and the vice president.
5. Neither Susan nor Lisa are on the committee.
6. This is the employee's parking lot.
7. Either the computers or the printer is malfunctioning.
8. The benefits of this health insurance policy is obvious to employees.
9. We review the client's system of internal control. Then we will recommend ways to improve it.
10. Three new procedures were used to improve the internal control system. This was the responsibility of Hugh Tran.

## Exercise 5–10 [General]

Revise the memo in Figure 5–1, using the guidelines you've studied in this and other chapters. Your goal is to produce a more effective memo.

**FIGURE 5–1**   Memo to Accompany Exercise 5–10

To:      Miss Elaine Jacobs
From:    Jonathan Brooks
Subject: Banquet for Veteran Employees
Date:    March 12, 2011

How are you doing? I am fine.

I have been asked by the Human Resources Department to organize a banquet for employees who have been with our firm ten years or more we are considering scheduling the event for May 8, which will be a convenient time for most people. Each of the honorees have already agreed that the date will work with his schedules. Being that you have experience in setting up events for our department. We hope you will take charge of the arrangement with the caterer the florist and the printer for the program. All these cost covered by the Human Resources Department.

In the past, we give special gifts to the honorees, therefore they has something tangible as a reward for their service. Please ask somebody to look into this, coordinate with Human Resources about the amount of money we can spend on each persons' gift. How many honoree's we have will effect the amount we can spend on each gift.

We want to ensure that each honoree realizes how much the firm appreciate's his service.

Please let me know if you can do this. Also can you suggest names of other people who might be willing to work on a committee for this banquet. I'm too busy with more important work to spend much time on this project.

# NOTES

1. By permission. From MERRIAM-WEBSTER'S COLLEGIATE® DICTIONARY, 11TH EDITION © 2010 by Merriam-Webster, Incorporated (www.Merriam-Webster.com).

2. Financial Accounting Standards Board, "Notice to Constituents About the Codification," *Accounting Standards Codification*™ (v. 4.1), (Stamford, Conn.: FASB, April 30, 2010), 4.

3. Ibid.

# CHAPTER

## Format for Clarity: Document Design

**6**

How a document looks at first glance can make a big difference in how the reader reacts to it. An attractive document generally gets a positive response, but a paper that is not pleasing to the eye may never be read. A good design does more for the readers than appeal to them visually. A well-planned format also contributes to the clarity of documents by making them easier to read. In fact, the SEC stresses the importance of document design to make financial statement disclosures useful to investors. According to an SEC Commissioner, "not only is the choice of words critical, but a document's format and placement of information on the page are equally important elements of getting the message across."[1] Good design also helps a document look polished and professional after final revision, which is the seventh tip for effective writing (refer to Figure 1–2 in Chapter 1).

This chapter looks at techniques of document design that make letters, memos, and reports more attractive. These techniques can be used for any kind of document. We consider ways to make documents look professional and attractive, such as the choice of paper and print and the use of white space. We also show how techniques of formatting, such as headings, lists, and graphic illustrations, can make your documents clearer and more readable. Later chapters cover the conventions and formats specific to particular kinds of documents, such as the standard parts of letters, memos, and reports.

## GOOD DESIGN: AN ILLUSTRATION

To illustrate the difference good design can make in the readability of a document, study the example in Figures 6–1 through 6–3, which are three versions of the same memo. Figure 6–1 shows straight text, with no divisions for paragraphs, headings, or other features of good document design; Figure 6–2 divides the text into readable paragraphs with a little more white space; and Figure 6–3 uses additional white space, headings, and a set-off list. Which version of the memo do you think is most effective? Does the version in Figure 6–3 suggest formatting techniques you can use in your own writing?

**FIGURE 6–1** Memo for Comparison (see Figures 6–2 and 6–3)

TO: Paul J. Streer, Partner

FROM: Billie Sanders

DATE: April 17, 2011

SUBJECT: Tax implications of Robert Burke's prospective joint purchase of rental real estate.

Our client, Robert Burke, has expressed concern about the tax implications of a venture he is considering, a joint purchase of real estate with Anne Simmons. The issue that must be considered is whether Mr. Burke will be subject to a deduction limitation because the property will be used as a residence by Ms. Simmons. The conclusion is that because the rental agreement is a shared equity financing agreement, Mr. Burke will not be subject to a deduction limitation. On January 1, 2012, Ms. Simmons and Mr. Burke plan to purchase rental real estate, which Ms. Simmons will occupy as her residence. They will enter into an agreement whereby Mr. Burke will provide the down payment and one-half of the monthly mortgage payment. Ms. Simmons will pay the remaining portion of the monthly mortgage, monthly rental payments to Mr. Burke, and the monthly operating costs of the home. They will split the property taxes evenly. Mr. Burke will receive one-half of the appreciation value of the home upon its sale and has the option to demand that his interest in the property be paid to him after five years. The issue to be settled is whether Mr. Burke is subject to the deduction limitation in 280A(c)(5) because the rental property was used as a residence by the taxpayer. The agreement between Ms. Simmons and Mr. Burke qualifies as a shared equity financing agreement under 280A(d)(3)(C). Because the agreement can be classified as such, 280A(c)(5) will not apply and cannot limit the deductions attributable to the rental of Mr. Burke's share of the property to the gross income derived from the rental. This conclusion was also reached by the IRS in Private Letter Ruling 8410038. To override the limitation of 280A(c)(5), the shared equity financing agreement must meet certain requirements: (1) under 280A(d)(3)(D), both Ms. Simmons and Mr. Burke must have a qualified ownership interest in the property (an undivided interest for more than fifty years in the entire property) and (2) the rent Ms. Simmons pays to Mr. Burke must be the fair rental at the time the agreement is entered, taking into account Ms. Simmons' qualified interest. Because Mr. Burke will be allowed the deductions and Ms. Simmons will not (except for expenses allowable even if the dwelling were not rented), payment of expenses should be the responsibility of Mr. Burke. The agreement can contain a provision that compensates Mr. Burke for this additional encumbrance. If those expenses were paid by Ms. Simmons, the deduction would go unused. The joint purchase Mr. Burke proposes to enter into is sound. The agreement will not have unfavorable tax implications for him if he is careful to follow these recommendations.

**FIGURE 6–2**   Memo for Comparison (see Figures 6–1 and 6–3)

TO:        Paul J. Streer, Partner

FROM:    Billie Sanders

DATE:     April 17, 2011

SUBJECT: Tax implications of Robert Burke's prospective joint
               purchase of rental real estate.

Our client, Robert Burke, has expressed concern about the tax implications of a venture he is considering, a joint purchase of real estate with Anne Simmons. The issue that must be considered is whether Mr. Burke will be subject to a deduction limitation because the property will be used as a residence by Ms. Simmons. The conclusion is that because the rental agreement is a shared equity financing agreement, Mr. Burke will not be subject to a deduction limitation.

On January 1, 2012, Ms. Simmons and Mr. Burke plan to purchase rental real estate, which Ms. Simmons will occupy as her residence. They will enter into an agreement whereby Mr. Burke will provide the down payment and one-half of the monthly mortgage payment. Ms. Simmons will pay the remaining portion of the monthly mortgage, monthly rental payments to Mr. Burke, and the monthly operating costs of the home. They will split the property taxes evenly. Mr. Burke will receive one-half of the appreciation value of the home upon its sale and has the option to demand that his interest in the property be paid to him after five years.

The issue to be settled is whether Mr. Burke is subject to the deduction limitation in 280A(c)(5) because the rental property was used as a residence by the taxpayer.

The agreement between Ms. Simmons and Mr. Burke qualifies as a shared equity financing agreement under 280A(d)(3)(C). Because the agreement can be classified as such, 280A(c)(5) will not apply and cannot limit the deductions attributable to the rental of Mr. Burke's share of the property to the gross income derived from the rental. This conclusion was also reached by the IRS in Private Letter Ruling 8410038.

To override the limitation of 280A(c)(5), the shared equity financing agreement must meet certain requirements: (1) under 280A(d)(3)(D), both Ms. Simmons and Mr. Burke must have a qualified ownership interest in the property (an undivided interest for more than fifty years in the entire property) and (2) the rent Ms. Simmons pays to Mr. Burke must be the fair rental at the time the agreement is entered, taking into account Ms. Simmons' qualified interest.

Because Mr. Burke will be allowed the deductions and Ms. Simmons will not (except for expenses allowable even if the dwelling were not rented), payment of expenses should be the responsibility of Mr. Burke. The agreement can contain a provision that compensates Mr. Burke for this additional encumbrance. If those expenses were paid by Ms. Simmons, the deduction would go unused.

The joint purchase Mr. Burke proposes to enter into is sound. The agreement will not have unfavorable tax implications for him if he is careful to follow these recommendations.

**FIGURE 6–3**   Memo for Comparison (see Figures 6–1 and 6–2)

TO:        Paul J. Streer, Partner

FROM:      Billie Sanders

DATE:      April 17, 2011

SUBJECT:   Tax implications of Robert Burke's prospective joint purchase
           of rental real estate.

Our client, Robert Burke, has expressed concern about the tax implications of
a venture he is considering, a joint purchase of real estate with Anne Simmons.
The issue that must be considered is whether Mr. Burke will be subject to a deduction limitation because the property will be used as a residence by Ms. Simmons.
The conclusion is that because the rental agreement is a shared equity financing
agreement, Mr. Burke will not be subject to a deduction limitation.

Client's Situation

On January 1, 2012, Ms. Simmons and Mr. Burke plan to purchase rental real
estate, which Ms. Simmons will occupy as her residence. They will enter into an
agreement whereby Mr. Burke will provide the down payment and one-half of the
monthly mortgage payment. Ms. Simmons will pay the remaining portion of the
monthly mortgage, monthly rental payments to Mr. Burke, and the monthly operating costs of the home. They will split the property taxes evenly. Mr. Burke will
receive one-half of the appreciation value of the home upon its sale and has the
option to demand that his interest in the property be paid to him after five years.

Tax Issue

The issue to be settled is whether Mr. Burke is subject to the deduction limitation
in 280A(c)(5) because the rental property was used as a residence by the taxpayer.

Tax Implications

The agreement between Ms. Simmons and Mr. Burke qualifies as a shared
equity financing agreement under 280A(d)(3)(C). Because the agreement can be
classified as such, 280A(c)(5) will not apply and cannot limit the deductions
attributable to the rental of Mr. Burke's share of the property to the gross
income derived from the rental. This conclusion was also reached by the IRS in
Private Letter Ruling 8410038.

Recommendations

To override the limitation of 280A(c)(5), the shared equity financing agreement must meet certain requirements:

   (1) Under 280A(d)(3)(D), both Ms. Simmons and Mr. Burke must have a
       qualified ownership interest in the property (an undivided interest for
       more than fifty years in the entire property).
   (2) The rent Ms. Simmons pays to Mr. Burke must be the fair rental at the
       time the agreement is entered, taking into account Ms. Simmons' quali-
       fied interest.

Because Mr. Burke will be allowed the deductions and Ms. Simmons will not
(except for expenses allowable even if the dwelling were not rented), payment of
expenses should be the responsibility of Mr. Burke. The agreement can contain a
provision that compensates Mr. Burke for this additional encumbrance. If those
expenses were paid by Ms. Simmons, the deduction would go unused.

The joint purchase Mr. Burke proposes to enter into is sound. The agreement
will not have unfavorable tax implications for him if he is careful to follow these
recommendations.

# A PROFESSIONAL APPEARANCE

If you already have a job, you may find models of well-designed documents by looking at papers written by people with whom you work. In fact, your employer may expect all documents to be written a certain way—in a standard format, for example, and on the company's letterhead and standard stock paper. You'll seem more professional if you learn your employer's expectations for document design and adhere to them.

Often, whether you're on the job or still in school, you'll have some leeway in how you design documents. The remainder of this chapter looks at techniques you can use to give your documents a professional appearance. To ensure that your documents look professional, choose high-quality material: the best paper and the best print. Plan your pages so that they have an attractive use of margins and white space, and be sure they are perfectly neat.

## Paper and Print

If you're already employed, you might not have any choice about the paper; you'll probably use your company's letterhead stationery and standard stock for all your documents. If you are still a student, however, you should select a paper that makes a good impression. For the final copy of a paper you submit for a grade, your instructor may prefer that you use 8½; × 11-inch paper of a high-quality bond, about 24-pound weight, in white or off-white.

The print of your document is another consideration. After you prepare your final manuscript on a computer, print it on a good printer that gives a professional appearance.

Whatever word processing program and printer you use, you will probably have a choice of type sizes and font styles. Choose a 12-point type size and a standard font such as Times New Roman throughout your document. Type sizes and fonts should be easy to read, and they should not draw attention to themselves, so be conservative in your choices. Never use unusual fonts for business documents.

## White Space and Margins

White space is any part of a page without print. White space includes margins, the space between sections, and the space around graphic illustrations.

A document with visual appeal will have a good balance between print and white space. White space also makes a document easier to read. The space between sections, for example, helps the reader see the paper's structure.

No hard-and-fast rules apply to margin widths or the number of lines between sections. As a general guideline, plan about a 1-inch margin for the sides and bottoms of your papers. The top of the first page should have about a 2-inch margin; subsequent pages should have a 1-inch margin at the top.

Leave an extra line space between the sections of your document. A double-spaced page, for example, would have three lines between sections.

For any document that is single-spaced, be sure to double-space between paragraphs.

## Neatness Counts!

Sloppiness in a document is unprofessional and careless. The use of a computer, especially one with a spell-checker, enables you to find errors and make corrections with ease. (Remember, spell-checkers don't distinguish between homonyms, such as *bear* and *bare*. Chapter 5 discussed this problem more fully.) Always proofread the final print-out because it's possible for errors to appear on the printed page that don't show up on a computer screen.

# FORMATTING

Some writers think of their document's format only in terms of straight text: page after page of print unbroken by headings or other divisions. If you look at almost any professional publication, including this handbook, you'll see how various formatting devices, such as headings, lists, and set-off material, make pages more attractive and easier to read.

## Headings

For any document longer than about a half page, you can use headings to divide the paper into sections. Headings make a paper less intimidating to readers because the divisions break up the text into smaller chunks. Headings give readers a chance to pause and reflect on what they've read.

Headings also help readers by showing them the paper's structure and the topics it covers. In fact, many readers preview the contents of a document by skimming through to read the headings. For this reason, headings should be worded so that they indicate the contents of the section to follow. Sometimes headings suggest the main idea of the section, but they should clearly identify the topic discussed. If you look through this book, you'll see how the headings suggest the chapters' contents.

Headings can be broken down into several levels of division. Some headings indicate major sections of a paper and others indicate minor divisions. In other words, a paper can have both headings and subheadings. In this chapter, for example, "A Professional Appearance" indicates a major section of the chapter; "Paper and Print" marks the beginning of a subtopic, because it's just one aspect of a document's appearance. Generally, a short document needs only one heading level, but this rule can vary depending on what you are writing.

The style of the heading (how the heading is placed and printed on the page) varies with the levels of division. Some styles indicate major headings; other styles indicate subheadings. As an example, the major headings might be printed in a boldface font in all capital letters at the left margin, and subheadings might be indented, bold-faced, with only the initial letter of each main word capitalized, as follows:

**FIRST LEVEL: BOLD FONT, LEFT MARGIN, ALL CAPS**
> **Second Level: Bold Font, Initial Letters Capitalized, Indented**
> *Third Level: Indented, Italicized*

Here is another example of heading styles and the corresponding levels of division:

**FIRST LEVEL: CENTERED, ALL CAPS, BOLDFACED**

**Second Level: Left Margin, Boldfaced**
> *Third Level: Indented, Italicized*

If you use fewer than three levels, you can follow this last system of headings, using any of the three styles, as long as they are in descending order. For example, you might use second-level headings for main topics and third-level headings for subtopics. If you are using only one level of headings, any style is acceptable.

It's possible to overuse headings. You should not normally use a heading for every paragraph, for example.

## Lists and Set-Off Material

Another formatting technique that can make a document easier to read is set-off material, especially lists. Mark each item on the list with a number, a bullet, or some other marker. Double-space before and after the list. The items can be single-spaced or double-spaced.

Here is an example of a list using bullets:

Your firm should update its systems in these areas:

- Budgets
- Payrolls
- Fixed assets
- Accounts payable
- Accounts receivable

Set-off lists not only improve the paper's appearance by providing more white space, but they also make the paper more readable. The following examples present the same information as straight text and in a list format. Which arrangement do you prefer?

The meeting will discuss the new vacation policy. First, we'll explain who is eligible for extended vacation leave. Next we'll discuss when the policy will take effect. Finally, we'll discuss how to get vacation requests approved.

*or*

The meeting will discuss the new vacation policy:
- Eligibility for extended leave
- Effective date
- Approval process

Remember that set-off lists should be written with parallel grammatical structure (see pages xx–xx). The set-off list in the previous example uses noun phrases.

Occasionally, you'll use set-off material purposes other than lists. Long direct quotations are set off, and on rare occasions you might set off a sentence or two for emphasis. Chapters 2 through 6 use this technique to emphasize the guidelines for effective writing. Chapter 8 discusses the use of direct quotations.

### Pagination

The next formatting technique is a simple one, but it's overlooked surprisingly often. For every document longer than one page, be sure to include page numbers. They can be placed at either the top or the bottom of the page, in the center, or in the right-hand corner. Begin numbering on page 2.

## GRAPHIC ILLUSTRATIONS

Graphic illustrations—such as tables, graphs, and flowcharts—can make a document more interesting and informative. They enable you to summarize a great deal of information quickly and help readers identify and remember important ideas.

Tables are an efficient way to summarize numerical data in rows and columns. When you use a table, be sure you label the rows and columns, indicate the units of measure you are reporting, and align the figures. Table 6–1, which shows the consolidated statements of income of The Northeastern Beverage Company and Subsidiaries, is an example of a table.

A pie chart shows how a whole is divided into parts, just as a pie is divided into slices. When you use a pie chart, label the wedges and show what percentages of the whole they represent. The pie chart in

TABLE 6–1    The Northeastern Beverage Company and Subsidiaries Consolidated Statements of Income

| | Year ended December 31 | | |
| | 2010 | 2009 | 2008 |
|---|---|---|---|
| (In millions except per share data) | | | |
| **NET OPERATING REVENUES** | **$41,879** | $38,563 | $34,121 |
| Cost of goods sold | **12,173** | 11,924 | 9,945 |
| **GROSS PROFIT** | **29,706** | 26,639 | 24,176 |
| Selling, general, and administrative expenses | **15,674** | 12,949 | 11,811 |
| Other operating charges | **401** | 357 | 332 |
| **OPERATING INCOME** | **13,631** | 13,333 | 12,033 |
| Interest Income | **163** | 302 | 283 |
| Interest Expense | **315** | 408 | 413 |
| Equity income (loss)–net | **666** | 15 | 27 |
| Other income (loss)–net | **39** | 31 | (4) |
| **INCOME BEFORE INCOME TAXES** | **14,184** | 13,273 | 11,926 |
| Income taxes | **3,429** | 2,761 | 2,173 |
| **CONSOLIDATED NET INCOME** | **$10,755** | $10,512 | $9,753 |
| Less: Net income attributable to Noncontrolling interests | **98** | 76 | 61 |
| **NET INCOME ATTRIBUTABLE TO SHAREOWNERS OF THE NORTH- EASTERN BEVERAGE COMPANY** | **$10,657** | $10,436 | $9,692 |
| **BASIC INCOME PER SHARE** | **$3.02** | $3.01 | $2.87 |
| **DILUTED NET INCOME PER SHARE** | **$3.00** | $2.99 | $2.85 |
| **AVERAGE SHARES OUTSTANDING** | **3,528** | 3,472 | 3,891 |
| Effect of dilutive securities | **26** | 19 | 17 |
| **AVERAGE SHARES OUTSTANDING ASSUMING DILUTION** | **3,554** | 3,491 | 3,398 |

Refer to Notes to Consolidated Financial Statements.

Figure 6–4 shows The Northeastern Beverage Company's case volume by state for 2010. The circle represents the total volume, and the slices show the percentages of that total for each state.

Graphs, which can take several forms, are useful for comparisons. Two of the most common types of graphs are bar graphs and line graphs. Bar graphs compare quantities or amounts. The bar graph in Figure 6–5 shows total revenue for Southeastern Sporting Goods.

A line graph, which also compares quantities, is helpful for showing trends. A line graph may contain a single line or multiple lines. The line graph in Figure 6–6 compares the performance of AT&T stock to

**FIGURE 6–4** The Northeastern Beverage Company Case Volume by State

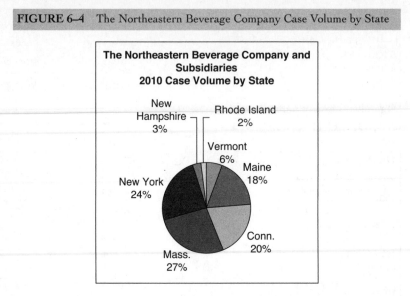

the Standard and Poor's 500 Index, a Peer Group, and the Standard and Poor's 500 Integrated Telecom Index.

Another type of graphic illustration is a flowchart, which shows the steps in a process or procedure. If you use a flowchart in your documents, use boxes or other shapes to show activities or outcomes; label each box or shape and arrange them so that the process flows from left to right and from the top to the bottom of the page.

**FIGURE 6–5** Southeastern Sporting Goods Total Revenue

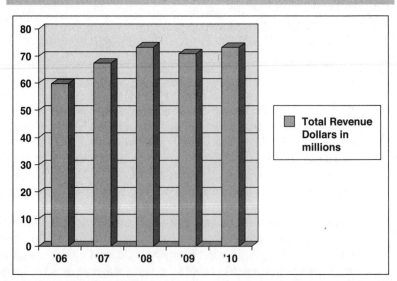

**FIGURE 6–6**   AT&T Stock Performance Graph

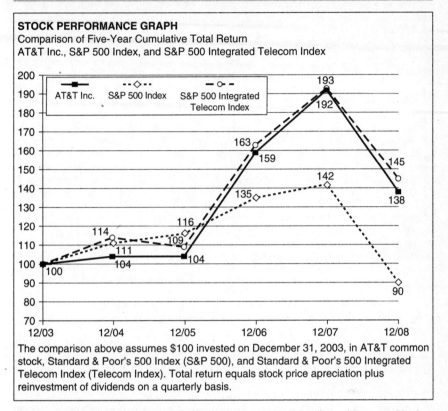

**STOCK PERFORMANCE GRAPH**
Comparison of Five-Year Cumulative Total Return
AT&T Inc., S&P 500 Index, and S&P 500 Integrated Telecom Index

The comparison above assumes $100 invested on December 31, 2003, in AT&T common stock, Standard & Poor's 500 Index (S&P 500), and Standard & Poor's 500 Integrated Telecom Index (Telecom Index). Total return equals stock price apreciation plus reinvestment of dividends on a quarterly basis.

AT&T. "2006 AT&T Annual Report," 2008. Courtesy of AT&T Intellectual Property. Used with permission.

Use arrows to show the direction of the flow. Figure 6–7 shows a typical example.

Systems analyses often include very sophisticated flowcharts to show how a system works, with established symbols and formats to represent different components of the system.

If you include graphic illustrations in the documents you write, whether flowcharts, graphs, or tables, you should follow certain guidelines. Be sure to number the graphic illustrations and give them descriptive titles. Tables should be called Tables (such as Table 6–1), and graphs and flowcharts should be called Figures (such as Figure 6–7). Graphic illustrations should be labeled sufficiently so that they are self-explanatory, but they should also be discussed in the text of the document. This discussion should refer to the illustration by description, name, and number. The discussion should precede the illustration. The illustrations can be placed either in the body of the document, close to the place in the text where they are discussed, or in an appendix.

**FIGURE 6–7** The Cash Flow Estimation Process in Capital Budgeting

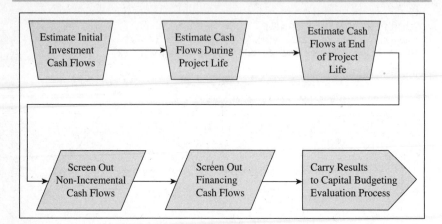

Andrew, Jr., Joseph D., and Timothy Gallagher, *Financial Management: Principles and Practice* (Upper Saddle River, NJ: Prentice-Hall, Inc. © 1996, p. 281). Copyright © 1996 by Textbook Media. Reprinted with permission.

In addition, if you use a graphic illustration from another source, identify the source fully at the bottom of the illustration.

## DOCUMENT DESIGN AT THE COMPUTER

Many of the formatting techniques we've talked about in this chapter are easily applied with a computer and appropriate software, which make changing margins, arranging set-off materials, adding white space, and designing headings easy. In addition, graphics software can help you produce high-quality illustrations. With these tools you can make corrections to the text just before you print your final draft, and you can submit a document that is flawless and professional.

This chapter has completed the guidelines for effective writing.

1. **Analyze the purpose of the writing, the accounting issues involved, and the needs and expectations of the readers.**
2. **Organize your ideas so that readers will find them easy to follow.**
3. **Write the draft and then revise it to make the writing polished and correct.**
4. **Make the writing unified. All sentences should relate to the main idea, either directly or indirectly. Eliminate digressions and irrelevant detail.**
5. **Use summary sentences and transitions to make your writing coherent.**
6. **Write in short paragraphs that begin with clear topic sentences.**
7. **Develop paragraphs by illustrations, definition, detail, and appeals to authority.**
8. **Be concise—make every word count.**
9. **Keep it simple—use simple vocabulary and short sentences.**
10. **Write with active verbs and descriptive nouns.**

11. **Use jargon only when your readers understand it. Define technical terms when necessary.**
12. **Be precise—avoid ambiguous and unclear writing.**
13. **Be concrete and specific. Use facts, details, and examples.**
14. **Use active voice for most sentences.**
15. **Vary vocabulary, sentence lengths, and sentence structures. Read the writing aloud to hear how it sounds.**
16. **Write from the reader's point of view. Use tone to show courtesy and respect.**
17. **Proofread for grammar, punctuation, spelling, and typographical errors.**
18. **Use formatting techniques to give your writing clarity and visual appeal.**

---

# EXERCISES

## Exercise 6–1 [General]

Review several annual reports issued by publicly traded corporations during the most recent year. Identify some reports that are examples of good document design and some that are examples of poor document design. Discuss the design strengths and weaknesses of these statements.

## Exercise 6–2 [General]

Assume you are the president of your school's chapter of Beta Alpha Psi (the national accounting honorary society). The chapter wishes to request funding from the school's Dean of Student Affairs for a job fair, and you have been asked to write a letter to the Dean. What topics should the letter include? What tone will be appropriate for a letter to the Dean? Write the letter, using effective document design. Chapter 9 discusses letters.

## Exercise 6–3 [General]

Assume you are the supervisor of your company's accounting department. Write a memo to the staff suggesting ways they might improve the design of the internal documents they write. Chapter 10 discusses memo writing.

## Exercise 6–4 [Tax]

A client, Hal Mueller, wants to give his sister a house he has owned for several years as a second home. His sister would be allowed to live in it during her lifetime. Upon her death the title to the house would pass to a local university. Mr. Mueller has asked you what the effects of this transaction would be on his personal income tax. Write a letter to Mr. Mueller responding to his inquiry, using the principles of effective document design discussed in this chapter. Chapter 9 discusses letter writing.

### Exercise 6–5 [Tax]

One of your retired clients, George Young, is a very active volunteer with the Red Cross in its disaster services. He has asked you, as his tax advisor, what type of deductions he can take for income tax purposes for expenses associated with his Red Cross activities. He also wants to know what sort of records he should keep to support such deductions. Write a letter to Mr. Young in response to his request, paying attention to good document design. Chapter 9 discusses letter writing.

### Exercise 6–6 [Auditing/Financial]

Assume you are an auditing partner in a regional CPA firm. Write a memo to all audit staff members explaining how subsequent events may or may not affect a compilation and review engagement. Your memo should illustrate effective document design. Chapter 10 discusses memo writing.

### Exercise 6–7 [Auditing]

As a member of the auditing standards team of your CPA firm, you have been asked to write a memo to all audit staff to discuss the distinction between technical compliance with GAAP and "fair presentation." You are expected to also include a discussion of what an auditor's obligation is when these two concepts conflict. Write the memo, paying attention to good document design. Chapter 10 discusses memo writing.

### Exercise 6–8 [Auditing/Ethics]

As a member of the ethics standards team of your CPA firm, you have been asked to write a memo to all audit staff to discuss the importance of ethics in auditing in general, and of compliance with Rule 501 of the AICPA's *Code of Professional Ethics* in particular. Write the memo, paying attention to good document design. Chapter 10 discusses memo writing.

### Exercise 6–9 [Systems]

You are a systems consultant. One of your clients, Elaine Joseph of Joseph Electrical Supply, wants to enter e-commerce. She has expressed concern about control and accounting issues. Write a letter to Ms. Joseph explaining some of the control and accounting issues involved in e-commerce. Your letter should demonstrate effective document design. Chapter 9 discusses letter writing.

## Exercise 6–10 [Systems]

You are a systems consultant. One of your clients, Ben Hill of Hill Manufacturing, is concerned about protecting his company from fraud. He has recently learned that fraud detection software is available and has asked you whether or not he should be using such software and what it might do for his company. Write a letter to Mr. Hill responding to his request. Your letter should demonstrate effective document design. Chapter 9 discusses letter writing.

## Exercise 6–11 [Systems]

As a partner in a regional financial services consulting firm, you have been asked to address a meeting of accounting honor students at a large local university. Your topic will be the importance of studying Accounting Information Systems (AIS) and the value of AIS to all companies. Outline your speech, and design the graphic illustrations you will use to present your ideas. Chapter 15 discusses how to prepare a speech.

---

## NOTES

1. Cynthia A. Glassman, "Speech by SEC Commissioner: Remarks at the Plain Language Association International's Fifth International Conference," Securities and Exchange Commission, 2005. www.sec.gov/news/speech/ spch110405cag.htm (6 December 2010).

# CHAPTER

## Critical Thinking

*7*

In earlier chapters we've noted how important critical thinking
skills are to the analysis and communication of accounting information. We defined critical thinking as fair, open-minded thinking
that asks appropriate questions and considers all relevant information
before reaching a conclusion. Critical thinkers consider problems
from multiple points of view before reaching a decision, and they are
careful to avoid reasoning errors, which are called logical fallacies.
They also use precise, clear language to construct unambiguous arguments that readers can understand and, in turn, evaluate fairly. In
other words, critical thinkers are responsible in their analysis of issues
and communication of ideas; critical thinking is thus a component of
ethical responsibility. And critical thinking is inseparable from effective communication.

In this chapter we will consider in more detail the critical thinking topics introduced in earlier chapters and investigate additional
topics that will help you become a careful thinker as well as a more
responsible and effective communicator. We will discuss the process
of constructing an argument, two approaches to logical reasoning,
and some of the fallacies you should learn to recognize and avoid.
We will then show how you can use critical thinking to resolve ethical dilemmas.

## MAKING AN ARGUMENT: THE PROCESS

As a practicing professional, you will sometimes be asked to recommend a course of action for your firm or your clients. To derive a
sound recommendation, you must construct an argument. This
process can be divided into steps, some of which have been introduced
in earlier chapters. Here is a summary of this process:

1. Identify the key issues.
2. Anticipate all sides to an argument.
3. Research all sides, using authoritative sources.
4. Weigh the evidence for all sides, and build support for your position.
5. Identify and respond to counterarguments.
6. Communicate your conclusions.

To illustrate the process, consider this hypothetical scenario. You are an accountant employed by a medium-size accounting firm in a southern city. The firm has 20 accountants on its staff, in addition to technical and clerical support staff. The firm has had its offices in a grand old office building in the downtown heart of the city for the past 60 years. However, the owners of the building have decided to convert the building to residential condominiums, forcing your firm to relocate. You have been asked to recommend the best alternative for the new office. After researching the alternatives, you will present your recommendation in the form of a memo to the firm's partners. How do you form and communicate your recommendation? The process listed previously will help you, as you construct an argument to support your conclusions.

A word of caution is in order here: Remember that it's always important to consider the expectations of your readers and the purpose of the document you are writing. What are the expectations of the partners who asked you to investigate the relocation problem? Do they expect you to identify the one best site for the firm, or have they asked you to recommend several viable locations, giving the advantages and disadvantages of each choice? In the latter case, the partners themselves would make the final selection, based on the information you have provided. You would have narrowed the field, then, through your analysis and research. For the purposes of this hypothetical example, assume that the partners have delegated this responsibility to you: You will decide on the best site and then defend your choice for the partners' final approval.

1. *Identify key issues.* The first step in constructing an argument is to identify the key issues. In the situation just described, the most important issues might be, first, where in the city the new office should be located and, second, whether the firm should lease office space, purchase an office condominium, or purchase or construct its own building. Each of these major issues could be further analyzed. You should consider the availability and costs of suitable space, the suitability of potential sites for the firm's business, and the accounting implications of the decision to lease, purchase, or construct.

2. *Anticipate all sides to the argument.* Before you reach your conclusions, you need to identify all the reasonable alternatives. With preliminary research, you'll gather information about the obvious choices. You also need to identify the preferences of other people involved in the decision and take account of their knowledge, experience, assumptions, and biases. It's especially important to consider the views of those who will make the final decision, in this case the firm's partners. Listen carefully to what other people say, read carefully what they have written on the issues in question, and, where appropriate, ask them to clarify their views or make preliminary suggestions for the best solution to the problem. For example, before you suggest a lease, purchase, or construction in this scenario, find out if the partners are willing to consider

all three possibilities. You should also determine which sections of the city they believe to be viable locations for the firm. Are they determined to maintain the firm's office in the center of the city, or would they consider moving to a midtown or suburban location?

3. *Research all sides, using authoritative sources.* After you have identified the alternative solutions to your problem, you can research the possibilities, including sources for both accounting and nonaccounting information. Consider your firm's needs and how alternative sites would accommodate those needs. Is the location convenient to the firm's employees and clients, and is the location suitable for business? Is adequate parking or public transportation available for the firm's employees and clients? What other businesses are located in this area? Would proposed buildings require renovation? What are the costs of these renovations in both time and money as well as other moving costs? All these decisions involve accounting considerations, which you also must research. What are the accounting and tax implications of the decision to lease, purchase, or construct? Refer to specific GAAP for these scenarios. (For more information on using authoritative accounting sources, see Chapter 8.)

4. *Weigh the evidence for all sides, and build support for your position.* After you've analyzed the information found in your research, the solution to your problem may be obvious. In this example, assume that you have identified the best site for the firm's relocation after weighing the pros and cons of the alternatives, and that you are ready to give the reasons for your conclusions. Building support for your conclusion involves organizing your ideas and materials in a logical order. This organization might take the form of an outline: the key issues, the recommendation, and the reasons to support your recommendation, from most to least important.

5. *Identify and respond to counterarguments.* In this office relocation example, some of the partners may have initial preferences for a different location, or they may raise objections to the site you've selected. At this point in the construction of your argument, the analysis becomes somewhat more complicated: You must identify in advance the reasons why other concerned people might disagree with your conclusions; That is, you must identify the *counterarguments* (arguments against your position). You must also decide how you will respond to these objections—whether you will agree with them (concede the counterarguments) or argue against them (refute the counterarguments).

The response to a counterargument may be a combination of concession and refutation. For instance, one of the partners in this example may object that the site you've recommended requires extensive, costly renovation. You might concede that those costs will be high, but also point out that over time the costs will be more than made up because the cost of the new lease (or purchase) will be considerably lower than the firm's current lease expense.

Sometimes people constructing an argument believe that presenting both sides (or all sides) of the argument will weaken their position. Just the opposite is the case, however. By presenting all sides, you'll create the impression that you are a responsible person who has carefully considered all sides of an issue before reaching a conclusion. Thus people will find you credible and fair and will take your argument seriously.

To complete this step successfully, keep an open mind and imagine the situation from multiple points of view. Review the questions you asked in step 2 or ask additional questions. Would it be appropriate for you to seek preliminary feedback on your conclusions, before you present the final recommendation?

6. *Communicate your conclusions to the appropriate decision makers.* In this step, you present your conclusions and your reasons, along with the counterarguments you have anticipated and your response to them. You may present your conclusions orally, perhaps in a meeting, or in a written document such as a memo, letter, or report. In this example, you'll write the memo the partners have requested. For written documents, apply the effective writing techniques discussed in Chapters 1–14 of this book, as needed. For oral presentations, follow the guidelines given in Chapter 15. You may, of course, be asked to present your recommendations in both oral and written formats. For both formats, remember the importance of a coherent, logical arrangement of ideas (Chapter 3); precise, clear language (Chapters 4 and 5); and attractive visual aids—in this case, perhaps maps and photographs (Chapter 6).

## Reaching Sound Conclusions: Two Approaches to Logic

Critical thinking is the construction of an argument, often in a manner such as the process outlined in the preceding section. It may also be thought of as an exercise of logic, which is defined as the practice of good reasoning. The science of logic is often divided into inductive and deductive reasoning. Recall that Chapter 3 discussed deductive and inductive structures for paragraphs. Deductive paragraphs begin with the main idea, or topic sentence, and then give support for or details of this idea. Inductive paragraphs offer the support and the details before the conclusion, which is presented at the end of the paragraph. This section of the chapter further examines these forms of critical thinking, as well as some of the more commonly made reasoning errors, which are called fallacies.

### *Inductive Reasoning*

The process used to construct an argument in the office relocation scenario discussed previously demonstrates one form of inductive reasoning: gathering evidence and then reaching a conclusion. More formally, inductive reasoning is defined as reaching conclusions about the entirety of something (the whole) from a study of representative examples (parts of that whole). The scientific method of research is one example of inductive reasoning: observing samples, gathering data, and drawing tentative conclusions, or hypotheses, which are then further tested for verification. Some variations of inductive reasoning include making comparisons (drawing analogies), analyzing causes, conducting surveys, referring to authoritative sources, and citing statistics. In short, inductive reasoning begins with specific facts and from these facts derives general conclusions or principles.

*Deductive Reasoning*

With inductive reasoning, you gather specific information and then reach a general conclusion. With deductive reasoning, you apply reasoning in the opposite direction; you begin with one or more general principles and arrive at a specific conclusion through reasoning. Consider these examples:

> All accounting majors at this university must take a course in tax accounting.
>
> Jenny is an accounting major at this university.
>
> Therefore, Jenny must take a course in tax accounting.

Deductive reasoning is often stated in the form of a syllogism. A *syllogism* consists of a major premise, a minor premise, and a conclusion. In the preceding example, the first line is the major premise, the second line is the minor premise, and the third line is the conclusion.

Here's another example of a syllogism:

MAJOR PREMISE: Asset account balances increase with debits.
MINOR PREMISE: The asset account was debited.
CONCLUSION: The asset account balance increased.

To reach sound conclusions using deductive reasoning, you must be sure your arguments are both valid and sound. The terms *valid* and *sound* will become clearer with examples. First, a *valid* argument is one in which the conclusion has been correctly drawn from the premises. Study the following examples:

*Example 1:* Valid argument

MAJOR PREMISE: All the students in this class have passed the placement test.
MINOR PREMISE: Robert is a student in this class.
CONCLUSION: Therefore, Robert has passed the placement test.

*Example 2:* Invalid argument

MAJOR PREMISE: All the students in this class have passed the placement test.
MINOR PREMISE: Robert has passed the placement test.
CONCLUSION: Therefore, Robert is a student in this class.

In the valid argument in Example: 1, the conclusion has been correctly drawn from the premises, unlike the invalid argument in Example 2. In Example 2, even though Robert has passed the placement test, he might not be a student in the class for any number of reasons. He might have taken the class in an earlier semester, postponed the class until a later semester, be enrolled in a different section of the class, changed his major, or transferred to another school.

Let's look at two more examples. Example 3 is a valid argument—the conclusion has been correctly drawn from the premises—but Example 4 is invalid:

*Example 3:* Valid argument

MAJOR PREMISE:  All publicly held companies must construct financial statements following GAAP.
MINOR PREMISE:  Brite Company is a publicly held company
CONCLUSION:  Therefore, Brite Company must construct its financial statements following GAAP.

*Example 4:* Invalid argument

MAJOR PREMISE:  All publicly held companies must construct financial statements following GAAP.
MINOR PREMISE:  Brite Company constructs its financial statements following GAAP.
CONCLUSION:  Brite Company is a publicly held company.

Many companies that are not publicly held also construct financial statements following GAAP. Thus, Brite Company might not be publicly held.

Deductive reasoning must be sound, as well as valid, for the conclusions to be true. *Sound* reasoning requires not only that (a) the conclusion has been correctly drawn from the premises, but also that (b) the premises are themselves true. For a sound conclusion, both the major and minor premises must be true. For instance, in the preceding Example 1, the conclusion would not be sound if either the major or minor premise is not true: (1) Some students in the class have not passed the placement test, or (2) Robert is not a student in the class.

Sometimes, the use of a syllogism will help you spot errors in reasoning. Consider the following example:

The SEC has filed charges against The Gigantic National Corporation for cheating its former employees out of their pension benefits. Larry Womack, the CEO, issues this statement to the press: "The buck stops here. As CEO, I must accept responsibility for the fraud uncovered by the SEC. A few unscrupulous middle managers have violated company policy and the law by authorizing and carrying out this fraud. Those responsible will be identified and will no longer work for this corporation. I deplore what has happened, but I will not resign."

What is wrong with the reasoning expressed in Womack's statement? We can analyze his argument in the form of a syllogism such as this one:

MAJOR PREMISE:  The person(s) responsible for the fraud will no longer work for this corporation.
MINOR PREMISE:  I am responsible for the fraud.
CONCLUSION:  I will not resign.

You can see that the conclusion in this case does not follow logically from the major and minor premises. This argument is invalid. Put another way, the CEO has contradicted himself.

## Fallacies: Mistakes in Reasoning

To reach sound conclusions, you must be careful to avoid mistakes in reasoning; that is, you must learn to recognize and avoid fallacies in the arguments you make or those made by others. We have already considered the requirements that a deductive argument be both valid and sound; that is, the argument must avoid the fallacies of drawing improper conclusions from the premises, or reasoning from false premises. Some other common fallacies that you should also avoid are listed here along with examples of each:

- *Fallacies involving language:* Using ambiguous word choices (vague or undefined), loaded language, labels, and slogans

  Anyone who favors the passage of this legislation is unpatriotic.

  (What does *unpatriotic* mean in this case? This word, as it is used here, is vague and loaded. That is, it may generate an emotional response unrelated to critical thinking about the legislation in question.)

- *Fallacies involving appeals to emotion:* Appealing to fear, pity, anger, or prejudice

  If we change our pension plan, widows and orphans will suffer.

  (This argument illustrates an appeal to pity. Of course, decision makers should consider the effects of the proposed change on pension recipients, but other reasons should also be evaluated. It might be, for example, that the company will go bankrupt if it doesn't change its pension plan.)

- *Fallacy of appeal to tradition:* Arguing for something only because it's customary

  We shouldn't promote Joanne Risling to a partner position. Her degree is from a private university. It's tradition that our partners graduate from the state university.

- *Fallacy of false authority:* Using authorities that are unidentified, irrelevant, or lacking proper credentials

  Experts agree that Whiz Kid makes the best computers.

  (Who are these experts?)

  We should invest in this stock because all our friends are buying it.

  (This statement illustrates a type of false authority called the bandwagon fallacy: "Get on the bandwagon and do what everybody else is doing.")

- *Ad hominem fallacy:* Attacking opponents' character, rather than their arguments

  Don't listen to what he's saying. He's an idiot.

- *Post hoc fallacy:* Assuming that because one circumstance happens before another, the first circumstance is the cause of the second

After we hired Stan Sterling, our company's profits increased. Clearly Stan is the reason for our increased profitability.

(Hiring Stan may indeed have affected the company's profits; however, we need more information before reaching this conclusion. What is Stan's position? What other factors, such as changes in the market, might be responsible for the growth in profits?)

- *Hasty generalization fallacy:* Using poor or inadequate sampling techniques

Professor Brown is a poor teacher. I know this because my roommate took his tax accounting course and complained about it every day.

Clearly, Jan Smith will be elected class president. I asked three of the people on my hall, and all of them plan to vote for Smith.

- *Either/or fallacy (false dilemma):* Assuming there are only two choices, when there may be several

You're either for me or against me.

(I may support you as a general rule but disagree with you on this particular point.)

Either we adopt this measure, or we face bankruptcy.

(We might adopt a different measure and avoid bankruptcy.)

- *Slippery slope fallacy:* Arguing that if one event occurs, a series of undesirable events will inevitably occur as a result

If we provide cell phones to our sales staff, the next thing you know they'll demand their own laptop computers, then company cars, and then chauffeurs to drive those cars. They'll then want unlimited expense accounts for trips to Las Vegas. The company will go bankrupt.

Earlier, we defined critical thinking as fair, open-minded thinking that asks appropriate questions and considers all relevant information before reaching a conclusion. Although there is no formula for achieving critical thinking, if you keep in mind the factors we have discussed in this chapter, your thinking will be much more responsible, enabling you to be a more effective communicator.

## Critical Thinking and Ethical Dilemmas

Chapter 1 of this handbook discussed the importance of ethics in the practice of accounting. We saw that accountants are expected to uphold a high standard of ethics in the practice of their professional responsibilities. They find guidance for making ethical decisions in legal requirements, codes of ethics (such as the AICPA's Code of Professional Ethics), and their personal ethical values. Often what constitutes ethical behavior is obvious, but sometimes accountants face complex situations for which the ethical solution is not immediately clear. Critical thinking can help resolve these ethical dilemmas.

The process to resolve ethical dilemmas resembles the steps you take to make a strong argument, as discussed earlier in this chapter. Indeed, identifying and defending a course of action as the most ethical among several alternatives is itself a kind of argument even if one you have only with yourself. When you are faced with a situation that requires you to make an ethical decision, follow these steps:

1. Obtain all the facts relevant to the situation.
2. Identify the ethical issues.
3. Determine who will be affected by the way these issues are resolved. Consider individuals as well as groups, such as shareholders, employees, and the general public.
4. Identify alternative solutions to the issues, including arguments that might be used to support each alternative.
5. Analyze how the individuals and groups identified in step 3 would be affected by the alternative solutions.
6. Consider guidelines for ethical decisions, such as applicable legal requirements, codes of ethics, and your own ethical values. Be careful to avoid logical fallacies in your thinking.
7. Decide on the appropriate action and, when necessary, communicate your decision to the appropriate parties. If the situation is potentially contentious, be prepared to provide the reasons for your decision. When you write or speak to someone about the ethical issues, be especially tactful, courteous, and respectful to all parties concerned.

As you can see, resolving ethical dilemmas depends on critical thinking, as well as effective communication.

---

## TEST YOURSELF

The following statements contain mistakes in reasoning (fallacies). Which fallacies are illustrated here? (Some statements may illustrate more than one fallacy.)

1. Ever since I moved into this new building last month, my allergies have been worse. The building is clearly the cause of the allergies.
2. Give them an inch, and they'll take a mile.
3. Our country: Love it or leave it.
4. Don't listen to him. He's just a money-grabbing capitalist (or bleeding-heart liberal).
5. Three out of four accountants agree: *The Daily Balance Sheet* is the best source of financial news.
6. We don't need more public transportation in our city. Everyone in my office agrees they'd rather drive their own cars.
7. In our family, we eat pizza, potato chips, and ice cream every Friday night. I wouldn't feel right changing this custom even though my doctor tells me to lose weight.
8. We shouldn't hire Jim Blankenship. He's from Hick City, and everybody knows people from there are just a bunch of ignorant buffoons.

## TEST YOURSELF ANSWERS

1. Post hoc fallacy. Something in the building *might* be causing the allergy problem, but other causes are possible as well, including the season of the year.
2. Slippery slope.
3. False choice. This statement also illustrates the fallacy of using slogans rather than arguments.
4. Ad hominem and loaded language.
5. False authority. What is the origin of this statistic?
6. False authority and hasty generalization.
7. Appeal to tradition.
8. Appeal to emotion (prejudice), loaded language, ad hominem.

## EXERCISES

### Exercise 7–1 [General]

Your school is considering a new attendance policy. If this policy is adopted, students will be allowed only three absences for each class during the term. After the fourth absence, the registrar's office will suspend the student. Suspended students will be allowed to appeal the suspension if they can offer documented evidence that they missed the classes for legitimate reasons, such as illness, a death in the family, or jury duty.

Do you believe the new attendance policy should be adopted? Following the guidelines for critical thinking discussed in this chapter, decide where you stand on this issue. (Remember the importance of identifying and responding to counterarguments.) After you have formed your conclusions, write your argument in the form of a letter to the Dean of Students at your school. Chapter 9 discusses letters.

### Exercise 7–2 [General]

Some administrators in your school have proposed a change in grading policy for major level courses (i.e., beyond the principles or introductory level). They propose that instructors be required to apply a normal curve (normal distribution) to grades, rather than scaling the grades. What would be the advantages and disadvantages of this proposed policy? Consider both sides of this question, using critical thinking to analyze the pros and cons of the proposal. Then write a letter to the editor of your school's newspaper, or the local newspaper where your school is located, in which you summarize your findings. Chapter 9 discusses letters.

### Exercise 7–3 [Financial/Ethics]

You are a staff accountant at Outrageous Corporation. The controller of the company, Howard Eino, is concerned that profits reported in the annual report will not meet those forecast at the beginning of the year. He has asked you to decrease the amount of annual depreciation charged on certain equipment by revising the estimated life. When you tell Mr. Eino that revision of useful life solely to "manage" profit is not appropriate, he responds by saying, "Oh, everybody does it." You realize that if you fail to do what your boss wants, you may receive an unfavorable annual performance evaluation. How will you resolve this dilemma?

To help yourself think through this problem, you've decided to write an outline in which you'll record the issues, relevant information, your reasoning, and the course of action you finally decide to take. You won't show the outline to anyone else, but you want it to be complete and well-organized so that your thinking will be clear. Write the outline.

### Exercise 7–4 [General]

Look for illustrations of the fallacies discussed in this chapter in print media, on radio or television, on the Internet, or in the conversations you hear. Quote or paraphrase the passage that illustrates the fallacy, giving a citation of the source. Then identify the fallacy and explain the error in reasoning the passage demonstrates. Chapter 8 discusses how to document sources.

### Exercise 7–5 [Financial/Theory]

Some people would argue that historical costs should no longer be used in accounting because they are not relevant. Others argue that departing from historical costs introduces too much subjectivity into accounting. Write out a detailed outline for a presentation to your class providing a defense of both points of view and then explain why in many cases the FASB has chosen to depart from historical cost in many of its accounting standards.

To prepare for this assignment, you may wish to review Chapter 15 on oral presentations.

### Exercise 7–6 [Auditing/Theory]

Some have suggested eliminating the provision of Rule 203 of the AICPA's professional ethics that permits nonconformance with GAAP if, in the opinion of the CPA, following GAAP would result in misleading financial statements. Thoroughly discuss the pros and cons of eliminating this provision of Rule 203 and present a convincing argument as to whether it should or should not be eliminated.

Prepare your argument in the form of a memo to the managing partner of your CPA firm, Elaine Morgan. Chapter 10 discusses memos.

## Exercise 7–7 [Financial/International]

In 2010 the International Accounting Standards Board (IASB) changed its constitution to emphasize the adoption of International Financial Reporting Standards (IFRSs), rather than simply convergence of those standards with standards issued by individual countries. Write an essay on whether the SEC should support convergence between United States GAAP and IFRSs, or whether the SEC should support adoption of IFRSs. Your essay should demonstrate your understanding of critical thinking. Assume the audience for your essay is accounting students in your class. Chapter 11 discusses essays.

## Exercise 7–8 [Tax]

Write an essay that addresses the purpose, structure, and recent activities of the IRS Oversight Board. Include a discussion of its strategy to reduce the "tax gap" — that is, to reduce the amount of uncollected taxes. Your essay should demonstrate your understanding of critical thinking. Assume the audience for your essay is accounting students in your class. Chapter 11 discusses essays.

## Exercise 7–9 [Systems]

Write a brief article for your accounting honorary society's Web page about why an accounting student should study accounting information systems. Your purpose is to give a logical argument to persuade students to elect to take an advanced systems course. Chapter 14, which discusses writing for publication, will help you prepare your article.

## Exercise 7–10 [Managerial]

Your accounting honorary society's Web page is running a series of articles about various careers in accounting that accounting students might choose. You have been asked to write an article about the advantages of a career in management accounting. Write the article with the purpose of persuading students to seek a career in management accounting without discouraging them from considering other career choices. Chapter 14 discusses writing for publication.

# CHAPTER

# Accounting 8 Research

Accountants and business services professionals often do research to solve technical accounting or tax problems or to gather information on some general topic of interest, such as the feasibility of offering a new service to their clients. This chapter discusses how to conduct research and write a research paper or technical memorandum. If you have written documented papers or reports before, much of this material will be review. However, the suggestions should be helpful to anyone who must conduct research and write a summary of the results.

The first part of the chapter discusses basic guidelines for all research, including using electronic and printed sources of information, taking and using notes, using direct quotations and paraphrases, and documenting sources. The remainder of the chapter focuses on specific steps in the technical accounting research process, including determining relevant facts, identifying key issues, researching the literature, considering alternative solutions, and communicating results. These steps in the research process are similar to the guidelines given in the Chapter 7 for critical thinking and resolving ethical dilemmas. Accountants need all these skills to solve problems encountered in practice.

## RESEARCH: BASIC GUIDELINES

If your project requires research, chances are you already know something about the topic you will research. If you don't, you may need to do some initial reading so that you have a basic familiarity with your subject. After you have a general idea of what your topic involves, you're ready to begin your research in more depth.

One author said this about research:

> Research . . . is the process of obtaining information systematically. That process is deliberate and is conducted carefully and with diligence. Usually, research implies an exhaustive search for and collection of information to resolve a problem and includes the collection of that pertinent information.[1]

The key is that good research requires deliberation, care, and diligence. You should look at all possible sources of information so that you don't overlook something important.

Often it's a good idea to write out a research plan before you begin your research. In your research plan, you can list known information sources and references to consult to determine additional resources. For example, let's assume your research topic is "forensic services" and that you are aware that the AICPA has published a report on this topic. You also realize that professional journals have published articles on forensic services. Initially, your research plan might list the following:

- Check the AICPA Web site to see if the report on forensic services is posted. You can also check the Web site for other information on forensic services or links to such information.
- Check the *Journal of Accountancy* and other professional journals for past articles.
- Do a keyword search of any electronic literature indexes available at the library for articles or reports from the past two years.
- Do a topical and keyword search of the Web.

As you begin to follow your research plan, you should modify it to include references to other resources you find. Thus, you may add references to specific articles, reports, Web sites, indexes, or searchable databases. As you come across specific sources, such as published articles and reports, look at the bibliographical, footnote, or endnote references they contain. These will often lead you to useful material you may not find otherwise.

As you conduct your research, keep track of what you have done by checking off the steps listed in your plan. If your research includes a keyword search of an electronic index or database, be sure to keep a log of the keywords and keyword combinations you have used in your search and the results you obtained. Keeping good records will increase the efficiency of your research because you can avoid duplicating searches; at the same time, you can critique the search process you have followed to determine what you may have missed or how to refine the process. Keeping records of your sources will also help you write the citations for your final document.

### *FASB Accounting Standards Codification*™

In 2009 the Financial Accounting Standards Board (FASB) released a new codification system for Generally Accepted Accounting Principles (GAAP) called the *FASB Accounting Standards Codification*™ (often referred to as "ASC" or "Codification"). The FASB now refers to the Codification as "the single source of authoritative nongovernmental U.S. Generally Accepted Accounting Principles (US GAAP)." The Codification supersedes all existing non–Securities and Exchange Commission (non-SEC) standards. The FASB now issues all authoritative US GAAP in the form of Accounting Standards Updates (ASUs), rather than FASB Statements, FASB Interpretations, EITF Abstracts, and such. Accounting Standards ASUs are used to revise the Codification and are not by themselves considered to be authoritative.[2]

The FASB's new Codification will affect the way you cite accounting standards for papers you prepare for your accounting courses or for any other accounting writing you may complete. The Codification uses a system of Topic numbers, Subtopic numbers, Section numbers, and Paragraph numbers. So, for example, the definition of *goodwill* may be found in Topic 310 ("Intangibles—Goodwill and Other"), Subtopic 10 ("Overall"), Section 05 ("Overview and Background"), Paragraph 01, and it would be cited as "FASB ASC par. 310-10-05-01."

The Codification is available in both printed and electronic form. (See "CD-ROM and Online Databases," p. 129, and Appendix 8–B at the end of this chapter, for more information on this source.)

## Electronic Sources of Information

Electronic sources of information include the Internet, online databases (including the electronic version of the *FASB Accounting Standards Codification*™), and CD-ROM databases. The quantity and availability of these electronic sources, along with how quickly and easily they can be searched, should place them high on your list of resources for most research.

### The Internet

One step in your research plan should be to search the Internet for material related to your topic. Search engines such as Google enable you to locate documents ("pages") on the Web. Tailor the search to your needs by using keywords or phrases associated with your research topic.

The Internet may lead you to publications available at your library or to documents that you can download. Read the material you find on the Internet carefully and take accurate notes of your findings, including references to the sources you are using. (A later section of this chapter discusses note taking and how to properly indicate references in more detail.) Print out useful material you find, unless the length of a particular source makes this impractical, in which case you should save it on a disk or burn it on a CD and record the Web address (URL).

Appendix 8-A at the end of this chapter shows some of the better Web sites available on the Internet that offer information related to accounting and finance as well as links to other useful sites.

*CD-ROM and Online Databases*

Many information databases are available on CD-ROM or online. The FASB Accounting Standards and AICPA Professional Standards are both available in this manner. You can use the Financial Accounting Research System (FARS), available from the FASB, to search FASB and AICPA publications.

The *FASB Accounting Standards Codification™ Research System* covers accounting literature issued by several standard setters. FASB publications included are Statements, Interpretations, Technical Bulletins, Staff Positions, Staff Implementation Guides, and Statement 138 Examples. Abstracts and Topic D of the Emerging Issues Task Force are included, as are Derivatives Implementation Group Issues, Accounting Principles Board Opinions, Accounting Research Bulletins, and Accounting Interpretations. AICPA Statements of Position, Audit and Accounting Guides, Practice Bulletins, and Technical Inquiry Service issuances are also available here, along with "relevant portions of authoritative content issued by the SEC and selected SEC staff interpretations and administrative guidance."[3]

*CCH's Accounting Research Manager®* contains "analytical accounting, auditing, governmental, internal controls, and SEC information as well as primary source data."[4] The *CCH® Tax Research NetWork™* or CCH's *Standard Federal Tax Reporter*, which is available in print or is accessible electronically through CCH's *IntelliConnect®*, can be indispensable for tax research.[5] Thomson Reuters' *Checkpoint* is another good on-line research database for tax research.[6]

Many other databases are available on CD-ROM or online. Appendix 8–B at the end of this chapter lists many of the most useful computerized references and databases available for accounting and finance research.

## Printed Sources of Information

Although electronic media can provide excellent sources for your research, don't limit your research to electronic sources; some important information may not be available in electronic form. Printed information sources will require conventional library research. When electronic sources are unavailable, you'll have to use printed resources.

Even if your library doesn't have specialized electronic databases, it most likely has a general database, which lists articles published in most periodicals, including accounting periodicals. You'll access this database by a keyword search, so be imaginative in looking for articles on your topic; consider the different headings under which articles might be listed.

One print source of information about technical accounting topics is official accounting standards. The *FASB Accounting Standards Codification™* is available in printed form as well as electronic. You can also study printed versions of government regulations or laws to find out how to handle a client's technical problem. In either case, read the material carefully and take accurate notes of your findings, including references to the sources you use.

Appendix 8–C at the end of this chapter lists some of the popular printed sources of accounting information. The library probably has other references that you may find helpful as well. For example, many newspapers publish an index. Many of these indexes are available both as reference books and as computerized reference services.

A librarian can help you find references that will help you to prepare your paper.

## Note Taking

After you have located a useful source, take notes on what you read. You may decide to take notes on a computer, particularly if you have a laptop that you can take to the library or keep next to the computer terminal at which you are conducting an electronic search. Using a computer can help you write your notes and organize them at the same time, which will save you time later. Any good word processing or database program can be used to take notes.

Some people prefer to handwrite their notes rather than use a computer. Most of the techniques discussed here apply in either case.

If you take notes on a computer, you'll need two computer files: one for the bibliography (the list of sources you used) and another for your notes. (If you handwrite your notes, you can use two sets of cards: 4 × 6-inch cards for your notes and 3 × 5-inch cards for your bibliography.)

Be sure to include in the *bibliography file* all the information you will need for the bibliography (see the section on documentation later in this chapter). The following are examples of entries you might make in your bibliography file:

1. Financial Accounting Standards Board (FASB). *Accounting Standards Codification*™, Topic 350, "Intangibles—Goodwill and Other." Stamford, Conn.: FASB, 2010.

2. Financial Accounting Standards Board (FASB). *Objectives of Financial Reporting by Business Enterprises, Statement of Financial Accounting Concepts No. 1.* Stamford, Conn.: FASB, 1978.

Give each of your sources a number. The number will save time when you take notes from that source and later when you draft your paper. The source just illustrated is numbered *1*.

The *note file* contains the information you will actually use in your paper. Notice the parts of this note file entry:

II.  A. 1.—Goodwill definition
[1] Subtopic 10, Sect. 05, Par. 01

"An asset representing the future economic benefits arising from other assets acquired in a business combination or an acquisition by a not-for-profit entity that are not individually identified and separately recognized."

The first line of the note file entry gives an outline code (II. A. 1.), which corresponds with the section in your outline where the note fits, and a short description of what the note is about. The second line gives the number of the source for this note as contained in your bibliography file and the page or paragraph numbers where this information was found ([1] Subtopic 10, Sect. 05, Par. 01). The note itself is taken from the source and is the material you will use in your paper.

## Direct Quotation and Paraphrase

You can take notes in two ways: as a direct quotation (the exact words from the source) or as a paraphrase (your own words and sentence structures). If you take notes as direct quotations, you can decide later whether to use a direct quotation or paraphrase in your paper. However, if you're sure you won't need a direct quotation in your paper and you take the time to paraphrase as you research, you'll save time when writing the draft. Remember, too, that no more than about 10% of most papers should be direct quotations.

Here's a good way to paraphrase. Read a section from your source (or quotation copied earlier into your notes)—perhaps several short paragraphs. Then look away and try to remember the important ideas. Write them down. Then look back to check your notes for accuracy.

If you take notes as quotations, use quotation marks so you'll know later that these are someone else's words. Copy the quotation exactly, including capitalization and punctuation. It's important that direct quotations be accurate in every way and that paraphrases be your own words and sentence structures, not just a slight variation of your source.

## Plagiarism

It's important to give credit for material you borrow from another writer, whether you paraphrase or quote directly, and whether you've used electronic or printed sources. If you don't, you'll be guilty of plagiarism. The *Prentice Hall Handbook for Writers* contains the following discussion of plagiarism:

Plagiarism consists of passing off the ideas, opinions, conclusions, facts, words_in short, the intellectual work_of another as your own. . . .

* * *

The most obvious kind of plagiarism occurs when you appropriate whole paragraphs or longer passages from another writer for your own paper. . . . No less dishonest is the use of all or most of a single

sentence or an apt figure of speech appropriated without acknowl-
edgment from another source.

* * *

. . . even though you acknowledge the source in a citation, you are also
plagiarizing when you incorporate in your paper faultily paraphrased or
summarized passages from another author in which you follow almost
exactly the original's sentence patterns and phrasing. Paraphrasing
and summarizing require that you fully digest an author's ideas and
interpretations and restate them in your own words_and you must reference the source. It is not enough simply to modify the original
author's sentences slightly, to change a word here and there.[7]

Plagiarism, therefore, can involve the unacknowledged (undocu-
mented) use of someone else's *idea*—not just the use of the person's
exact words.

The key to avoiding plagiarism is to document your sources adequately with either internal documentation or notes (see the section
on documentation). In actual practice, however, sometimes you
might not know whether you should identify the source of information you want to use in your paper. The difficulty arises because
information that is considered common knowledge in a given field
need not be documented.

Obviously the problem is to decide what is common knowledge.
One guideline says that if you can find the same information in three
different sources, that information is considered common knowledge
and, therefore, needs no documentation.

There are many gray areas when it comes to issues of plagiarism.
Perhaps the safest rule is to document your sources whenever there is
any question of plagiarism.

Remember: Plagiarism is theft of another person's words or ideas.
In some situations, it's punishable by law. If you plagiarize at school,
the repercussions are very serious: You may fail the assignment, fail
the course, or be expelled, depending on your school's policies.
Plagiarism on the job may lead to termination.

## Organizing Your Notes and Ideas

As you take notes, you will probably form some idea of the major
divisions of your paper; that is, you should be getting a rough idea of
its outline.

Go ahead and write down your ideas for an outline. The more
reading you do, the more complete the outline will become. Stop and
evaluate the outline from time to time. Are you covering all the
important areas of your topic? Is the outline getting too long? Should
you narrow the topic? Are some sections of the outline irrelevant to
the topic? Answering these questions will guide you as you continue
your research.

## Writing Your Research Report or Memo

When your research is complete, you are ready to begin writing your report or memo. Your first step should be to refine your outline. Be sure that your topic is completely covered and that the ideas are arranged in the most effective order. Think about the introduction and conclusion to your paper, as well as any other relevant parts. Do you want to include charts, tables, or graphs?

Next, arrange your notes in the order of the outline and write the appropriate outline code beside each note.

With a completed outline and an orderly arrangement of your notes, you're ready to write the draft of your report or memorandum.

## Integrating Notes Into Your Writing

The draft of a research paper is written just like that of any other kind of writing, except you are incorporating notes taken from your sources into your own ideas. If you have already paraphrased the notes, your task is much easier.

Indicate the source of your notes in your draft—you must give credit for words or ideas that are not your own. In the final version of your paper, these references will be footnotes, endnotes, or parenthetical citations. In the draft, you can indicate your sources with a parenthetical notation such as this: ([1] p. 403). The numbers come from your notes and refer to the source and page or paragraph number of each note.

## Revising

After you have completed the draft, you'll need to revise it to perfect the organization, development, style, grammar, and spelling. You might also ask a colleague to review your paper and suggest ways it can be improved.

## Documentation

As noted earlier, any information you get from a source other than your own knowledge must be documented; that is, you must say where you got the information. Styles for documentation vary, but two of the most common are internal documentation and notes.[8] The format we illustrate for both styles is consistent with *The Chicago Manual of Style*[9] and Kate L. Turabian's *A Manual for Writers of Term Papers, Theses, and Dissertations*[10] or, in the case of electronic citations, Walker and Taylor's *The Columbia Guide to Online Style*.[11] You may want to consult one or more of these works as you write your paper.

### *Internal Documentation*
Many writers prefer to use internal documentation, which places abbreviated information about sources within the text, using parentheses ( )

or brackets [ ], followed by a list of references at the end of the paper. What goes within the parentheses or brackets depends on the kind of source you are using. Appendix 8–D at the end of this chapter gives sample citations and reference list entries for sources typically used by accounting professionals.

It's a good idea to introduce quotations or paraphrases within the text itself, as in this example:

> According to the *FASB Accounting Standards Codification™*, current assets are "cash and other assets or resources commonly identified as those that are reasonably expected to be realized in cash or sold or consumed during the normal operating cycle of the business." (FASB ASC, par. 210-10-45-01).

Note that the end punctuation for the quotation, in this case the period, comes after the parentheses. The numbers shown in this citation refer to Codification Topic (210), Subtopic (10), Section (45), and Paragraph (01). This is the standard way of citing the Codification. If readers check the reference list at the end of the paper, they will find the following:

> Financial Accounting Standards Board (FASB), 2010. *Accounting Standards Codification™*. Stamford, Conn.: FASB.

It is important to consider whether the readers of your paper will be familiar with the literature cited. If they won't be, you should identify the source more fully and briefly explain its significance.

### *Endnotes or Footnotes*

The other style of documentation in wide use is endnotes or footnotes. The difference between these two note forms is that footnotes come at the bottom of the page where the references occur, whereas endnotes come at the end of the paper. Most authorities consider endnotes acceptable. If you prefer footnotes, your word processor should be able to place footnotes on the correct pages in the acceptable format. With either endnotes or footnotes, you have the option of adding a bibliography at the end of your paper, listing your sources in alphabetical order. Appendix 8–E at the end of this chapter gives examples of notes and bibliographical entries for typical accounting sources.

As with internal documentation, you should introduce your paraphrased or quoted material:

> According to an article in *The Wall Street Journal*, many accounting firms find the poor writing skills of their new employees to be a serious problem.[12]

The introduction to this paraphrase tells generally where the information came from; the note and bibliographical entry give complete information about the source.

*Citing Electronic Sources*

Electronic sources have become so important to the research process that you'll probably need to cite material that you have found online or on CD–ROM.

An acceptable form of citation for documents available from electronic sources usually resembles the pattern of citations for hard-copy sources, but you need to provide additional information so that your readers can find the file or document online.

It's important to provide the date you accessed the document since the document may be modified or even removed from online availability after you have accessed it. For the same reason, it's also a good idea to print out and keep a hard copy of the document you are citing unless the size of the document makes this impractical.

Examples of citations for electronic sources are illustrated in Appendices 8–C and 8–D at the end of this chapter.

## CRITICAL THINKING AND TECHNICAL ACCOUNTING RESEARCH

In Chapter 7 we discussed critical thinking in general. In this section, we examine its importance and application to accounting research.

In *An Introduction to Applied Professional Research for Accountants,* Professor David A. Ziebart has this to say about technical accounting research:

> ... [technical accounting] research ... is a process, and its result is a defensible solution to the problem or issue at hand. By process we mean a systematic routine of identifying the problem or issue, specifying alternative plausible solutions, conducting an inquiry into the propriety of the alternatives, evaluating the authoritative literature found, making a choice among the alternatives, and communicating the results. Since the solution must be defensible, the accounting professional must be certain that the search of the professional literature is exhaustive and the reasoning employed in determining the solution is sound.[13]

Notice the importance of critical thinking skills to the process of accounting research. Professor Ziebart specifies these steps of the research process that involve critical thinking: identifying the issues or problems; identifying alternative solutions; evaluating the best solution; and communicating the recommended solution, giving reasons for its preference.

Technical accounting research is most often done in either financial or tax accounting. The following discussion, which focuses on financial accounting, will give you an idea of the complexity of this kind of research, as well as a strategy you can use when faced with a difficult accounting problem.

## Financial Accounting Research

Research in financial accounting is often necessary (particularly in larger accounting firms and industry) because financial transactions may not always be directly covered by generally accepted accounting principles (GAAP). In other words, you may not always be able to find guidance in published accounting standards that fits a particular transaction or that fairly represents the conditions under which the transaction occurred. When this situation occurs you must devise an accounting solution that can be defended based on accounting theory and logic found elsewhere in GAAP. The following section suggests a procedure you can use for this research.

## Steps in the Financial Accounting Research Process

Financial accounting research involves the following steps:

1. Determine all the relevant facts.
2. Identify all the issues involved.
3. Research the issues in the accounting literature.
4. Identify alternative solutions and arguments for and against each.
5. Evaluate alternative solutions and choose the one that can be best defended.
6. Communicate the results of your research to the interested parties.

Note that these steps are similar to those presented in Chapter 7, but they are applied more directly to financial accounting research. Let's discuss these steps one at a time.

### Determine all the Relevant Facts

Determining the relevant facts is often fairly straightforward. If you realize that research is necessary, you're probably already aware of most facts of the transaction. Be sure you have *all* the facts before you begin your research. Do you fully understand the transaction and the conditions under which it was made? If the transaction is supported by a contract or other documents, be sure you have examined them thoroughly. Are there any hidden contingencies, liabilities, or unperformed duties on the part of any participants? What motivated the parties to make the transaction?

### Identify All the Issues Involved

It often comes as a surprise to many people that identifying the issues can be one of the more difficult steps in the accounting research process. It's not uncommon for facts (or a lack of facts), terminology, and researcher bias to obscure some issues rather than clarify them. Ethical issues may also become apparent as you gather additional information and consider alternative solutions. Attention to critical thinking will help you ensure that all the issues are identified.

Consider the case of a custom machine parts manufacturer that routinely manufactures more parts than its customers order, expenses the cost of these extra parts as part of cost of goods sold, and physically holds the parts in inventory at a carrying value of zero. If a customer later has an emergency need for another part or two, the parts can be delivered immediately; however, this almost never happens, and the additional revenue from the sale of these extra parts is of no consequence. The question is whether the manufacturer's method of accounting for this situation is appropriate. What are the issues?

A quick reading of the facts presented may suggest that the issue is whether the cost of manufacturing the extra parts is properly accounted for by expensing it as part of cost of goods sold and carrying the inventory at zero, or whether the cost of the extra parts should be attributed to the inventory. Certainly the questions of inventory valuation and accounting for cost of goods sold will be answered by our research and the conclusions we draw from it. However, the central issue is best stated quite differently.

The basic issue in this case is the nature of the expenditure involved in producing the extra parts. That is, which one of the elements discussed in *Statement of Financial Accounting Concepts No. 6* best describes the expenditure? Does the expenditure result in an asset (not necessarily the physical parts)? This is the question to start with because definitions of the other elements depend on the definition of an asset. If an asset has resulted from the expenditure, the type of asset is still in question: Is it inventory, goodwill, or some other intangible asset? If an asset has not been the result, has an expense been incurred? If so, is it appropriate to include it as part of cost of goods sold, or is it some other type of expense? If an expense has not been incurred, it must be accounted for as a loss.

*Research the Issues in the Accounting Literature*
After you have identified the issues, the next step is to research the accounting literature to gather all relevant material. If the issues involve theoretical questions, as most probably will, you should consult relevant parts of the *Statements of Financial Accounting Concepts*. Certainly you should review the *FASB Accounting Standards Codification*™ to identify GAAP bearing directly or indirectly on the issues.

Sometimes you may find useful information in GAAP covering an unrelated area. For example, if an issue involves revenue recognition of an entity in the software industry, GAAP covering the music industry or some industry even further removed from the software industry may contain logic or guidance that could serve as a basis for a solution.

It's possible that your research may take you beyond the materials just discussed. Regulations of the SEC, regulations of other federal agencies, accounting books, and articles in accounting journals all may prove useful. SEC regulations may be controlling if the entity involved falls under SEC jurisdiction. Online and CD-ROM databases such as those listed in Appendix 8-B at the end of this chapter are good sources for much of this material.

### Identify Alternative Solutions and Arguments for and Against Each

It's important to realize that if you're engaged in technical accounting research, you're probably dealing with issues for which there are no solutions established. You must identify all alternative solutions, determine the best solution, and defend that solution against all others.

### Evaluate Alternative Solutions and Choose the One That Can be Best Defended

In the end, you must be able to present a well-reasoned defense of your accounting method. Although accounting is not law (except as governed by the SEC), just as a lawyer may prepare a well-reasoned defense of an issue using legal precedent and logic, an accountant doing technical accounting research must use many of the same skills in preparing a defense of a proposed solution to an accounting issue. Indeed, it's possible that the solution you choose may have to be defended in a court during some legal proceeding.

If you anticipate that your readers will oppose your recommended treatment or will prefer an alternative, your written document should anticipate and answer their objections. You should explain the reasons that support your recommendation as well as why alternatives are not acceptable.

### Communicate the Results of Your Research to the Interested Parties

You will usually communicate the results of your research in a report, letter, or a memo although occasionally you also may report orally. However you report your research, incorporate all the elements of effective communication discussed in this book. Audience analysis, precision, clarity, and logical development are particularly important.

---

## EXERCISES

### Exercise 8–1 [General]

Choose one of the following topics and narrow it, if necessary. Write a documented research paper on your topic, using the steps discussed in this chapter.

- The CPA's role in forensic accounting
- The Public Company Accounting Oversight Board (PCAOB)
- The International Auditing and Assurance Standards Board (IAASB) and its role in establishing International Standards on Auditing (ISAs)

- The use of fair value measurements in GAAP
- The importance of ethics in public and private accounting
- The role and importance of the Conceptual Framework in the accounting standard setting process
- The impact of the Sarbanes-Oxley Act (SOX) on accounting career opportunities
- The role of judgment in the application of accounting standards and whether that role should be reduced or expanded
- The impact of the Committee of Sponsoring Organizations' (COSO) Internal Control–Integrated Framework
- Indexing the capital gains tax for inflation

## Exercise 8–2 [Financial]

American Petroleum Company (AP Oil) owns and operates deep-water drilling rigs in international waters off the coast of Euromania, a country in Western Europe. Several months ago AP Oil experienced a disastrous explosion and fire at one of its rigs that resulted in a monumental oil spill that has yet to be contained. The spill is expected to have dire effects on hundreds of miles of the Euromanian coastline, putting untold thousands of people in fishing, tourist, and supporting industries out of work. Since the disaster occurred in international waters, the ability of the Euromanian courts to impose liability judgments against AP is probably limited to its ability to seize whatever AP assets are located within its jurisdiction. These assets are carried on AP's books at $20 billion. In addition, Euromanian law limits liability in such cases to a maximum of €96 million ($115 million). However, due to a feeling of ethical obligation and in an effort to salvage the good name of the company, AP's board of directors has agreed to honor all damage claims in an unlimited fashion. It is estimated that the value of such claims could reach €83 billion ($100 billion).

Your firm has served as the auditors for AP for several years. AP's board of directors has requested that your firm prepare a report for the board discussing how its decision should be reflected in AP's financial statements under US GAAP. Your supervisor, Charles Brogan, has asked you to research the technical issues involved and prepare a memo for him recommending how the issues should be handled; he will subsequently prepare the report for AP. He has told you not to be concerned with the issue of foreign currency translation, as that is well understood by AP. Prepare the memo for Mr. Brogan. (Chapter 10 discusses memos.)

## Exercise 8–3 [Financial]

Columbia Power Company has entered into several long-term purchase contracts with fuel suppliers for its power plants. Most of these contracts were for five years. By October 2010, the market price of fuel had plummeted so that contractual price commitments exceeded current market prices and market prices projected through the end of the contracts by $200,000,000. Consequently, Columbia Power booked a $200,000,000 loss in the fourth quarter of 2010 with the following entry:

| | | |
|---|---|---|
| Estimated Loss on Purchase Commitments | 200,000,000 | |
| Estimated Liability for Purchase Commitments | | 200,000,000 |

During the first two quarters of 2011, Columbia Power ran into severe cash flow problems unrelated to the purchase commitment problem of the previous year. As a consequence, Columbia filed for bankruptcy protection from its creditors.

Columbia's lawyers have determined that in similar situations the bankruptcy court typically grants relief to the petitioner by reducing its obligations to creditors by 50 percent. In many cases, the court has nullified purchase agreements altogether, arguing that to the extent that such contracts are unfulfilled they are executory contracts.

If the court reduced Columbia's obligations to creditors by only 25%, the entire $200,000,000 estimated liability for purchase commitments booked the previous year would be eliminated. (None of the originally booked liability has been reduced by payments to suppliers.) In the opinion of Columbia's lawyers, Columbia will probably never have to pay any of the estimated liability. Your own CPA firm's legal staff agrees. In fact, in their words "it is inconceivable" that Columbia will have to pay more than current market price for any fuel it has purchased or will purchase after the bankruptcy court has ruled.

Columbia Power wants to eliminate the estimated liability for purchase commitments in its second-quarter financial statements. Should this be permitted? As a member of the CPA firm responsible for auditing Columbia Power's financial statements, you have been asked by your boss, Susan Chase, to research this technical accounting problem and to prepare a memo recommending what should be done and why. (Chapter 10 discusses memos.)

## Exercise 8–4 [Financial]

The president of High Roller Ball Bearing Corporation, a closely held corporation, has directed that the company purchase $1,000 worth of state lottery tickets each week in the company's name. The state holds a lottery every other month. At the fiscal year-end, the company has $6,000 worth of lottery tickets on hand for the lottery to be held the following month. The president wants to show these tickets as a deferred charge.

As High Roller's CPA, would you go along with this? Write a memo to your boss, John Sampson, recommending what position your firm should take with this client and why. (Chapter 10 discusses memos.)

## Exercise 8–5  [Financial]

Your client, Smooth Brew Company, has just purchased a brewery known for the unique taste of its beer. This taste is primarily the result of using sparkling spring water that flows from a particular stream made famous in the brewery's advertisements. The brewery is located on 20 acres at the foot of a large mountain. The famous stream flows down the mountain out of North Carolina and through the brewery's property in Georgia.

Your client paid a high price for these brewing operations—$1 million above the fair market value of the tangible assets acquired. The president of Smooth Brew has made it clear that the main reason he agreed to pay the price is to get access to the special water. Accordingly, he has requested that an account entitled "Water" be set up in the balance sheet and valued at $1 million.

As Smooth Brew's CPA, you know your firm will have to take a position on this issue. Should your firm allow the client to account for the $1 million the way he suggests? If not, what will be the position of your firm on how the transaction should be accounted for?

Write a memo to your boss, Claire Sanders, recommending what position your firm should take with this client and why. (Chapter 10 discusses memos.)

## Exercise 8–6  [Auditing]

Prepare a research report on the subject of independence in auditing. Cover the necessity for independence in general, what professional standards say about independence, what the SEC's role has been to foster independence, and anything else you may find appropriate. Assume your report will be distributed to entry-level accountants recently hired by your firm, as part of their in-house training materials. (Chapter 11 discusses reports.)

## Exercise 8–7  [Financial/Systems]

You are employed by a large CPA firm and have been asked to prepare a research report on the use and effect on financial reporting of Extendable Business Reporting Language (XBRL). Write the report assuming it will be provided to your firm's clients. (Chapter 11 discusses reports.)

## Exercise 8–8  [Managerial]

Prepare a research report on the use of Grenzplankostenrechnung (GPK) and Activity Based Costing (ABC) cost systems. Discuss some actual experiences of companies as well as some advantages and disadvantages of using each system. Assume your report will be made available to your manufacturing clients. (Chapter 11 discusses reports.)

## Exercise 8–9 [Tax]

William owns a building that is leased to Lester's Machine Shop. Lester requests that William rewire the building for new equipment Lester plans to purchase. The wiring would cost about $4,000, but it would not increase the value of the building because its only use is in connection with the specialized equipment. Rather than lose Lester as a lessee, William agrees to forego one month's rent of $1,000 if Lester will pay for the wiring. Because Lester does not want to move, he agrees. William has asked you, as his CPA, what amount, if any, he will have to include in his gross income for tax purposes as a result of this arrangement. Research the issue and write a letter to William explaining your findings.[14] (Chapter 9 discusses letters.)

---

# NOTES

1. David. A. Ziebart, et al., *An Introduction to Applied Professional Research for Accountants*, 2nd ed. (Upper Saddle River, NJ: Prentice Hall, 2002), 2.
2. This information is taken from the "FASB Accounting Standards Codification™, Notice to Constituents (v 4.1), About the Codification."
3. Ibid.
4. "timely complete interpretive," CCH, 2010. www.accounting researchmanager.com/ARMMenu.nsf/vwHTML/ARMSplash?Open Document (7 December 2010).
5. For CCH's *Tax Research Network* or CCH's *IntelliConnect*, see http://tax.cchgroup.com/default (7 December 2010).
6. See http://ria.thomsonreuters.com/IntegratedSolutions (7 December 2010).
7. Melinda G. Kramer, Glenn Leggett, and C. David Mead, *Prentice Hall Handbook for Writers*, 12th ed. (Englewood Cliffs, NJ: Prentice Hall, 1995), 503.
8. Many documentation styles are in current use. The sample entries in this chapter illustrate acceptable usage, but you may use another acceptable style as long as you're consistent within each paper.
9. *The Chicago Manual of Style*, 15th ed. Chicago: The University of Chicago Press, 2003.
10. Kate L. Turabian, *A Manual for Writers of Term Papers, Theses, and Dissertations*, 6th ed. Chicago: The University of Chicago Press, 1996.
11. Janice R. Walker and Todd Taylor, *The Columbia Guide to Online Style*, 2nd ed. New York: Columbia University Press, 2006.
12. Lee Burton, "Take Heart, CPAs: Finally a Story That Doesn't Attack You as Boring," *The Wall Street Journal* (13 May 1987), 33.
13. David. A. Ziebart, et al. *An Introduction to Applied Professional Research for Accountants*, 2nd ed. (Upper Saddle River, NJ: Prentice Hall, 2002), 3.
14. Adapted and modified with permission from Thomas R. Pope, Kenneth E. Anderson, and John L. Kramer, *Federal Taxation 2005* (Upper Saddle River, NJ: Prentice Hall, 2005), 3–40.

# Appendix 8 – A

# *Sources of Accounting and Financial Information on the Internet*[*]

Accounting Organizations
    Academy of Accounting Historians        http://aahhq.org/
    Advancing Government Accountability    www.agacgfm.org/
      (Formerly: Association of Government   homepage.aspx
      Accountants)
    American Accounting Association       http://aaahq.org/
    American Institute of CPAs           www.aicpa.org/
    Financial Accounting Standards Board   www.fasb.org/
    Governmental Accounting Standards Board  www.gasb.org/
    Institute of Internal Auditors, The      www.theiia.org/
    Institute of Management Accountants    www.imanet.org/

Business and Accounting News Network Services
    Accounting Today for the WebCPA     www.accountingtoday.com
    CNNMoney.com                http://money.cnn.com/
    MSN                      http://moneycentral.msn.com/
                                home.asp

Business Newspapers
    *Investor's Business Daily* (Investors.com)  www.investors.com/
    *Barron's Online*              http://online.barrons.com/
                               home-page
    *Financial Times of London*       www.ft.com/home/us
    *Wall Street Journal, The*        http://india.wsj.com/home-page

Business Magazines
    *Bloomberg BusinessWeek*       www.businessweek.com/
    *Business 2.0*              http://money.cnn.com/magazines/
                                business2
    *CPA Journal, The*           cpaj.com
    *Fortune Magazine*          http://money.cnn.com/magazines/
                                fortune
    *Money Magazine* (CNNMoney.com)    http://money.cnn.com/magazines/
                                moneymag
    *Worth*                    www.worth.com/

Data on the Economy, Industries, Market Indexes,
and Financial Statistics—Domestic and Foreign
    Bloomberg.com               www.bloomberg.com/
    Briefing.com                www.briefing.com/
    Dow Jones                 www.dowjones.com/

---

[*]These web addresses were accurate when this book went to press. However, web addresses change frequently.

| | |
|---|---|
| International Monetary Fund (IMF) | www.imf.org/external/index.htm |
| New York Federal Reserve Bank—exchange rates | www.ny.frb.org/markets/fxrates/ noon.cfm |
| World Bank, The | www.worldbank.org/ |

**Information About Stocks—Company Performance; Corporate Financial Data, Charts, Company Home Pages, and Such**

| | |
|---|---|
| Internetnews.com | www.internetnews.com/bus-news |
| *INVESTools* | www.investools.com/ |
| Morningstar.com | www.morningstar.com/ |
| NASDAQ | www.nasdaq.com/ |
| NYSE | www.nyse.com/ |
| OTC Bulletin Board | www.otcbb.com/ |
| StockMaster | www.stockmaster.com/ |

**Information About Bonds**

| | |
|---|---|
| Bonds Online | www.bonds-online.com/ |

**Information About Mutual Funds**

| | |
|---|---|
| Morningstar.com | www.morningstar.com/ |
| Standard and Poor's Rating Service | http://www.standardandpoors. com/home/en/us |
| *StockMaster* | www.stockmaster.com/ |

**Academic Research**

| | |
|---|---|
| Social Science Research Network | www.ssrn.com/ |

**Securities Exchanges**

| | |
|---|---|
| NASDAQ | www.nasdaq.com/ |
| New York Stock Exchange (NYSE) | www.nyse.com/ |

**Government Sites**

| | |
|---|---|
| Federal Citizen Information Center (National Contact Center) | www.info.gov/ |
| Fed World (National Technical Information Service) | www.fedworld.gov/ |
| Internal Revenue Service (IRS) | www.irs.ustreas.gov/ |
| Securities and Exchange Commission (SEC) | www.sec.gov/ |
| Thomas (Library of Congress) | http://thomas.loc.gov/ |
| U.S. Government Accountability Office (GAO) | www.gao.gov/ |
| U.S. House of Representatives | www.house.gov/ |
| U.S. Senate | www.senate.gov/ |

**Links to Other Organizations, Firms, Journals, and a Wealth of Other Excellent Sites**

| | |
|---|---|
| AccountantsWorld | www.accountantsworld.com/ |
| AICPA Store (accounting publications) | www.cpa2biz.com/index.jsp/ |
| Rutgers Accounting Web | http://accounting.rutgers.edu/ |
| SmartPros Accounting | www.accountingnet.com/ |

| | |
|---|---|
| Thomson Reuters | http://ppc.thomson.com/ |
| WebCPA | www.webcpa.com/ |

**International Accounting and Finance Organizations and Sites**

| | |
|---|---|
| International Accounting Standards Board | http://www.ifrs.org/Home.htm |
| International Association of Financial Executive Institutes | www.iafei.org/ |
| International Federation of Accountants | www.ifac.org/ |
| International Monetary Fund | www.imf.org/ |
| World Bank | www.worldbank.org/ |

# Appendix 8 – B

# *Computerized Reference and Database Services**

## CD-ROM Databases

- *Business Source*, by EBSCO Information Services. Provides citations and abstracts to articles in about 600 business periodicals and newspapers. Full text is provided from selected periodicals, covering accounting, communications, economics, finance, management, marketing, and other business subjects. For additional information go to www2.ebsco.com.
- *FARS (Financial Accounting Research System)*, by the Financial Accounting Standards Board (FASB). Provides access to all FASB and AICPA pronouncements, including *Current Text, Original Pronouncements, EITF Abstracts*, and *Implementation Guidelines*. For additional information go to www.fasb.org/fars.
- *WILSONDISC: Wilson Business Abstracts*, by H. W. Wilson Co. Provides CD-ROM "cover-to-cover" abstracting and indexing of hundreds of prominent business periodicals. Indexing is from 1982 to present, and abstracting is from 1990 to present. For additional information go to library.dialog.com/bluesheets/html/bl0553.html.

## Online Databases

- *ABI/INFORM* (ProQuest) provides online indexing to business-related material occurring in over 900 periodicals from 1971 to the present. For additional information go to www.proquest.com/en-US/catalogs/databases/detail/abi_inform.shtml.
- *Accounting Research Manager®*, by Commerce Clearing House (CCH) contains "analytical accounting, auditing, governmental, internal controls and SEC information as well as primary source data." For additional information go to www.accountingresearchmanager.com/ARMMenu.nsf/vwHTML/ARMSplash?OpenDocument.
- *Accounting Standards Codification™ Research System*, by the FASB, covers accounting literature issued by several standard setters. FASB publications included are Statements, Interpretations, Technical Bulletins, Staff Positions, Staff Implementation Guides, and Statement 138 Examples. Abstracts and Topic D of the Emerging Issues Task Force are included as are Derivatives Implementation Group Issues, Accounting Principles Board Opinions, Accounting Research Bulletins, and Accounting Interpretations. AICPA Statements of Position, Audit and Accounting Guides, Practice Bulletins, and Technical Inquiry Service issuances are also available here, along with "relevant portions of authoritative content issued by the SEC and selected SEC staff interpretations and administrative guidance."[†] For additional information go to fasb.org.

---

*These web addresses were accurate when this book went to press. However, web addresses change frequently.

[†]Financial Accounting Foundation, "Notice to Constituents (v 4.1) — About the Codification," 2010. (Stamford, Conn.: Financial Accounting Foundation, 2010), 8.

- *Annual Reports—Corporate (AICPA)*, formerly known as *NAARS Annual Reports*, contains "portions of annual reports to shareholders and information extracted from SEC filings, including financial statements, footnotes, auditor's opinions, material incorporated by reference and management responsibility letters." For additional information go to libguides.mit.edu/content.php?pid=63012&sid=466611
- *Banking Information Source* provides indexing and abstracting of periodicals and other literature from 1982 to present, with weekly updates. Covers the financial services industry, including banks, savings institutions, investment houses, credit unions, insurance companies, and real estate organizations. Emphasis is on marketing and management. For additional information go to www.proquest.com/en-US/catalogs/databases/detail/pq_banking_info.shtml.
- *Capital IQ Compustat*, by Standard and Poor's. Financial data for the most recent 20 years on publicly held U.S. and some foreign corporations. For additional information go to www.compustat.com/?gclid= COL10NyyvaACFUFM5QodxDySUQ.
- *Checkpoint*, by Thomson Reuters, is a good online research database for tax research. For additional information go to ria.thomsonreuters.com/ IntegratedSolutions.
- *Development Research Institute (DRI) at New York University* contains U. S. and international statistical data relating to money markets, interest rates, foreign exchange, banking, and stock and bond indexes. For additional information go to http://dri.as.nyu.edu/object/dri.pub_database.
- *Disclosure Database®*, by Dialog, LLC, provides information from records filed with the SEC by approximately 14,000 publicly owned corporations. The database is updated weekly. For additional information go to http:// library.dialog.com/bluesheets/html/bl0101.html.
- *EconLit* by the American Economic Association covers the worldwide literature of economics. Subjects include microeconomics, macroeconomics, economic history, inflation, money, credit, finance, accounting theory, trade, natural resource economics, and regional economics. For additional information go to www.aeaweb.org/econlit/index.php.
- *IntelliConnect®*, by Commerce Clearing House (CCH), provides access to the *CCH® Tax Research NetWork™* xand CCH's *Standard Federal Tax Reporter*, which is indispensable for tax research. For additional information go to tax.cchgroup.com/default.
- *Investext® Archive,* by Dialog, LLC, contains full text of investment research reports from hundreds of sources, including leading brokers and investment bankers. Reports are available on approximately 60,000 publicly traded companies. Separate industry reports are available. For additional information go to http://library.dialog.com/bluesheets/html/ bl0545.html.
- *U.S. Basic Economics Database* presents more than 6,000 statistical series relating to business, industry, finance, and economics. Time period is 1947 to present, with daily updates. For additional information go to www.bsu. edu/mcobwin/econ/database/dri/index.html.

# Appendix 8 – C

# *Other Printed Sources of Accounting and Financial Information*

Business News, Articles, Market Data;
Stock, Bond, and Mutual Fund Price Quotes

| | |
|---|---|
| *Barron's* | *Investor's Business Daily* |
| *USA Today* | *The Wall Street Journal* |

Business News, Articles

| | |
|---|---|
| *Business Week* | *Fortune Magazine* |
| *Forbes Magazine* | *Money Magazine* |

Data on the Economy and Industries;
Financial and Economic Statistics

| | |
|---|---|
| *Business Conditions Digest* | *Standard & Poor's Statistical Surveys* |
| *Economic Report of the President* | *Statistical Abstract of the United States* |
| *Federal Reserve Bulletin* | *US Industrial Outlook* |
| *Standard & Poor's Industry Surveys* | *World Almanac* |

Summary Data About Industries, Companies; Advice
on Industries, Stocks; Analysis and Forecasts

| | |
|---|---|
| *Standard & Poor's Outlook* | *Value-Line Investment Survey* |

Stock Information, Company Performance;
Corporate Financial Data

| | |
|---|---|
| *Annual reports of companies* | *Moody's OTC Manual* |
| *Moody's Bank & Finance Manual* | *Moody's Public Utility Manual* |
| *Moody's Bond Record* | *Moody's Transportation Manual* |
| *Moody's Bond Survey* | *Standard & Poor's Corporation Records* |
| *Moody's Handbook of Common Stocks* | *Standard & Poor's Stock Reports* |
| *Moody's Industrial Manual* | |
| *Moody's International Manual* | |

Bond Information

| | |
|---|---|
| *Moody's Bond Record* | *Moody's Bond Survey* |

Mutual Fund Information

*Morningstar Mutual Funds*

# Appendix 8 – D

# *Internal Documentation Style*

C = Citation within the text
R = Entry in reference list

Book — Single Author
C      (Pacter 1994, 12)
R      Pacter, P. 1994. *Reporting financial information by segment.* London, UK: International Accounting Standards Committee.

Book — Single Editor
C      (Frankel 1994, 64)
R      Frankel, J. A., ed. 1994. *The internationalization of equity markets.* Chicago: University of Chicago Press.

Book — Two Authors
C      (Romney and Steinbart 2003, 621)
R      Romney, Marshall B., and Paul John Steinbart. 2003. *Accounting Information Systems,* 9th ed. Upper Saddle River, NJ: Prentice Hall.

Book — More than Two Authors
C      (Ahrens, Elder, and Beasley 2005, 84)
R      Ahrens, Alvin A., Randal J. Elder, and Mark S. Beasley. 2005. *Auditing and Assurance Services,* 10th ed. Upper Saddle River, NJ: Prentice Hall.

Book — Author Is an Association, Institution, or Organization
C      (AICPA 1993, 2)
R      American Institute of Certified Public Accountants (AICPA). 1993. *The information needs of investors and creditors: A report on the AICPA special committee's study of the information needs of today's users of financial reporting, November, 1993.* New York: AICPA.

Article in a Journal — Single Author
C      (Schwartz 1996, 20)
R      Schwartz, Donald. 1996. The future of financial accounting: Universal standards. *Journal of Accountancy* 181, no. 5 (May): 20–21.

Article in a Journal — Two Authors
C      (May and Schneider 1988, 70)
R      May, G. S., and D. K. Schneider. 1988. Reporting accounting changes: Are stricter guidelines needed? *Accounting Horizons* 2, no. 3 (September): 68–74.

Article in a Journal — More Than Two Authors
C      (Barth, Landsman, and Rendleman 1998, 75)
R      Barth, Mary E., Wayne R. Landsman, and Richard J. Rendleman, Jr. 1998. Option pricing-based bond value estimates and a fundamental components approach to account for corporate debt. *The Accounting Review* 73, no. 1 (January): 73–102.

**Article in a Magazine**
C     (Blinder 1988, 25)
R     Blinder, Alan S. 1988. Dithering on hill is crippling a key agency.
        *Business Week,* 26 September, 25.

**Article in a Newspaper — Author Not Identified**
C     (*The Wall Street Journal,* 16 July 1986)
R     Words count. *The Wall Street Journal,* 16 July 1986.

**Article in a Newspaper — Author Identified**
C     (May 1987)
R     May, Gordon S. No accounting for poor writers. *The Wall Street Journal,*
        29 May 1987.

**Primary Source Reprinted in a Secondary Source**
C     (FASB, *SFAC 1,* par. 3)
R     Financial Accounting Standards Board (FASB). 1978. *Objectives of*
        *financial reporting by business enterprises, statement of financial*
        *accounting concepts no. 1.* Stamford, CT: FASB. Reprinted in
        *Original Pronouncements, As Amended, 2005/2006 Edition:*
        *Accounting Standards as of June 1, 2006,* Vol. II. New York:
        John Wiley & Sons, 2006.

**FASB Accounting Standards Codification™\***
C     (FASB ASC par. 350-10-05-01)
R     Financial Accounting Standards Board (FASB), 2010. *Accounting*
        *Standards Codification™* . Stamford, Conn.: FASB.

**Legal Citation**
C     (*Aaron v. SEC,* 446 U.S. 680, 1980)
R     Aaron v. SEC, 446 U.S. 680 (1980).

**Internal Revenue Code Section**
C     (*Internal Revenue Code* Sec. 6111(a))
R     *Internal Revenue Code.* Sec. 6111(a).

**Government Document**
C     (SEC 1995, 3)
R     United States Securities and Exchange Commission (SEC). 1995.
        *Self-regulatory organizations; notice of filing and order granting*
        *accelerated approval of proposed rule change by the National*
        *Association of Securities Dealers, Inc., relating to an interim extension of*
        *the OTC Bulletin Board (R) service through September 28, 1995.*
        Securities Exchange Act Release No. 35918, 60 FR 35443. Washington,
        DC. (July 7).

---

\*The numbers shown in the in-text citation refer to the Codification Topic (350), Subtopic
(10), Section (05), and Paragraph (01). The date in the accompanying reference list entry is
the date of the edition of the ASC. Since the ASC is continuously updated, this will usually be
the date you consulted it.

Federal Register
C    (61 Fed. Reg. 1996, 208:55264)
R    "Revision to NASA FAR supplement coverage on contractor financial
      management reporting." *Federal Register* 61, no. 208 (25 Oct. 1996): 55264.

World Wide Web
C    (Aguilar, 2004)
R    Aguilar, Melissa Klein. "PCAOB Found 'Significant Audit and Accounting
      Issues' in Big Four Inspections." Accountants Media Group. 2004.
      www.accountingtoday.com/news/4698-1.html (23 December 2010).

E-mail
C    May, Gordon S. "The PCAOB." Personal e-mail (3 Aug. 2004).
R    Personal e-mail messages are usually not included in reference lists.

More than One Work in Reference List by Same Author or Authors—Different Years
C    (Lang and Lundholm, 1993)
R    Lang, M., and R. Lundholm. 1993. Cross-sectional determinants of
      analyst ratings of corporate disclosures. *Journal of Accounting Research*
      31, no. 2 (Autumn): 246–271.
      _____. 1996. Corporate disclosure policy and analyst behavior.
      *Accounting Review* 71, no. 4 (October): 467–492.

More Than One Work in Reference List By Same Author or Authors—Same Year
C    (Frost and Pownall, 1994b, 61)
R    Frost, C. A., and G. Pownall. 1994a. Accounting disclosure practices in the
      United States and United Kingdom. *Journal of Accounting Research* 32,
      no. 1 (Spring): 75–102.
      _____. 1994b. A comparison of the stock price response to earnings
      measures in the United States and the United Kingdom. *Contemporary
      Accounting Research* 11, no. 1 (Summer): 59–83.

# *Endnotes or Footnotes and Bibliography Style*

N = Endnote or footnote (Endnotes are numbered with full-size Arabic numerals in a Notes section at the end of each chapter.)
B = Bibliographical entry

Book—Single Author
N        [1]P. Pacter, *Reporting Financial Information by Segment* (London, UK: International Accounting Standards Committee, 1994), 12.
B        Pacter, P. *Reporting Financial Information by Segment.* London, UK: International Accounting Standards Committee, 1994.

Book—Single Editor
N        [1] J. A. Frankel, ed., *The Internationalization of Equity Markets* (Chicago: University of Chicago Press, 1994), 64.
B        Frankel, J.A., ed. *The Internationalization of Equity Markets.* Chicago: University of Chicago Press, 1994.

Book—Two Authors
N        [1]Marshall B. Romney and Paul John Steinbart, *Accounting Information Systems*, 11th ed. (Upper Saddle River, NJ: Pearson Prentice Hall, 2009), 622.
B        Romney, Marshall B., and Paul John Steinbart. *Accounting Information Systems*, 11th ed. Upper Saddle River, NJ: Pearson Prentice Hall, 2009.

Book—More than Two Authors
N        [1]Alvin A. Ahrens, Randal J. Elder, and Mark S. Beasley, *Auditing and Assurance Services*, 13th ed. Upper Saddle River, NJ: Pearson Prentice Hall, 2010.
B        Ahrens, Alvin A., Randal J. Elder, and Mark S. Beasley. *Auditing and Assurance Services,* 13th ed. Upper Saddle River, NJ: Pearson Prentice Hall, 2010.

Book—Author Is an Association, Institution, or Organization
N        [1]American Institute of Certified Public Accountants (AICPA), *The Information Needs of Investors and Creditors: A Report on the AICPA Special Committee's Study of the Information Needs of Today's Users of Financial Reporting, November, 1993.* (New York: AICPA, 1993), 2.
B        American Institute of Certified Public Accountants (AICPA). *The Information Needs of Investors and Creditors: A Report on the AICPA Special Committee's Study of the Information Needs of Today's Users of Financial Reporting, November, 1993.* New York: AICPA, 1993.

Article in a Journal—Single Author
N    [1]Donald Schwartz, "The Future of Financial Accounting: Universal
       Standards," *Journal of Accountancy* 181, no. 5 (May 1996): 20.
B      Schwartz, Donald, "The Future of Accounting: Universal Standards."
       *Journal of Accountancy* 181, no. 5 (May 1996): 20(21.

Article in a Journal—Two Authors
N    [1]G. S. May and D. K. Schneider, "Reporting Accounting Changes: Are
       Stricter Guidelines Needed?" *Accounting Horizons* 2, no. 3 (Sept. 1988): 70.
B      May, G. S., and D. K. Schneider. "Reporting Accounting Changes: Are
       Stricter Guidelines Needed?" *Accounting Horizons* 2, no. 3 (Sept. 1988):
       68–74.

Article in a Journal—More than Two Authors
N    [1]Mary E. Barth, Wayne R. Landsman and Richard J. Rendleman, Jr.,
       "Option Pricing-Based Bond Value Estimates and a Fundamental
       Components Approach to Account for Corporate Debt," *Accounting
       Review* 73, no. 1 (January 1998): 75.
B      Barth, Mary E., Wayne R. Landsman, and Richard J. Rendleman, Jr.
       "Option Pricing-Based Bond Value Estimates and a Fundamental
       Components Approach to Account for Corporate Debt." *Accounting
       Review* 73, no. 1 (January 1998): 73–102.

Article in a Magazine
N    [1]Alan S. Blinder, "Dithering on Hill Is Crippling a Key Agency,"
       *Business Week*, 26 September 1988, 25.
B      Blinder, Alan S. "Dithering on Hill Is Crippling a Key Agency."
       *Business Week*, 26 September 1988, 25.

Article in a Newspaper—Author Not Identified
N    [1]*The Wall Street Journal*, 16 July 1986, "Words Count."
B      *The Wall Street Journal*, 16 July 1986, "Words Count."

Article in a Newspaper—Author Identified
N    [1]Gordon S. May, "No Accounting for Poor Writers," *The Wall Street Journal*,
       29 May 1986.
B      May, Gordon S. "No Accounting for Poor Writers," *The Wall Street Journal*,
       29, May 1986.

Primary Source Reprinted in a Secondary Source
N    [1]Financial Accounting Standards Board (FASB). *Objectives of
       Financial Reporting by Business Enterprises, Statement of Financial
       Accounting Concepts No. 1.* (Stamford, Conn.: FASB, 1978), par. 3;
       reprinted in *Original Pronouncements, As Amended, 2005/2006 Edition:
       Accounting Standards as of June 1, 2005,* Vol. II. (New York: John Wiley
       & Sons, 2005), 1005–1020.
B      Financial Accounting Standards Board (FASB). *Objectives of
       Financial Reporting by Business Enterprises, Statement of Financial
       Accounting Concepts No. 1.* Stamford, Conn.: FASB. Reprinted in
       *Original Pronouncements, As Amended, 2005/2006 Edition: Accounting
       Standards as of June 1, 2005,* Vol. II, 1005–1020. New York: John Wiley &
       Sons, 2005.

N ¹Financial Accounting Standards Board (FASB). *Accounting for Income Taxes, Statement of Financial Accounting Standards No. 109.* (Stamford, Conn.: FASB, 1992), par. 17; available in *Financial Accounting Research System (FARS)*. Stamford, Conn.: Financial Accounting Standards Board, 2010.

B Financial Accounting Standards Board (FASB). *Accounting for Income Taxes, Statement of Financial Accounting Standards No. 109.* Stamford, Conn.: FASB. Available in *Financial Accounting Research System (FARS)*. Stamford, Conn.: Financial Accounting Standards Board, 2010.

Legal Citation

N ¹*Aaron v. SEC.* 446 U.S. 680 (1980).
B *Aaron v. SEC.* 446 U.S. 680 (1980).

Internal Revenue Code Section

N ¹*Internal Revenue Code* Sec. 6111(a).
B *Internal Revenue Code*. Sec. 6111(a).

Government Document

N ¹United States Securities and Exchange Commission (SEC), *Self-Regulatory Organizations; Notice of Filing and Order Granting Accelerated Approval of Proposed Rule Change by the National Association of Securities Dealers, Inc., Relating to an Interim Extension of the OTC Bulletin Board® Service Through September 28, 1995.* Securities Exchange Act Release No. 35918, 60 FR 35443 (7 July 1995): 3.

B United States Securities and Exchange Commission (SEC). *Self-Regulatory Organizations; Notice of Filing and Order Granting Accelerated Approval of Proposed Rule Change by the National Association of Securities Dealers, Inc., Relating to an Interim Extension of the OTC Bulletin Board (R) Service Through September 28, 1995.* Securities Exchange Act Release No. 35918, 60 FR 35443 (7 July 1995).

Federal Register

N ¹"Revision to NASA FAR Supplement Coverage on Contractor Financial Management Reporting." *Federal Register* 61, no. 208 (25 Oct. 1996): 55264.

B "Revision to NASA FAR Supplement Coverage on Contractor Financial Management Reporting." *Federal Register* 61, no. 208 (25 Oct. 1996): 55264.

World Wide Web

N ¹Melissa Klein Aguilar, "PCAOB Found 'Significant Audit and Accounting Issues' in Big Four Inspections," Accountants Media Group. 2004. www.accountingtoday.com/news/4698-1.html (23 December 2010).

B Aguilar, Melissa Klein. "PCAOB Found 'Significant Audit and Accounting Issues' in Big Four Inspections," Accountants Media Group. 2004. www.accountingtoday.com/news/4698-1.html (23 December 2010).

E-Mail

N ¹Gordon S. May, "The PCAOB." Personal e-mail (3 Aug. 2009).
B May, Gordon S., "The PCAOB." Personal e-mail (3 Aug. 2009).

**More than One Work in Bibliography by Same Author or Authors**

N    [1] M. Lang and R. Lundholm, "Cross-Sectional Determinants of Analyst Ratings of Corporate Disclosures," *Journal of Accounting Research* 31, no. 2 (Autumn 1993): 246–271.

B    Lang, M., and R. Lundholm, "Cross-Sectional Determinants of Analyst Ratings of Corporate Disclosures," *Journal of Accounting Research* 31, no. 2 (Autumn 1993): 246–271.

————. "Corporate Disclosure Policy and Analyst Behavior," *The Accounting Review* 71, no. 4 (October 1996): 467–492.

# CHAPTER
# 9
# Letters

Accountants write letters to a variety of people, including clients, government agencies, and fellow professionals. Auditors, for example, write a variety of letters: engagement letters, letters regarding deficiencies in internal control, management letters, and other letters to clients. Tax accountants may write letters seeking data about a client's tax situation, or to clarify issues for a client. Accountants may also write letters to communicate the results of research into a technical accounting problem or for a wide variety of other reasons.

For any letter to get the best results, of course, it must be well written. This chapter begins with some principles of good letter writing: organization, style, tone, and format. We then look at some typical letters that accountants write.

## PRINCIPLES OF LETTER WRITING

Effective letters have the characteristics of any good writing: They contain correct, complete information, and they are usually written with specific readers in mind. They are also written in an active, direct style. In other words, they are coherent, clear, and concise. The letters are also neat and attractive, with a professional appearance.

### Planning a Letter

A letter can vary in length from one paragraph to several pages although many business letters are no longer than a page. Whatever the length, think carefully about what the letter should cover before you begin so that you won't forget something important.

As in other writing tasks, analyze the purpose of the letter before you write it. If you are answering another person's letter, keep that letter on hand and note any comments for which a reply is needed. Jot down a brief outline to organize the material logically.

It's also important to think about the reader of your letter, especially when writing about a technical topic. The reader's knowledge and experience should determine how much detail you use when explaining the technical material in the letter.

Sometimes you must explain complex accounting procedures in words that a non-accountant can understand. *Tax Research Techniques*, a study published by the AICPA, discusses user needs in writing letters to clients about tax problems:

> Like a good speaker, a good writer must know the audience before beginning. Because tax clients and their staff vary greatly in their tax expertise, it is important to consider their technical sophistication when composing a tax opinion letter. The style of a letter may range from a highly sophisticated format, with numerous technical explanations and citations, to a simple composition that uses only layperson's terms. In many situations, of course, the best solution lies somewhere between the two extremes.[1]

## Organization

Like other kinds of writing, a letter is organized into an introduction, a body, and a conclusion. Each section uses summary sentences to emphasize main ideas and help the reader follow the train of thought.

The *introduction* of a letter establishes rapport with the reader and identifies the subject of the letter or the reason it was written. You can mention previous communication on the subject, such as an earlier letter or phone call, or remind the reader of a recent meeting or shared interest. The introduction should also briefly summarize the main ideas or recommendations discussed in the letter. If the letter is longer than about a page, it's also a good idea to identify in the introduction the main issues or topics the letter will cover.

The *body* of the letter is divided logically into discussions of each topic. Arrange the topics in descending order of importance *from the reader's point of view*. Start with the most important issue and work your way down to the least important. Begin the discussion of each issue with a summary sentence stating the main idea or recommendation.

Paragraphs should be short, usually a maximum of four or five sentences, and each should begin with a topic sentence that summarizes the paragraph's main idea.

The letter's *conclusion* may be a conventional courteous closing:

> Thank you very much for your help.

The conclusion is also a good place to tell your correspondent exactly what you want him or her to do, or what you will do to follow up on the subjects discussed in the letter:

> May I have an appointment to discuss this matter with you? I'll be in Chicago next week, October 7–11. I'll call your administrative assistant to see whether we can arrange a time that is convenient for you.

If your letter is very long, the conclusion may also summarize your main ideas and recommendations.

## Conciseness and Clarity

Conciseness and clarity, two qualities of all good writing, are particularly important in letters. You don't want to waste your readers' time, nor do you want them to miss important ideas. Come to the point quickly and say it in a way they will understand.

Many techniques already presented in this handbook are useful for writing short, clear letters. Your writing should be unified: Each paragraph should contain a central idea that is easy to spot. The letter should also be as brief and simple as possible, while still conveying an unambiguous, precise meaning.

## Tone

One of the most important characteristics of a well-written business letter is its tone, or the way it makes the reader feel. Chapter 4 discussed writing from your reader's point of view, emphasizing the reader's interests and needs. Courtesy and respect are important qualities of business letters, as they are in all forms of communication.

In general, effective letters reflect a personal, conversational tone. However, the best tone to use for a given letter depends to some extent on the purpose and reader of that letter. Review the discussion of tone in Chapter 4 to see how the content of the letter and your relationship with the reader can affect the tone you choose for your correspondence.

## Form and Appearance

One of the primary characteristics of an effective letter is a neat appearance. Good stationery is important: 8½ × 11-inch, unlined paper of a high-quality bond, about 24-pound weight. Envelopes, 4 × 10 inches, should match the stationery. White or cream is usually the best color choice. Software programs now make it possible to design and print your own letterhead stationery. If you design your own letterhead, be conservative when you select font styles and sizes.

Business letters should be printed on a good-quality printer. Envelopes should also be printed. Both the letter and the envelope should be free of errors. Neatness is essential!

A letter is usually single-spaced, with double-spacing between paragraphs although letters can be double-spaced throughout (see the sample formats in Figures 9–1 and 9–2). Margins should be at least 1 inch on all sides and as even as possible without justifying the right margin although a shorter letter may allow you to set wider margins.

One-page letters should be placed so that the body of the letter, excluding the heading, is centered on the page or slightly above center. A computer makes it easy to experiment with margins and spacing until you get the best arrangement.

**FIGURE 9–1**   Diagram of a Letter Format—Block Style

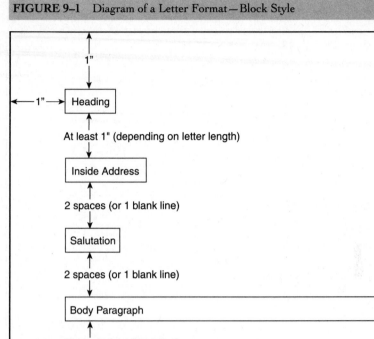

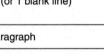

**FIGURE 9–2**    Diagram of a Letter Format — Modified Block Style

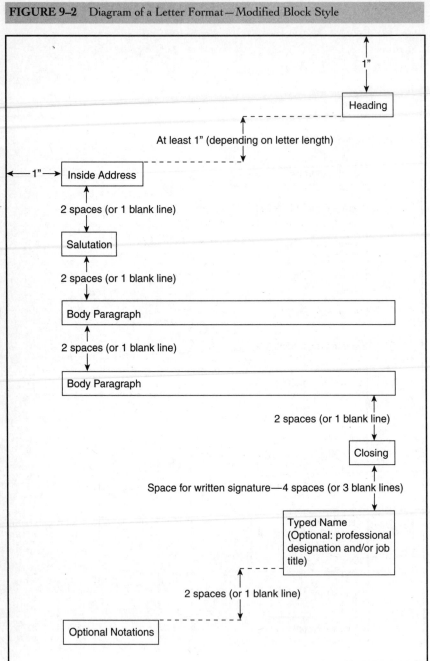

## Parts of the Letter

Study the diagrams in Figures 9–1 and 9–2, which illustrate the parts of a letter and their proper placement for two formats: the block and the modified block styles. The following sections describe each part of the letter in more detail. Remember also that formatting techniques, such as headings and set-off lists, can make your letters attractive and easy to read.

### *Heading*

The heading contains your address (not your name) and the date of the letter. If you use stationery without a letterhead, place the heading on the left margin (for block style) or next to the right margin (for modified block style). If you use letterhead stationery, omit the heading except for the date. Center the date below the letterhead or place it next to the left margin for block style.

### *Inside Address*

The inside address is a reproduction of the address on the envelope. Place the title of the person to whom you are writing either on the same line as his or her name, or on the following line:

Anna O'Rourke, President
Excellent Consulting Services
2110 Winners Circle
Atlanta, GA 30378

*-or-*

Anna O'Rourke
President
Excellent Consulting Services
2110 Winners Circle
Atlanta, GA 30378

It's usually better to address a letter to a specific person rather than to an office or title. You can usually find the name of the person to whom you are writing by phoning the company or organization or, possibly, by consulting its Web page. You should also verify the spelling of the name and the gender of the person, if gender isn't obvious from the name.

### *Salutation*

If possible, address your correspondent by name:

Dear Ms. O'Rourke:

*or*

Dear Mr. Smith:

For a female correspondent, use Ms. unless she prefers another title. If you know your correspondent well, you may use his or her first name in the salutation:

Dear Anna:

Be careful with the use of first names, however, especially when writing to someone you haven't met in person. A title and last name may be especially appropriate for an older person or one in a position of greater authority than yours. In many situations, a respectful, courteous tone requires using a title and last name.

If you don't know the name of the correspondent, use a salutation such as the following:

Dear Human Resource Division:
Dear Registrar:

Note that a colon (:) always follows the salutation in a business letter.

### Closing

The letter's formal closing is placed at the left margin for a block-style letter and next to the right margin for the modified block style. Capitalize the first word of the closing and put a comma at the end. Either of the following closings is correct:

Sincerely yours,
Sincerely,

### Signature

Your name should be printed four lines below the closing; your position or professional designation (or both) can be added in one of the ways shown below:

Sincerely,

*Anna O'Rourke*

Anna O'Rourke
President

*or*

Sincerely yours,

*Anna O'Rourke*

Anna O'Rourke, CPA
Managing Partner

The space between the closing and printed name is for your handwritten signature.

*Optional Parts of a Letter*

Sometimes you'll need additional notations, which are placed below the signature at the left margin. First, if someone else types your letter, a notation is made of your initials (all capital letters) and the typist's (all lowercase):

AO'R:lc

*or*

AO'R/lc

Second, if the letter includes an enclosure, make a notation:

Enclosure(s)

Finally, if you will distribute copies of the letter to other people, note the people who will receive a copy:

cc: John Jones

*Second Page*

Many business letters are only one page long. If you need to write additional pages, each should have a heading identifying the addressee, the date, and the page number. This information is usually printed at the left margin:

Mr. Richard Smith
November 18, 2011
Page 3

A second page (and any subsequent pages) should have at least three lines of text, in addition to the heading and closing.

## RESPONDING TO CORRESPONDENCE

When you reply to a letter written by someone else, it's important to respond in a way that will build a good working relationship between you and the correspondent. Many of the techniques for effective letters already discussed apply to responses. Here is a summary of those techniques, as well as a few pointers that apply particularly when you are answering someone else's letter:

1. Respond promptly, by return mail if possible.
2. Reread carefully the letter you received, noting questions that need answers or ideas that need your comment.
3. For the opening paragraph:
   - Refer to the earlier correspondence, such as the date of the letter you received.
   - If your letter is good news, or at least neutral, state clearly and positively the letter's main idea.

- If your letter contains bad news, such as the denial of a request, identify the subject of the letter in the opening paragraph. State the explicit refusal later in the body of the letter, after you have prepared the reader with some buffer material.
4. Answer all your correspondent's questions fully and cover all relevant topics in sufficient detail. However, the letter should be as concise as possible.
5. End with a courteous closing.

## TYPICAL ACCOUNTING LETTERS

Before we begin this section, we should note that many accounting firms have standardized letters for some situations. The management of a firm may have decided on the organization and even the specific wording that it requires its staff to use for engagement letters, management advisory letters, and the like. If your firm uses standardized letters, simply adapt the basic letter to the specific case you are concerned with, adding dates, names, figures, and other relevant facts.

Sample letters for various situations are presented in the following pages, along with some general comments on the content and organization of these letters.

### Engagement Letters

Engagement letters put into writing the arrangements made between an accounting firm and a client. Engagement letters can confirm the arrangements for a variety of services: audit, review, compilation, management advisory services, or tax. The main advantage of an engagement letter is that it clarifies the mutual responsibilities of the accountant and client and thus prevents possible misunderstandings.

Engagement letters can vary a great deal in content, depending on the firm writing the letter, the type of services to be provided, and the facts of the case. However, most engagement letters will include the following:

- A description of the objectives and nature of the service the accountants will provide, including any nonaudit services, such as the preparation of tax returns or management consulting.
- A description of the responsibilities of both the client and the auditor
- A description of any limitations, restrictions, or deadlines imposed on the work to be done
- A description of any assistance to be provided by the client
- A statement that an audit will possibly not uncover all acts of fraud

In addition to these elements, an engagement letter may also include other information, such as information about the fee and a space for the client to indicate acceptance of the arrangements outlined in the engagement letter.

Figure 9–3 shows a sample engagement letter for an audit.

FIGURE 9–3    Engagement Letter for an Audit (*Continued*)

**Yeo and Stockton**
**Certified Public Accountants**
**511 Avondale Avenue**
**Austin, Texas 78712**

July 15, 2011

Robert Martinez, President
Heritage Manufacturing Company
301 Planters Road
Austin, Texas 78712

Dear Mr. Martinez:

This letter will confirm our understanding of the arrangements for our audit of the financial statements of Heritage Manufacturing Company for the year ending December 31, 2011.

Our Responsibilities

We will audit the company's financial statements for the year ending December 31, 2011, for the purpose of expressing an opinion on the fairness with which they present, in all material respects, the financial position, results of operations, and cash flows in conformity with generally accepted accounting principles.

We will conduct our audit in accordance with generally accepted auditing standards. Those standards require that we obtain reasonable, rather than absolute, assurance that the financial statements are free of material misstatement, whether caused by error or fraud. Accordingly, a material misstatement may remain undetected. Also an audit is not designed to detect error or fraud that is immaterial to the financial statements; therefore, the audit will not necessarily detect misstatements less than this materiality level that might exist because of error, fraudulent financial reporting, or misappropriation of assets. If, for any reason, we are unable to complete the audit or are unable to form or have not formed an opinion, we may decline to express an opinion or decline to issue a report as a result of the engagement.

Although an audit includes obtaining an understanding of internal control sufficient to plan the audit and to determine the nature, timing, and extent of audit procedures to be performed, it is not designed to provide assurance on internal control or to identify significant deficiencies. However, we are responsible for ensuring that the audit committee is aware of any significant deficiencies that come to our attention.

*Source:* Adapted with permission from Alvin A. Arens, Randal J. Elder, and Mark S. Beasley, *Auditing and Assurance Service: An Integrated Approach,* 10th ed. (Upper Saddle River, NJ: Prentice Hall, Inc., 2010), 214.

**FIGURE 9–3** (*Continued*)

Robert Martinez, President
July 15, 2011
Page 2

Management Responsibilities

The financial statements are the responsibility of the company's management. Management is also responsible for (1) establishing and maintaining effective internal control over financial reports, (2) identifying and ensuring the company complies with the laws and regulations applicable to its activities, (3) making all financial records and related information available to us, and (4) providing to us at the conclusion of the engagement a representation letter that, among other things, will confirm management's responsibility for the preparation of the financial statements in conformity with generally accepted accounting principles, the availability of financial records and related data, the completeness and availability of all minutes of the board and committee meetings, and to the best of its knowledge and belief, the absence of fraud involving management or those employees who have a significant role in the entity's internal control.

The timing of our audit and the assistance to be supplied by your personnel, including the preparation of schedules and analyses of accounts, are described on a separate attachment. Timely completion of this work will facilitate the completion of our audit.

Other Services

As part of our engagement for the year ending December 31, 2011, we will also prepare the federal and state income tax returns for Heritage Manufacturing Company.

Our fees will be billed as work progresses and are based on the amount of time required at various levels of responsibility, plus actual out-of-pocket expenses. Invoices are payable upon presentation. We will notify you immediately of any circumstances we encounter that could significantly affect our initial estimate of total fees of $125,000.

If this letter correctly expresses your understanding, please sign the enclosed copy and return it to us. We appreciate the opportunity to serve you.

Accepted:                                    Yours very truly:

*Robert Martinez*                            *Mary Stockton*

By: Robert Martinez                          Mary Stockton
Date: July 27, 2011                          Partner

## Management Advisory Letters

At the conclusion of an audit, an accountant often writes a letter to the client suggesting ways the client can improve the business. This type of letter may contain suggestions on a variety of topics:

- Internal control
- The accounting and information system
- Inventory control
- Credit policies
- Budgeting
- Tax matters
- Resource management
- Operating procedures

Sometimes, if the auditor includes many recommendations in the management letter, the letter may be quite long. If you write a management letter that is more than three pages long, consider organizing it into a report with a transmittal letter. Address the transmittal letter to the president or board of directors of the client company and summarize in the letter the major recommendations made in the report. Chapter 10 provides information on report writing.

In any case, whether the management letter is a single document or a report with a transmittal letter, remember that long letters are more attractive and easier to read if they contain headings. These headings divide the letter into logical sections.

Whatever the format of the management letter, write it in a way that is helpful to the client and builds a good professional relationship between the client and your firm. The techniques for effective writing discussed so far in this book certainly apply to management letters: clear and logical organization, readable style, and specific and concrete explanation.

An article in the *Journal of Accountancy* has noted that management letters may anger clients if they don't give enough specific information to support the accountants' suggestions.[2] The authors stress the importance of answering three questions about each recommendation:

- Why is the change needed?
- How can it be accomplished?
- What benefits will the client receive?

An example of a short, but effective, management advisory letter appears in Figure 9–4.

## Tax Research Letters

Accountants who provide tax services often write letters to their clients communicating the results of the research into some tax question. These letters can be for either tax planning or after-the-fact tax situations.

**FIGURE 9–4**    Management Advisory Letter (*Continued*)

JADAU AND HERNANDEZ
Certified Public Accountants
1553 W. Ellis Street
Atlanta, Georgia 30316

March 15, 2011

Arthur Sanders, President
Art Products, Inc.
24 N. Broad Street
Atlanta, Georgia 30327

Dear Mr. Sanders:

Our examination of Art Products' financial statements for the year ended December 31, 2010, revealed two areas where we believe you could improve your business:

- Stronger budgeting system
- Review of credit policies

The following paragraphs explain these recommendations in greater detail.

Budgets

Operating, selling, and general administrative expenses for 2010 as compared with 2009 increased from $1 million to $1,050,000, a change of 5 percent. Although management has been able to control expenditures, we believe efforts in this area would be assisted by implementation of a strong system of budgeting.

Under such a system, responsibility for actual performance is assigned to the employees most directly responsible for the expenditures involved. (It is best that such employees have a role in establishing the budgets.) Periodic reports reflecting actual and budgeted amounts, together with explanations of significant variances, should be provided to the management personnel responsible for approving the budgets initially. We cannot overemphasize the value of sound budgeting and planning in all areas of the company's activities

Credit Policies

The history of write-offs of bad accounts over the past few years indicates that the write-off percentage has declined. Considering the low net earnings margin under which the company operates (slightly less

*Source:* Robert T. Lanz and S. Thomas Moser, "Improving Management Letters," *Journal of Accountancy*, 149, no. 3 (March 1980): 41–42.

FIGURE 9–4    (*Continued*)

Arthur Sanders
March 15, 2011
Page 2

than 0.6 percent of net sales), it is most important that this favorable
record continue because a significant increase in bad debts could
have a substantial negative impact on net earnings.

In view of the high cost of money for business in general, management should consider reviewing its credit policies to reasonably
ensure that the risk inherent in continued sales to customers of ques-
tionable credit standing is justified. This is a delicate area of policy; it
is not desirable to so restrict sales representatives that profitable
sales are lost because of overly stringent credit policies. However, the
credit and collection department should exercise a reasonable
amount of control to ensure a minimum of bad accounts. For example, a limit could be set on the amount sales representatives could
extend to customers whose accounts have reached a certain balance.

We will be glad to discuss these suggestions with you and help you
implement them.

Sincerely,

*Juan Hernandez*

Juan Hernandez
Jadau and Hernandez
Certified Public Accountants

The content and organization of these letters can vary, but the following basic outline is a good one:

- The facts on which the research was based.
- Caution that the advice is valid only for the facts previously outlined.
- The tax questions implicit in these facts.
- The conclusions, with the authoritative support for the conclusions.
- Areas of controversy that the IRS might dispute. (Tax accountants do not
  all agree that the letter should identify the vulnerable areas in the client's
  situation. *Tax Research Techniques* suggests that if the letter does identify
  these weaknesses, the accountant should caution the client to control
  access to the letter.)[3]

In addition to a logical organization, such as the one outlined
here, tax research letters should be understandable to the client. Tax
questions are often highly technical, and you may need to explain the
conclusions in terms a businessperson will understand.

Figure 9–5 illustrates a letter written to a client to report the results of tax research. The letter, which is written to the chief administrator of a large hospital, deals with a technical tax question, but is clearly written with a friendly, courteous tone.

**FIGURE 9–5** A Letter Reporting the Results of Tax Research (*Continued*)

Professional Accounting Associates
2701 First City Plaza
Suite 905
Dallas, Texas 75019

December 12, 2011

Elizabeth Fegali, Chief Administrator
Mercy Hospital
22650 West Haven Drive
Arlington, Texas 75527

Dear Ms. Fegali:

It was great to see you at last Thursday's football game. If not for that last minute fumble, the Longhorns might have taken the conference championship!

In our meeting of December 6, you asked us to research whether the value of the meal vouchers that Mercy provides to its medical employees is taxable to the employees. I regret to inform you that if the vouchers are redeemed at MacDougal's, their value is likely to be taxable to the employees. On the other hand, if the vouchers are redeemed in the hospital cafeteria, their value is likely to be excludible from the employee's income.

In reaching this conclusion, we consulted relevant provisions of the Internal Revenue Code (IRC), applicable Treasury Regulations under the IRC, and a pertinent Supreme Court case. In addition, we reviewed the documents on employee benefits that you submitted to us at our earlier meeting.

Facts

The facts as we understand them are as follows: Mercy provides meal vouchers to its medical employees to enable them to eat while on emergency call. The vouchers are redeemable either in the hospital cafeteria or at MacDougal's. MacDougal's is a privately owned institution that rents business space from the hospital. Although Mercy's employees are not required to remain on or near the premises during their meal hours, they generally do.

*Source:* Adopted with permission from Pope, Thomas R., Kenneth E. Anderson, and John L. Kramer, *Prentice Hall's Federal Taxation 2010, Comprehensive* (Upper Saddle River, N.J.: Prentice Hall, Inc., 2010), A-7.

**FIGURE 9–5**    (*Continued*)

Elizabeth Fegali
December 12, 2011
Page 2

Applicable Laws

Under the IRC, the value of meals is excludible from an employee's income if two conditions are met: first, the meals are furnished "for the convenience of the employer," and second, they are provided "on the business premises of the employer." Although the IRC does not explain what is meant by "for the convenience of the employer," "business premises of the employer," and "meals," other authorities do. Specifically, the Treasury Regulations define "business premises of the employer" to be the place of employment of the employees. The regulations state that providing meals during work hours to have an employee available for emergency calls is "for the convenience of the employer."

Moreover, under the IRC, if more than half the employees satisfy the "for the convenience of the employer" test, all the employees will be regarded as satisfying the test. The Supreme Court has interpreted "meals" to mean food-in-kind. The Court has held that cash allowances do not qualify as "meals."

Analysis

Clearly, the meals furnished by Mercy are "for the convenience of the employer." They are furnished during the employees' work hours to have the employees available for emergency calls. Although the meals provided in the hospital cafeteria appear to be furnished "on the business premises of the employer," the meals provided at MacDougal's do not appear to be. The hospital is the place of employment of the medical employees. MacDougal's is not. What is unclear is whether the meal vouchers are equivalent to food-in-kind. On the one hand, they are redeemable at more than one institution and thus resemble cash allowances. On the other hand, they are redeemable only in meals and thus resemble food-in-kind.

Recommendation

Because of this lack of clarity, we suggest that you modify your employee benefits plan to allow for the provision of meals-in-kind exclusively in the hospital cafeteria. In this way, you will dispel any doubt that Mercy is furnishing "meals," "for the convenience of the employer," "on the premises of the employer."

Please call me at (817) 475-2020 if you have any questions concerning this conclusion. I also suggest that we meet next week to discuss the possibility of revising your employee benefits plan.

**FIGURE 9–5** (*Continued*)

Elizabeth Fegali
December 12, 2011
Page 3

U.S. Treasury Regulations require us to advise you that, unless otherwise specifically noted, any federal tax advice in this communication (including any attachments, enclosures, or other accompanying materials) was not intended or written to be used, and it cannot be used, by any taxpayer for the purpose of avoiding penalties; furthermore, this communication was not intended or written to support the promotion or marketing of any of the transactions or matters it addresses.

Very truly yours,

*Rosina Havacek*

Rosina Havacek, Junior Associate
Professional Accounting Associates

## STANDARDIZED LETTERS: A CAUTION

As already mentioned, many organizations have standardized letters that they use for situations that occur often, such as engagement letters. These form letters save time, and they also convey the message precisely and reliably. If your employer expects you to use these standardized letters, then, of course, you should do so.

One word of caution: Remember that in many situations personalized letters are more appropriate than standardized letters. If you use standardized letters, be sure they are responsive to the reader's needs and concerns.

If you know your correspondent personally, a friendly reference to a topic of mutual interest can add warmth to your letter. The opening paragraph of the letter in Figure 9–5 provides a friendly, personalized opening to a client letter:

> It was great to see you at last Thursday's football game. If not for that last minute fumble, the Longhorns might have taken the conference championship!

### Letters Sent via E-mail

In the past, business correspondence was always sent using the postal service. Today many organizations and individuals send their letters electronically, at least some of the time. A major advantage of sending letters by e-mail is, of course, the speed with which they are transmitted. The recipient can also reply quickly, thus completing the exchange of information in a timely manner.

E-mail letters carry risks. Security of the correspondence can be an issue. E-mail letters also present potential problems for writers who wish to communicate effectively. For one thing, many people are accustomed to a very informal writing style for e-mail, which may be inappropriate for many business letters. Also, e-mail writers may not give the necessary attention to detail that marks an effective business letter. Grammatical and mechanical conventions, such as correct spelling and punctuation, are as important for e-mail letters as they are for those sent in an envelope. In fact, we can say that most of the guidelines for effective letters covered in this chapter apply to all business letters, whether they are sent electronically or by conventional means.

Chapter 10 provides additional information about how to write effective e-mail.

## EXERCISES

### Exercise 9–1  [General]

You are considering a move to a distant city, and you would like to work with a local accounting firm there. You have three years' experience working as a CPA in the city where you now live.

Write a letter requesting an interview to discuss possible employment with the firm for which you wish to work. Use the proper format, effective organization, and appropriate style. Invent any information you feel is necessary to make your letter complete. You may also want to study Chapter 15: Writing for Employment.

### Exercise 9–2  [General]

Suppose you received the letter shown in Figure 9–6. How would you react? What, specifically, is wrong with this letter? What about it is effective?

After you have analyzed the strengths and weaknesses of the letter as it is shown in Figure 9–6, revise it so that it would make a better impression on a reader.

### Exercise 9–3  [General]

A friend of yours, Greg Burleson, has a daughter, Elaine, who wants to major in accounting. She believes that the only skills she needs for success as an accountant are technical skills: knowledge of accounting

**FIGURE 9–6** Letter for Exercise 9–2

Smith, Barnum, and Bailey
Certified Public Accountants
301 MacDonald Place
Atlanta, Georgia 36095

Members
American Institute of          Telephone: (306) 782-5107
Certified Public Accountants

May 21, 2011

Mr. John W. Simmons
234 Myers Hall, UGA
Athens, Georgia 30609

Dear John:

After considerable debate about our needs, we have
decided to offer the internship to someone else. Our offer was
excepted, so the position is now filled. I enjoyed talking with
you and felt you would of been a positive impact to our firm
and would work well with our present staff. Upon graduation
we would be most interested in talking with you regarding full-
time employment. If I can be of assistance in the near future,
please feel free to call.

Sincerely,

*Jason A. Smith*

Jason A. Smith
JASjr/mlk
Enclosures

principles, the ability to research accounting issues, and computer
expertise. Your friend Greg suspects that success in accounting
requires a wider range of skills than Elaine realizes. However, Elaine
isn't receptive to suggestions from her father.

You are a successful CPA who has been in practice for over 20
years, and your family has been friends with the Burleson family for a
long time. Greg asks you to write a letter to Elaine about the skills
necessary to become a successful accountant. He is sure Elaine will
take your advice seriously.

Write a letter to Elaine, a freshman at State University.

## Exercise 9–4 [Tax]

Assume you are a CPA specializing in tax accounting for individuals in your community. One of your clients, Alicia Evans, has sent you the following e-mail:

> As you know, I have recently returned to work full time and need to hire someone to help me with house cleaning. I need to know what, if any, obligations I will have for withholding Social Security. Will I have any other tax or reporting obligations? I am considering the following possibilities:
>
> 1. Hiring an individual who has a business license and is self-employed as a contractor. This person would clean my house weekly. In return, I would pay this person $100 a week for 50 weeks of the year.
> 2. Using a cleaning service, who would send one of its employees to my home. I would use this service biweekly at $125 per visit, for a total of 26 visits per year.
> 3. Hiring my neighbor who does not have a business license. She would clean my house biweekly, and I would pay her $75 each visit, for a total of 26 visits each year.
>
> I have one more question. Can I deduct any of the above expenses for house cleaning from my own income tax? After all, if I were not working I would not need to hire someone else to clean my house. It seems to me the house cleaning should be a legitimate business expense.
>
> Please send the answer to the above questions to my home by registered mail. You have my address on file.

Write a letter to Ms. Evans in which you answer her questions.

## Exercise 9–5 [General/Auditing]

In the process of completing a tax return, your client, Sam Rhodes, refused to provide evidence to support some rather large deductions for business travel, saying, "Oh, I don't know about receipts. Just put it down, and if and when the IRS questions me, I'll worry about receipts then."

Write a letter to Mr. Rhodes explaining why you cannot prepare a tax return showing these deductions unless he can provide the receipts. Remember the importance of tact and diplomacy in an awkward situation such as this. Use the proper format, effective organization, and appropriate style. Invent any information you feel is necessary to make your letter complete.

## Exercise 9–6 [Auditing]

You are a partner in the firm of Shipley, Pyburn & Bynum, a local CPA firm. Your firm has received a letter from George Rayburn of

Rayburn Industries, a potential audit client asking the following questions:

- What are the objectives of auditing your firm follows?
- How much responsibility does your firm take for the financial statements you produce as a result of an audit? Will your firm guarantee the accuracy of financial statements following your audit?
- What sort of guarantee does your firm provide that it will find any and all errors and fraud during the completion of an audit?

It is evident that Mr. Rayburn has sent a similar letter with the same questions to several CPA firms and plans to select a firm based upon the answers he receives.

Write a letter to Mr. Rayburn responding to his questions. Invent any information you feel is necessary to make your letter complete.

### Exercise 9–7  [Auditing]

During your first audit of a new client, Capital Food Supplies, a small restaurant food supply company, you become aware of a major weakness in internal control: One employee keeps the accounts receivable and payable records, pays bills, and does the bank reconciliation each month. When you casually mention the problem to Scott Devin, the owner and general manager, he dismisses the issue. He says he trusts all his employees, has never had any problems, and can't afford to hire another employee just to deal with such a small internal control technicality.

Write a letter to your client tactfully explaining why you do not consider the problem to be "a small technicality." Explain the possible ramifications of not dealing with the issue, both in terms of the audit and in terms of asset protection. Use the proper format, effective organization, and appropriate style. Invent any information you feel is necessary to make your letter complete.

### Exercise 9–8  [Financial/Theory]

Your boss, John Creedy, is a partner in the small local CPA firm for which you work. One morning a client, Jeff Altman, the owner of Altman Manufacturing, storms into Mr. Creedy's office and delivers a complaint. An edited version follows:

> This morning at my breakfast club I spoke with my competitor, Tony Dodd. He uses the LIFO inventory method just as I do. He boasted that his accountant had told him that by speeding up his purchases of raw materials at year-end he could significantly increase reported profits. If he can do that, why can't I? And why haven't you discussed this gimmick with me? I don't expect to rely on Dodd for financial advice; I pay you for that.

After Altman's departure, Mr. Creedy calls you, the accountant-in-charge of the Altman account, into his office to discuss Mr. Altman's complaint. You explain to your boss that your concern is your client's very large raw material inventory and slow turnover rate caused by years of overbuying. Mr. Creedy advises you that Altman needs new capital in his business and is trying to interest another local businessperson in becoming a limited partner. An increase in reported profits could be advantageous to Mr. Altman's plans and, therefore, left to his own devices, Mr. Altman would likely follow Mr. Dodd's accountant's advice.

Mr. Creedy asks you to draft a letter to Mr. Altman. The letter should provide a discussion of the problems of maintaining an overly large inventory as well as the disadvantage of a low turnover rate. Although you are not familiar with Mr. Dodd's company, you are reasonably certain his accountant would not have made the comment he did if Mr. Dodd's company had the same existing inventory problems as Altman Manufacturing. Use the proper format, effective organization, and appropriate style for your letter. Invent any information you feel is necessary to make your letter complete.

### Exercise 9–9  [Financial]

Your client, Lewis Dabbs, has written a letter to you. He is concerned because he has just received an offer to purchase his business for $1,000,000 more than the net carrying value of the assets as reported in the most recent financial statements that you had audited. He is not interested in selling the business, but he is now convinced that you have certified financial statements that do not properly reflect the value of his company.

Write a letter to your client explaining why the figures in the balance sheet should not be changed. You may assume your client is an astute businessman with no background in accounting. Use good format, effective organization, and appropriate style. Invent any information you feel is necessary to make your letter complete.

### Exercise 9–10  [Tax]

Jennifer Davies, one of your tax clients, is contemplating making the following gifts: $25,000 to her church, $30,000 to each of her two grandchildren, $10,000 to her sister, and $15,000 to the local symphony orchestra. Ms. Davies has asked your firm what the tax consequences of these gifts will be to her and her husband. Among the issues you will want to discuss is the possibility of splitting some or all of the gifts with her husband. Ms. Davies is already aware of the term "gift splitting" because one of her friends has mentioned it to her. However, she does not understand how it works or whether it may be advantageous to her. She has also asked why she can't simply treat the gifts as "charitable contributions."

Write a letter to Ms. Davies replying to her inquiry. Invent any information you feel is necessary to make your letter complete.

### Exercise 9–11 [Systems]

James Gipper, one of your consulting clients, is the CEO of Glassplex, a rapidly growing plexiglass manufacturing company. Because his company is quickly developing its Internet presence, he is becoming increasingly concerned about Internet security. At his request, you are to write a letter to him outlining the basics of Internet security. Write the letter using good format, effective organization, and appropriate style. Invent any information you feel is necessary to make the letter complete.

### Exercise 9–12 [Cost/Managerial]

One of your clients is Corporate Sentry, Inc., which manufactures alarms and other security devices. Due to competitive pressures, it plans to reduce costs so that it can more competitively price its products. In preparation for its internal deliberations, the CFO of the company, Charles Sargent, has asked your consulting firm to write a letter to him explaining the difference between engineered costs and discretionary costs and how such a distinction may be relevant to their downsizing plans. Write the letter using proper format, effective organization, and appropriate style. Invent any information you feel is necessary to make your letter complete.

### Exercise 9–13 [Systems]

One of your clients, Jim Vaught, owns a very successful regional medical supply business. He has recently become interested in implementing an image processing system to improve cash collections. Mr. Vaught has asked you to write a letter to him describing the basics of a good image processing system. Write the letter using proper format, effective organization, and appropriate style. Invent any information you feel is necessary to make your letter complete.

## NOTES

1. Robert L. Gardner, Dave N. Stewart, and Ronald G. Worsham, Jr., *Tax Research Techniques*, 8th ed. (New York: American Institute of Certified Public Accountants, 2008), 185–186. This source provides additional information on other letters that tax accountants may write, such as tax protest letters and requests for rulings.

2. Robert T. Lanz and S. Thomas Moser, "Improving Management Letters," *Journal of Accountancy 149*, no. 3 (March 1980): 39–42.

3. These points are discussed in Gardner, Robert L., Dave N. Stewart, and Ronald G. Worsham, Jr., *Tax Research Techniques*, 8th ed. (New York: American Institute of Certified Public Accountants, 2008), 186–187.

# CHAPTER

# 10

# Memos and E-mail

Memos, also called memoranda or memorandums, are often used for communication within an organization—between departments, for example, or between a supervisor and other members of the staff. Memos may be of any length, from one sentence to several pages. They are usually less formal than letters written to people outside the organization, but well-written memos have the same qualities as good letters: clarity, conciseness, coherence, and courtesy.

In this chapter we first discuss some general characteristics of effective memos. Then we look at two special kinds of memos that accountants often write: memos to clients' files and memos that are part of working papers. We conclude with a discussion of e-mail, which has replaced hard copy memos in many situations, especially for communication within an organization. Many of the techniques used for effective memos are also applicable to e-mail although some special considerations apply to electronic communication.

## MEMOS: SOME BASIC PRINCIPLES

Often memos are quite short—ranging in length from one sentence, perhaps, to several paragraphs. Figure 10–1 is an example. Notice the heading of the memo: the person or persons addressed, the writer, the subject, and the date. Often, the writer's initials replace a formal signature.

Sometimes memos are much longer than the one in Figure 10–1; in fact, they can be used for short reports. For longer memos, organization and structure are more complicated, so you need to think of writing the memo in terms of the writing process discussed in Chapter 2. You need to spend some time planning your memo: analyzing its purpose, considering the needs and interests of your readers, perhaps doing some research, and, finally, organizing the material to be covered into a good outline. After you have planned the memo, you can then draft and revise it using the techniques covered in Chapters 2 through 7.

**FIGURE 10–1** Sample Memo

To:       Fourth-floor employees

From:     Skip Waller   *SW*

Subject:  Scheduled painting

Date:     September 12, 2011

Our painting contractors are scheduled to repaint the offices and public areas on our floor next week, September 19–23. The contractors understand that we will continue to work in the offices during this time and will try to disturb us as little as possible. But the work is bound to be somewhat disruptive, so let's all stay flexible and keep a sense of humor during this time that is bound to be somewhat inconvenient.

Thanks for your cooperation as we complete this much-needed maintenance.

## The Parts of a Memo: Organizing for Coherence

Like most kinds of writing, a memo is organized into an introduction, a body, and a conclusion. Summary sentences are used throughout the memo to make it more coherent. Even very short memos have this structure. The memo shown in Figure 10–1, which contains only two paragraphs, begins by summarizing the main idea of the memo. The remainder of the first paragraph provides additional information, and the final paragraph, which is only one sentence, concludes by thanking the readers for their cooperation.

### *Introduction*

Most introductions range in length from one sentence to one paragraph although for a longer memo the introduction might be two or three short paragraphs. The introduction should identify what the memo is about and why it was written. If the memo will discuss more than one topic or be divided into several subtopics, the introduction should identify all of the most important issues to be covered. The introduction might contain a sentence such as the following to indicate the memo's contents:

This memo explains how to account for patents, copyrights, and trademarks.

An introduction should also identify the main ideas or recommendations of your memo. Sometimes the main idea can be summarized in one or two sentences, but for longer memos you might need an entire paragraph. If the summary of your main ideas is longer than a paragraph, it's often better to put it in a separate section immediately following the introduction. This section would have a heading such as "Summary" or "Recommendations."

*Body*

The body of the memo can be divided into sections, each with a heading that describes the contents of that section. Remember to begin by summarizing the main idea of the section.

A section can have one or many paragraphs. Paragraphs should usually be no more than four or five sentences long, and each should begin with a topic sentence.

*Conclusion*

Memos often end with a conclusion, which can be very brief. Consider this example:

> Let me know if you have any further questions about these procedures.

A conclusion such as this one brings the memo to a close and ends in a courteous, helpful tone. A word of caution, however, about conclusions like the one just given: Be careful not to end all your memos with the same sentence (or some slightly altered variation). The conclusion should be a meaningful addition to the memo, not just an empty string of words added out of habit. Also, be sure your conclusion (like the rest of the memo) is appropriate to your reader. Consider why the preceding conclusion example would be unsuitable for a memo you're sending to your boss. The sample memos in this chapter show several different kinds of conclusions; all are appropriate to the content of the memo and the reader.

One misconception some people have about conclusions is that they should always repeat the memo's main ideas. For short memos, this repetition is usually not necessary although for memos longer than about three or four pages, such an ending summary can be helpful.

Whatever the length of the memo, the conclusion is a good place to tell your readers what you want them to do, or what you will do, to follow up on the ideas discussed in the memo. The memo shown in Figure 10–1 has such a conclusion.

## Concise, Clear, Readable Memos: Style and Tone

Memos should be as concise as possible: no unnecessary repetitions, digressions, or wordiness. They should be written in clear, direct style, so that readers find them interesting and informative. In addition, memos should have flawless grammar and mechanics.

Memos can vary considerably in tone, depending on what they are about and how they will be circulated. Some memos, such as the one in Figure 10–1, are informal. For these memos, a conversational, personal tone is appropriate.

Other memos are more formal and might serve as short reports. Some memos, such as the one shown in Figure 10–3, may report the results of research or work performed and may thus become part of the permanent records in a client's file. These memos are usually written with a more impersonal, formal tone. Whether formal or informal, however, all memos should be clear and concise.

## Formats

Memos can be written in a variety of formats, as the examples in this chapter show. The memo in Figure 10–2 is typical of the format

---

**FIGURE 10–2** A Memo

MEMORANDUM                                    August 16, 2011

TO:          FLOYD JONES
FROM:        DENNIS SMITH *DS*
SUBJECT:     PURCHASING SHERATON MANUFACTURING

This memo is in response to your questions concerning the purchase of Sheraton Manufacturing. The memo will first explain goodwill and then discuss how to determine its value. After you determine the value of Sheraton's goodwill, you will be better able to decide how much you want to offer for the company as a whole.

What Is Goodwill?

Goodwill is an intangible asset made up of items that may contribute to the value and earning power of a company but that are not other-wise listed on the company's balance sheet. Here are some possible items that may contribute to goodwill for Sheraton Manufacturing:

1. Highly capable engineering staff
2. Strong reputation for quality work
3. Good management
4. A large number of loyal customers

These items are not separately identified on Sheraton's balance sheet. However, they obviously have value and therefore should be included in the purchase price of the business.

Determining the Value of Goodwill

The value of goodwill is established by comparing the present value of future cash earnings (the purchase price of Sheraton Manufacturing) with the total value assigned to the separately identified assets acquired, less liabilities. The difference between the two is the value of goodwill.

The key to determining the value of goodwill is, of course, the deter-mination of the purchase price for Sheraton (estimating the present value of future cash earnings). We can do this by completing a cash-flow analysis similar to the ones we perform in our capital budgeting process.

Let me know if you have any further questions about goodwill or the Sheraton Manufacturing acquisition.

used in many organizations. Notice especially how the headings and set-off list make this memo attractive and easy to read.

Some organizations may prefer another format that has become customary within the organization. You should prepare your memos according to your employer's expectations. The examples in Figures 10–2 and 10–3 illustrate formats some CPA firms

---

**FIGURE 10–3**    A Memo to a Client's File (*Continued*)

**Memorandum to the File**

Date:     December 9, 2011

From:     Rosina Havacek *RH*

Re:       The taxability of meal vouchers furnished by Mercy Hospital to its medical staff.

**Facts**

Our client, Mercy Hospital ("Mercy"), provides meal vouchers to its medical employees to enable them to remain on emergency call. The vouchers are redeemable at Mercy's on-site cafeteria and at MacDougal's, a privately owned sandwich shop. MacDougal's rents business space from the hospital. Although Mercy does not require its employees to remain on or near its premises during their meal hours, the employees generally do. Elizabeth Fegali, Mercy's Chief Administrator, has asked us to research whether the value of the meal vouchers is taxable to the employees.

**Issues**

The taxability of the meal vouchers depends on three issues: first, whether the meals are furnished "for the convenience of the employer;" second, whether they are furnished "on the business premises of the employer;" and third, whether the vouchers are equivalent to cash.

**Conclusion**

Although it appears that the meals acquired by voucher in the hospital cafeteria are furnished "for the convenience of the employer" and "on the business premises of the employer," it is unclear whether the vouchers are equivalent to cash. If they *are* equivalent to cash, *or* if they are redeemed at MacDougal's, their value is likely to be taxable to the employees. On the other hand, if they are not equivalent to cash, *and* they are redeemed only in the hospital cafeteria, their value is likely to be excludible.

**Discussion**

*Applicable Law:* Section 119 provides that the value of meals is excludible from an employee's income if the meals are furnished for the convenience of, and on the business premises of, the employer. Under Reg. Sec. 1.119-1, a meal is furnished "for the convenience of the

Adapted with permission from Ray Sommerfeld, G. Fred Streuling, Robert L. Gardner, and Dave N. Stewart, *Tax Research Techniques*, 3rd ed., Revised (New York: American Institute of Certified Public Accountants, 1989), 161.

**FIGURE 10–3** *(Continued)*

Mercy Hospital File

December 9, 2011

Page 2

employer" if it is furnished for a "substantial noncompensatory business reason." A "substantial noncompensatory reason" includes the need to have the employee available for emergency calls during his or her meal period. Under Sec. 119(b)(4), if more than half the employees satisfy the "for the convenience of the employee" test, all employees will be regarded as satisfying the test. Regulation Sec. 1.119-1 defines "business premises of the employer" as the place of employment of the employee.

A Supreme Court case, *Kowalski v. CIR*, 434 U.S. 77, 77-2 USTC 9748, discusses what constitutes "meals" for purposes of Sec. 119. In *Kowalski*, the State of New Jersey furnished cash meal allowances to its state troopers to enable them to eat while on duty. It did not require the troopers to use the allowances exclusively for meals. Nor did it require them to consume their meals on its business premises. One trooper, R. J. Kowalski, excluded the value of his allowances from his income. The IRS disputed this treatment, and Kowalski took the IRS to court. In court, Kowalski argued that the allowances were excludible because they were furnished "for the convenience of the employer." The IRS contended that the allowances were taxable because they amounted to compensation. The U.S. Supreme Court took up the case and decided for the IRS. The Court held that the Sec. 119 income exclusion does not apply to payments in cash.

*Issue 1:* The meals provided by Mercy seem to be furnished "for the convenience of the employees." They are furnished to have employees available for emergency calls during their meal breaks. This is a "substantial noncompensatory reason" within the meaning of Reg. Sec. 1.119-1.

*Issue 2:* Although the hospital cafeteria appears to be the "business premises of the employer," MacDougal's does not appear to be. The hospital is the place of employment of the medical employees. MacDougal's is not.

*Issue 3:* Based on the foregoing authorities, it is unclear whether the vouchers are equivalent to cash. On the one hand, they are redeemable only in meals. Thus, they resemble meals-in-kind. On the other hand, they are redeemable at more than one institution. Thus, they resemble cash. Nor is it clear whether a court deciding this case would reach the same conclusion as the Supreme Court did in *Kowalski*. In the latter case, the State of New Jersey provided its meal allowances in the form of cash. It did not require its employees to use the allowances exclusively for meals. Nor did it require them to consume their meals on its business premises. In our case, Mercy provides its meal allowances in the form of vouchers. Thus, it indirectly requires its employees to use the allowances exclusively for meals. On the other hand, it does not require them to consume their meals on its business premises.

prefer when the memos are part of a client's file. Note that in Figures 10–3 the section labeled "Conclusion" appears before the section labeled "Discussion."

If you are free to design the format of your memos, be conservative; avoid oversize fonts and a great deal of inked space.

## SAMPLE MEMOS

The memo shown in Figure 10-2 was written in response to the hypothetical situation described here:

*Situation:*

> Floyd Jones is the proprietor of the firm for which you work. Mr. Jones wants to acquire a manufacturing business. The business he wants to acquire, Sheraton Manufacturing, is insisting that Floyd pay not only for the identifiable net assets of the business, but also for "goodwill." Floyd asks you: "What is goodwill? Should I pay for it? If I should pay for it, how much should I pay?"

Study the memo in Figure 10–2 to see how it illustrates the principles of memo writing already discussed. Do you think Mr. Jones will be pleased with the memo?

### Memos to Clients' Files

Accountants often record information about a client's situation in a memo that is placed in the client's file for later reference. Other members of the staff may refer to the information recorded in these memos months or even years later, so the information must be recorded clearly, accurately, and correctly.

For example, a client might write or call an accounting firm about a tax question. The person receiving the letter or handling the call then writes a memo to record the pertinent facts of the client's situation. Later, another member of the staff can research the question. The researcher needs adequate information to identify the issues and solve the client's problem.

A sample memo written for a client's file appears in Figure 10–3. This memo summarizes research into an accountant's tax question.

## E-MAIL

With the explosion of information technology, many memos are now written in the form of e-mail messages. Like paper memos, e-mails may be short and informal, or lengthy, formal documents that request or provide detailed information about a business's activities. To write effective e-mails, you should follow the guidelines for memos discussed earlier in this chapter: concise, clear writing with main ideas that are easy to spot. A few special tips are especially applicable to e-mails.

## Write a Strong Subject Line

Write a short, powerful subject line with key words near the beginning since your recipients' inboxes may truncate the subject line. You want to catch the attention of the recipients quickly and ensure that they open and read your message. Compare the following subject lines:

Subject: Meeting

vs.

Subject: Required staff meeting May 19, 3 PM

Which subject line is more likely to ensure attendance at the meeting?

## Put Important Ideas First

Begin your e-mail message with the most important idea(s), and arrange your message from most important to least important information. Remember that people often read e-mail hurriedly, scanning for what is important and closing the e-mail before reading it in entirety. Short paragraphs with clear topic sentences are especially important for longer e-mails.

## Use Conventional Grammar and Mechanics

Follow conventional usage for grammar and mechanics, including standard spelling, punctuation, and capitalization. Avoid the codes sometimes used for text messages sent via cell phone, such as all lowercase letters or abbreviations for frequently used words and phrases.

## A Few Cautions

The use of e-mail, while certainly convenient, requires caution. Be careful to avoid these risks:

*Address messages carefully.* We've all heard stories of messages being sent to unintended recipients. This often occurs when a memo is sent using a distribution list or some general address, rather than to an individual. The results are sometimes humorous, as when an employee invites the entire corporation to lunch; or they can be disastrous, as might occur when the plans for a new product are sent by mistake to the firm's competitors. The lesson is to "think twice and click once" when addressing e-mail messages.

When replying to an e-mail sent by someone using a distribution list, remember that if you click on the "Reply to All" button instead of the

"Reply" button, your reply will be sent to the entire distribution list. Is that necessary or what you intend?

***Compose your message as if it will be read by everyone.*** Remember that even though an e-mail message is addressed and sent to an individual, it may still be read by unintended recipients. E-mail messages are not private. They are sent over computer communication networks, where they can be easily intercepted. Moreover, e-mail files you delete from your computer may remain in storage on your organization's server. That nasty message you sent to your friend criticizing your boss might end up on your boss's desk without your knowledge! In general, you should assume that every e-mail message you write might be read by anyone and everyone else.

***Remember that there are no "off-the record" e-mails.*** All e-mail messages can be saved and used as proof that the communication took place. Usually you are sending the e-mail to record some information for the record, but occasionally people fall into the trap of treating e-mail like a phone call. For example, they may say in an e-mail something like "Steve thinks he's going to exercise his options for $4,000, but it'll never happen as long as I'm the CFO." Imagine how this CFO will feel if Steve turns up with a copy of the e-mail message. Again, the best advice is to assume that every e-mail message you write will be read by everyone else.

One more word of caution: E-mails can even become evidence in legal proceedings. An article that appeared in *The Economist* provides examples of problems that can occur when e-mails are subpoenaed for use in court:

> Catty or salacious gossip, the kind that was once swapped at the water cooler, is now often committed to e-mail. This is easy to subpoena and virtually impossible to erase. There is always a back-up somewhere, so even if you delete the e-mail privately denigrating a stock you are publicly urging your clients to buy, it will still be read out in court. If your firm is sued for sexual discrimination, expect the plaintiff to demand all the lewd e-mails your male executives have ever swapped with each other.[1]

***Avoid sending junk e-mail.*** Some people forward e-mail to people simply because they click on group addresses out of habit. "Tom, I'll be out of town Monday. Handle the meeting, will you? Thanks, Bill." is an example of a memo that has meaning only for Tom. What may happen, however, is that Bill will send the message to "Corporate Staff," or something similar, because that is the button he is used to clicking on when he sends e-mail. Consequently, perhaps 40 people will receive Bill's message and must take time to access it and then delete it (or worse—sometimes they will reply to it, perpetuating the problem).

***It may be best to deliver some kinds of messages in person.*** The chairman of one international law firm makes this point: "You should never engage in a disagreement electronically. . . . You want to do it face to face." He goes on to say:

... if you think you are going to have a difficult interaction with a colleague or a client, if you can do it face to face that's better, because you can read the body language and other social signals.

In texting and e-mails or even videoconferencing, you can't always gauge the reaction and sometimes things can have a tendency to be misunderstood, or they can ratchet up to a level of seriousness that you didn't anticipate ... In person, you see that somebody [is] reacting in a way that you didn't expect. Then you can stop and figure out what's going on, and adapt.[2]

***Think before you send.*** The ease and speed with which e-mails can be exchanged can be a hazard if writers send a hastily composed memo that contains emotional or politically volatile content. Don't use e-mail to express anger or frustration. Avoid the flames.

## TEXT MESSAGING

Because of content volume constraints, text messaging has only limited application in a business environment. However, it's worth noting that as in the case of e-mail, text messages do not disappear when deleted. Communications companies may store them for up to several weeks. A company that issues cell phones to its employees and pays the bills may have access to the text messages sent or received on those phones. Text messages may also be subject to subpoena in legal proceedings. So many of the same cautions relating to the use of e-mail may also apply to text messaging.

## EXERCISES

### Exercise 10–1  [General]

You are a partner in the local firm of Mueller, Britt, & Little, CPAs. It has come to your attention that several of the staff, both professional and support staff, have recently begun wearing political buttons and displaying political posters in the office.

Write a memo to be circulated to all personnel in your firm explaining that such activity should cease and explaining why it is inappropriate.

### Exercise 10–2  [General]

Recently you have noticed that your "inbox" on the local area network in your company accumulates eight to ten messages a day that are jokes and humorous stories downloaded from the Internet. Most of these messages are not very funny, but they all take time to delete, and sometimes in the process of deleting them you delete important messages by mistake. Clearly the situation has gotten out of hand. Write a memo to the staff about the problem, and ask that the practice of distributing humorous e-mail messages be discontinued. Be sure to explain your reasoning so you won't come across as dictatorial. You expect to send your memo as an e-mail message.

### Exercise 10–3 [General]

You are a manager in a local CPA firm, Barry, Peters, & Travis. While attending the symphony in your city you noticed in the program that a couple of other CPA firms in the area were listed among the donors; one had given $100,000, and another had given $40,000. As a fan of the symphony, you would like to see your firm also make a donation. However, beyond wanting to support the symphony, you want to encourage such a donation because you think it would enhance the image of your firm and be a good marketing move. You note that several of your firm's clients have also made donations.

Write a memo to the partner-in-charge of your firm, John Hoffman, persuading him to support such a donation.

### Exercise 10–4 [Financial]

You are newly hired as an accountant for the Chase Condominium Association, a condominium owners association of approximately 200 condo units. The Association is currently using the cash basis of accounting. The president, Brenda Galina, has asked that you explain what the accrual basis of accounting is, how it differs from the cash basis, and whether the Chase Condominium Association should switch from the cash basis to the accrual basis.

Write a memo to Ms. Galina that answers her questions. You will need to identify the facts and issues the association should consider before making the decision. Invent any facts necessary to do this.

### Exercise 10–5 [Financial]

You are newly hired as an accountant for Lanier Business Technologies, Inc., a small service business that has no formal capital budgeting system. The president of your company, Charles Lanier, has requested that you write a memo to him explaining what the net present value method of investment evaluation is, how it differs from the payback period method, and why Lanier Business Technologies should use the net present value method for capital budgeting purposes instead of the payback method. Write the memo.

## Exercise 10–6 [Systems]

Your company, Florodex, intends to contract with a systems consulting firm to develop a new database system. You are responsible for explaining to the consulting firm exactly what your company needs the system to do. However, you have very little understanding of database systems and think you should know more before you talk with the consultants. You have received an announcement about a two-day database overview seminar to be given by the local university and think it would be worthwhile to attend.

Write a memo to your boss, Peter Tolan, requesting that your company send you to the seminar. Invent any facts you think necessary.

## Exercise 10–7 [Managerial]

You are the controller of Beemer's Car Dealerships. Recently, you have become aware that your company needs to evaluate and perhaps redesign its internal control system. To familiarize the dealership's managers with the need for a good internal control system, you have decided to write a memo explaining what internal control is and why it's important to a business like Beemer's. Write the memo. You can make up hypothetical examples to illustrate it.

## Exercise 10–8 [Managerial]

You are a managerial accountant at Gourmet Restaurant Supplyies, which supply fresh produce, meat, seafood, and food staples to the area's finest restaurants. You have been asked by the controller to write a memo to the company's regional managers that will explain cost-volume-profit (CVP) analysis. In particular, the controller hopes that managers will understand how CVP analysis can help them perform their responsibilities.

Write the memo to Gourmet's three regional managers: Lupe Garcia, Sybil Alexander, and Paul Chan. You can make up hypothetical examples if needed to illustrate your memo.

## Exercise 10–9 [Financial]

You are the staff accountant for Harry Banister, who owns a small nursery and landscaping business. Mr. Banister is considering the purchase of a competing business, Rock Creek Nurseries. The sum of the fair market values of the separately identifiable assets of Rock Creek is $350,000. Mr. Banister determined this amount by having an appraisal made before making an offer. The offer he made was equal to this amount—that is, $350,000. The owner of Rock Creek has declined the offer and indicated he thinks his business is worth at least $400,000, considering the goodwill that exists. Mr. Banister cannot understand how the business can be worth more than $350,000, considering this was the amount of the appraisal.

Write a memo to Mr. Banister explaining what goodwill is, why it may exist for the business he wants to purchase, how to determine what to pay for it, and the effects on future financial statements he may expect.

### Exercise 10–10 [Tax]

The CPA firm you work for, Sutton, Alexander & Jones, has been in practice for five years. The majority of the tax work done for its clients, who are mostly small businesses, is the preparation of state and federal income tax returns. One of the firm's tax partners, Hugh Sutton, mentioned to you the possibility that the firm might expand its services to offer tax planning for the owners of small businesses. Write a memo to Mr. Sutton in which you discuss the advantages and disadvantages of offering tax planning as an additional service.

### Exercise 10–11 [Financial]

Daniel Gordon, the president of the Skinner Company, is considering a bond issue to raise $1,000,000 for the company. Mr. Gordon notes that long-term Treasury bonds yield 3% which he thinks is a good loan rate. Before proceeding with the bond issue, however, Mr. Gordon wants to know more about it. Specifically, he wonders what the annual interest payments would be on the bonds.

You are a financial analyst at Skinner Company. Write a memo to Mr. Gordon explaining what the interest payments on a $1,000,000, 20-year bond issue would be if the bonds were issued at a 3% yield. Also explain in your memo why the Skinner Company would probably not be able to issue the bonds at 3%.

### Exercise 10–12 [Systems]

You are a new employee at Southwest Parts Distributors, Inc. As a specialist in accounting information systems, one of your responsibilities is to recommend adequate controls to ensure the safety of Southwest's data, including the data it keeps on suppliers and customers. You recently recommended that the company adopt a new set of control procedures. However, Southwest's regional manager, Bill Tomlinson, has expressed impatience with your recommendations. He views the new procedures as "unnecessary red tape."

Write a memo to Mr. Tomlinson that explains the advantages of strong controls to protect the company's data.

### Exercise 10–13 [Systems]

You are employed by a regional systems consulting firm. Charles Drummond, the president of Drummond Industries, a successful local manufacturing company, has asked for your help. The company is experiencing systems problems, and he wants you to prepare a memo that he can use in a meeting with other top management that will address those problems.

Over the years Drummond has developed an accounting information system (AIS) that records the journal entries for sales along with the dates of the transactions. Other information about the sale is collected and processed by three other different AISs. This has led to a problem of redundancy and data discrepancies among systems.

Write a memo to Charles Drummond that recommends the development and implementation of an enterprise resource planning (ERP) system and explains how an ERP system can overcome the problems the company is experiencing. Invent any facts necessary to complete the memo.

## NOTES

1. "Electronic discovery—Of bytes and briefs," *The Economist*, 19 May 2007, 34.

2. "E-Mail Saves Time, But Being There Says More," *New York Times,* 20 January, 2010, B7.

# CHAPTER

# Reports

**11**

S ometimes accountants prepare formal reports, such as a report for a client that a CPA in public practice might prepare. Managerial accountants might prepare reports for other departments in their firm or perhaps for a group of managers with a particular need. Auditors prepare various reports to summarize their findings for auditing engagements. Figure 11–1 shows an example of an auditor's report, in this case, a standard unqualified report on comparative financial statements.

A report usually involves analyzing an accounting problem and applying auditing principles, accounting principles, or provisions of the tax code to a particular situation. It may also require researching professional literature or other material, so the research techniques discussed in Chapter 8 are often part of report preparation as well.

Reports vary in length, but all reports should meet certain basic criteria. The technical content should be accurate, the organization should be coherent, the report should be presented attractively, and the writing style should be clear and concise. Like all forms of writing, a report should be designed and written with the readers' needs and expectations in mind.

## PLANNING A REPORT

If you are preparing a report on the job, your company may have an established format for you to follow for all reports. Find out your organization's expectations and policies before you begin work on your report. Even if the organization doesn't require employees to follow a certain report format, you may find your job easier if you use several well-written reports as models.

If you are free to design your own report format, or if you are preparing the report for a class assignment, the format presented in this chapter can serve as a generic model that is typical of those used in business and industry.

When planning the report, you must also consider the purpose of the report and who its readers will be. Analyzing the purpose and audience for a report may be more difficult than it is for letters and memos because a report can have many groups of readers, and each group will have different interests and needs.

**FIGURE 11–1**    A Standard Auditor's Unqualified Report on Comparative Financial
Statements

**Coffey & Nelson, P.C.**
**Certified Public Accounts**
**2300 Peachtree St., Suite 100**
**Atlanta, GA 30000**

Independent Auditor's Report

To the Stockholders
DVD Enterprises, Inc.

We have audited the accompanying balance sheets of DVD
Enterprises, Inc., as of December 31, 2010 and 2009, and the related
statements of income, retained earnings, and cash flows for the years
then ended. These financial statements are the responsibility of the
company's management. Our responsibility is to express an opinion
on these financial statements based on our audit.

We conducted our audits in accordance with auditing standards generally accepted in the United States of America. Those standards
require that we plan and perform the audit to obtain reasonable
assurance about whether the financial statements are free of material
misstatement. An audit includes examining, on a test basis, evidence
supporting the amounts and disclosures in the financial statements.
An audit also includes assessing the accounting principles used and
significant estimates made by management, as well as evaluating the
overall financial statement presentation. We believe that our audits
provide a reasonable basis for our opinion.

In our opinion, the financial statements referred to above present fairly,
in all material respects, the financial position of DVD Enterprises, Inc.,
as of December 31, 2010 and 2009, and the results of its operations and
its cash flows for the years then ended in conformity with accounting
principles generally accepted in the United States of America.

*COFFEY & NELSON, P.C., CPAs*

February 23, 2011

For example, a report recommending that a firm invest in a new
computer system might be circulated to the Management Information
Systems (MIS) department, the accounting department, the departments that would actually use the system, and senior management.
The accounting department would be interested in the accounting
aspects of the acquisition as well as how the system could be used for

various accounting tasks. The MIS department would be interested in the technical features of the system and how it would affect MIS personnel. Other departments would want to know how the system would make their work easier or more difficult, whether it would affect their budgets, and what additional training, if any, their personnel would need to use the system. Senior management would be interested in the bigger picture, such as how the system would affect the firm's efficiency, competitiveness, and cash flow.

To write this report, you would need to identify clearly who the readers are and what information they want the report to include. You would obviously be writing to readers with different degrees of knowledge about the technical features of the new system and with different interests and concerns as well. The way to handle this complicated situation is to write different parts of the report for different groups of readers.

Fortunately, many reports are not as difficult to plan and write as this one, but this example shows how important it is to analyze carefully the needs and expectations of different groups of readers.

Most reports require a great deal of research. They may report the results of empirical studies or pilot projects, or report research involving generally accepted accounting principles or other technical literature. Organizing this research into a coherent outline is essential. Review the organization principles discussed in Chapter 3, and then apply the following questions to your report as you plan the outline and structure your draft.

1. Is the subject covered adequately?
   - Background information when necessary
   - Adequate explanations, supporting data, and examples
   - Citations from GAAP and other authorities, as needed
   - Application to the specific needs and interests of the readers
2. Is the report too long?
   - Digressions—off the subject
   - Too much explanation or detail
   - Repetitions or wordiness
3. Is the report logically organized?
   - In order from most to least important—from the readers' point of view
   - Summary sentences where helpful
   - Transitions to link ideas
   - Short, well-organized paragraphs with topic sentences

The format of a report—how its various parts are put together—also determines how coherent the report is.

# THE PARTS OF A REPORT

Reports can be presented in a variety of formats, but they are all designed to make the report easy to read. The format presented in this handbook is typical of how reports are structured.

A report may include these sections:

Transmittal document
Title page
Table of contents
List of illustrations
Summary section
Introduction
Body of the report
Conclusion
Appendices
Notes
Bibliography
Graphic illustrations

## Transmittal Document

The transmittal document can be either a cover letter or memo, depending on whether you are sending your report to someone inside or outside your organization. It presents the report to the people for whom it was written and adds any other information that will be helpful.

The transmittal document will not be long, but it should include essential information, such as the report's title, topic, and purpose. You should usually summarize the report's main idea or recommendation if you can do so in about one or two sentences. You may want to add other comments about the report that will be helpful to the readers, but you should always end with a courteous closing.

Whereas the style of the actual report is usually formal and impersonal, the transmittal document can usually be more conversational, including the use of personal pronouns.

## Title Page

In a professional report, the title page might look something like this:

Title of Report
Prepared for . . .
Prepared by . . .
Date

For a student's report, the instructor might prefer information such as this:

Title of Report
Student's Name
Course and Period
Instructor
Date

## Table of Contents

The table of contents appears on a separate page with a heading. The contents listed are the major parts of the report, excluding the transmittal document, with the appropriate page numbers.

## List of Illustrations

The list of illustrations, if applicable, includes titles and page numbers of graphs, charts, and other illustrations.

## Summary Section

All formal reports have a section near the beginning of the report that summarizes the main ideas and recommendations. This section can vary in length from one paragraph to several pages, and it can come either immediately before or immediately after the introduction. The summary section may be called an executive summary, abstract, synopsis, summary, or some other term.

An executive summary is especially helpful for long reports. This section gives the readers an overview of the report's contents without the technical detail. Busy managers may read the executive summary to decide whether they should read the entire report.

The executive summary identifies the purpose and scope of the report and possibly the methods used for research. It includes the major findings of the research, the conclusions of the researcher, and the recommendations, if any.

The length of an executive summary varies with the length of the report, but it's generally between one and three pages in length. The summary begins on a separate page following the table of contents or list of illustrations and is titled *Executive Summary*. The sample report at the end of this chapter uses this kind of summary.

For shorter reports, a section right after the introduction can provide a summary of the report's main ideas and recommendations. This section is labeled *Summary*; it's usually one or two paragraphs long.

## Introduction

The introduction of a formal report is longer than that of a letter or memo—usually at least two or three short paragraphs, and for long reports it may be longer than a page. The introduction identifies the subject of the report and states why it was written—who requested or authorized it or for whom it was prepared. The introduction states the purpose of the report in specific terms:

The purpose of this report is to discuss the feasibility of offering a stock bonus plan to employees of Gulf Coast Industries.

*Not:*

The purpose of this report is to discuss stock bonus plans.

Sometimes an introduction includes additional information to help the reader, perhaps a brief background of the report's topic. However, if it's necessary to include a great deal of background information, this material should be presented in a separate section in the body of the report.

In addition, the introduction of a report should end with a plan of development that gives the reader an overview or forecast of the topics the report covers and the order in which topics are presented. A simple plan of development can be in sentence form:

This report describes the proposed pension plan and then discusses its costs and benefits.

Sometimes a set-off list makes the plan of development easier to read:

This report discusses the following topics related to the proposed pension plan:

- Major provisions
- Benefits to employees
- Benefits to the corporation
- Cost
- Accounting for the plan

## Body of the Report

The body of the report should be divided into sections, and possibly subsections, each with an appropriate heading. Remember to begin each section with a statement that summarizes the main idea to be covered in that section.

The body of the report can also contain graphic illustrations, as discussed later.

## Conclusion

In addition to the summary section at the beginning, a report should have a conclusion to remind the reader of the report's main ideas and recommendations. This section may be from one paragraph to several pages in length.

## Appendices (Optional)

Depending on the report's audience and purpose, you may want to place technical information and statistics in appendices at the end of the report. If you use an appendix, give it a title and refer to it in the body of the report.

## Notes and Bibliography

What to put at the end of the report depends in part on the style of documentation you use. If you use endnotes, they should begin on a separate page and be labeled *Notes*.

Almost all reports have some sort of bibliography or reference list. This list identifies the sources you cited in your paper, and it may also include additional references the reader might want to consult. This section should begin on a separate page following the notes (if any), and it should have a title such as *Bibliography* or *References*.

Appendix 8–E in Chapter 8 demonstrates the proper form for endnotes or footnotes and bibliographical entries.

### Graphic Illustrations

Sometimes graphic illustrations, such as graphs or tables, make a report easier to read and more interesting, especially if you are presenting statistical or numerical data or if the subject of the report concerns a process. You can place graphic illustrations either in an appendix or in the body of your report, just after the place in the text where they are discussed.

Graphic illustrations are discussed more fully in Chapter 6.

## APPEARANCE

Presenting your report as attractively as possible is important. Use good quality paper and be sure that the report is printed on a high-quality printer.

Reports can be single-spaced or double-spaced, depending on the situation. Students' reports are usually double-spaced to provide space for annotations when they are graded. In all reports, the transmittal document and any set-off material are single-spaced. Pages should be numbered, using lowercase Roman numerals for front matter (table of contents, list of illustrations, executive summary) and Arabic numerals for the remainder of the report, from the introduction through the end matter.

## STYLE AND TONE

The tone of a formal report is usually just what its name implies: formal and, therefore, impersonal. You probably won't use personal pronouns or contractions in a formal report, for example. However, a formal style should still be readable and interesting, so you should use the effective style techniques discussed in Chapter 4. Even a formal document can be written simply, clearly, and concretely.

Unlike the actual report, the transmittal document may be written in a personal, more informal style.

The report in Figure 11–2 illustrates many effective report writing techniques.

**FIGURE 11–2** A Report (*Continued*)

B&H Financial Consultants
125 Easy Street
Athens, Georgia
August 8, 2011

Mr. Sam Hamilton
Hamilton Manufacturing
1890 Meerly Avenue
Atlanta, Georgia 30306

Dear Mr. Hamilton:

Enclosed is the report about convertible bonds that you requested in your letter of July 21. The report, titled *Convertible Bonds: Financial and Accounting Considerations*, examines the nature of convertible debt, the pros and cons of such an issue, and the accounting treatment of the securities.

The report shows that convertible bonds may represent a relatively less expensive method of raising capital than nonconvertible bonds. Another advantage is that should the convertible bonds be converted, the existing shares of common stock will not be diluted as severely as they would if common stock had been issued. However, as the report makes clear, these effects are by no means certain.

I believe the report will provide you with the information you need. If you have any further questions, however, don't hesitate to give me a call.

Sincerely yours,

*Joyce Samuels*

Joyce Samuels
jhw

FIGURE 11–2 *(Continued)*

CONVERTIBLE BONDS:
FINANCIAL AND ACCOUNTING CONSIDERATIONS

Prepared for Hamilton Manufacturing

by

JOYCE SAMUELS

AUGUST 8, 2011

**FIGURE 11–2** (*Continued*)

CONTENTS

FIGURE 11–2    *(Continued)*

## EXECUTIVE SUMMARY

This report provides information about convertible bonds for the managers of Hamilton Manufacturing. Included is information about the nature of convertible bonds, financial advantages and disadvantages of issuing such bonds, and their accounting treatment.

A convertible bond is a debt security that carries the option of exchange for an equity security, usually common stock. The bond indenture specifies when the bonds may be converted and a conversion ratio.

Convertible bonds would offer Hamilton several advantages:

- The company could issue the bonds at a premium or at a low stated interest rate, which investors would accept because of the conversion privilege.
- The company could avoid another stock issue now, when the price of Hamilton's stock is low.
- The company may avoid a decrease in share price caused by issuing a large number of new shares on the market at one time.
- Total stock issuance costs may be less.
- Management would avoid possible conflict with its major stockholder.

Management should consider the following potential disadvantages before issuing the convertible bonds:

- Before conversion, the uncertain conditions of the economy make a future increase in the market price of the company's stock uncertain. If conversion does not occur, Hamilton may have difficulty meeting the debt requirements.
- Bond conversion will reduce basic earnings per share. Conversion will also increase Hamilton's income tax liability because of the loss of interest expense.
- The required accounting treatment of convertible bonds may have an unfavorable effect on the company's financial statements: a high level of debt may be presented alongside a lowered diluted earnings per share (DEPS).

ii

FIGURE 11–2    (*Continued*)

## CONVERTIBLE BONDS:
## FINANCIAL AND ACCOUNTING CONSIDERATIONS

### Introduction

The purpose of this report is to provide information for the management of Hamilton Manufacturing about convertible debt as a means of financing. Convertible debt is an issue of debt securities (bonds) with the option to exchange those debt securities for equity securities (usually common stock).

Three major topics make up the report: (1) the nature of convertible bonds, (2) financial advantages and disadvantages Hamilton could expect if it issues the bonds, and (3) accounting treatment for the bonds.

### Nature of Convertible Bonds

When convertible bonds are issued, the bond indenture defines a time period after issuance during which the bonds may be converted. The indenture also gives a conversion ratio, which is the number of shares of stock for which each bond may be exchanged. The effective price of stock to the bondholder is determined by dividing the par value of the bond by the number of shares exchangeable for one bond.

The indenture usually includes a call provision so that the issuing entity can force bondholders to convert (usually at a premium over par). Thus, entities that issue convertible debt often do so as a means of raising equity capital. The following sections discuss why Hamilton might choose to issue convertible debt.

**FIGURE 11-2**    *(Continued)*

### Financial Advantages and Disadvantages

Advantages

Use of convertible debt would offer Hamilton advantages over straight debt or stock issues.

Investors in bonds that are convertible into stock are usually willing to accept a lower stated interest rate on such bonds, to pay a premium and accept a lower yield, or to accept less restrictive covenants. Thus, by issuing convertible debt, Hamilton will probably be able to obtain funds at a lower cost than if it issued debt that is not convertible.

Depending upon economic conditions, there may also be a timing advantage to issuing convertible debt. If current conditions make it unfavorable to sell stock because of depressed value, issuing convertible debt will allow Hamilton to raise capital debt now that may later be converted into stock when the stock price has recovered.

In addition, by issuing convertible debt, Hamilton may avoid a decrease in stock price caused by a large new issue of stock being made available on the market all at once.

Another advantage to Hamilton of issuing convertible bonds is that the company might avoid creating a conflict with major stockholders, who want to maintain their percentage interests. The stockholders might vote against a large issue of stock. However, the bond issue could be convertible into a number of shares small enough not to significantly injure the stockholders' interests.

Disadvantages

Most disadvantages of issuing convertible bonds are related to the uncertainty of conversion. If Hamilton's stock price does not rise, conversion may not occur without call, the company may not obtain the equity financing it desires, and Hamilton might then be saddled with long-term debt obligations.

Another disadvantage is the impact on either diluted earnings per share (DEPS) before conversion, or basic earnings per share (BEPS) after conversion. In either case the earnings per share figure will be reduced. After conversion, income tax expense will increase because of the reduction in interest expense.

2

FIGURE 11–2   (*Continued*)

### Accounting Treatment

According to Generally Accepted Accounting Principles (GAAP), if convertible bonds are "sold at a price or has a value at issuance not significantly in excess of the face amount . . . [n]o portion of the proceeds from the issuance . . . shall be accounted for as attributable to the conversion feature." (ASC pars. 470-20-25-10b and 470-20-25-12) In other words, the expectation that some or all of the bonds will be converted into stock is not recognized in the accounts.

Because convertible bonds are normally sold at a premium, the amount of the cash proceeds from the issue is usually greater than the face value of the bonds. The premium is amortized over the life of the bonds. The effect of the amortization is that the interest expense recorded by Hamilton each period would not equal the amount of the interest *payment*, but it would reflect the effective yield to the bondholders.

When the bonds are converted, Hamilton will remove from the accounts the balance associated with those bonds. Two methods can be used to record the common stock issued in exchange for the bonds. Under one method, the stock is assigned a value equal to the market value of the stock or the bonds. If this value differs from the book value of the bonds (the balance associated with the bonds, mentioned above), then a gain or a loss is recorded. Under the other method, which is more widely used, the value assigned to the stock equals the book value of the bonds and no gain or loss is recognized or recorded (Nikolai, Bazley, and Jones 2007, 658–659).

If Hamilton decides to retire its convertible bonds for cash before their maturity date, the transaction will be recorded in the same way as the early bonds, and the cash paid to retire them will be a gain or a loss on the income statement.

Although convertibles are accounted for solely as debt, Hamilton must also consider the equity characteristics of such issues in computing diluted earnings per share (DEPS). GAAP require that corporations having issued securities that are potentially dilutive of EPS, such as convertible bonds, must present both basic earnings per share (BEPS) and diluted earnings per share (DEPS) for income from continuing operations and for net income in the income statement "with equal prominence" (ASC par. 260-10-45-2).

3

**FIGURE 11–2**    (*Continued*)

The DEPS figure represents EPS *as if* the bonds had been converted into stock. If they had been converted, the removal of the bonds would have caused a reduction of interest expense, which would have increased earnings. However, the positive effect of the earnings adjustment may not offset the negative effect of the shares adjustment. Thus, convertibles reduce reported DEPS.

### Conclusion

In deciding whether to finance with convertible debt, Hamilton must consider whether it would benefit from using convertibles rather than straight debt or stock issues and, should conversion not occur as expected, whether it can meet the debt requirements. In addition, management should analyze carefully the effect of the issue on readers of the financial statements, because until the bonds are converted, a possibly high level of debt will exist alongside a lowered presentation of DEPS.

### WORKS CITED

Financial Accounting Standards Board (FASB), 2010. *Accounting Standards Codification.*™ Stamford, Conn.: FASB.

Nikolai, L. A., J. S. Bazley, and J. P. Jones. 2007. *Intermediate Accounting*, 7th ed. Mason, OH: Thompson South-Western.

4

# EXERCISES

## Exercise 11–1 [Financial]

A client, Manuel Rodriguez, has just inherited some money and has decided to invest it in stock. He is not interested in mutual funds because he prefers to have personal control over his stock investments. He currently has a diversified portfolio of stock to which this new investment will be added. Your client wants to invest about $25,000, but in keeping with his conservative investing strategy, he wishes to keep his risk as low as possible.

Mr. Rodriguez has asked you to evaluate the most recent annual reports of several corporations as possible investment options. Choose three corporations whose stock is listed on the NYSE or the NASDAQ and whose annual reports you can study. Compare the information found in these reports, and then write a report for Mr. Rodriguez that explains which of the companies is likely to be his best investment. Explain your conclusions thoroughly, quoting from the annual reports as necessary.

## Exercise 11–2 [Financial]

You have received an inquiry from a prospective client, Lazy Sofa, Inc., concerning the accounting for investments. Betty Jason, owner of Lazy Sofa, is considering investing some of her company's idle cash in either equity or debt securities. Write a report for Ms. Jason, explaining briefly how the types of investments and her purpose for investing might affect the accounting methods used. Remember that your client knows very little about accounting.

## Exercise 11–3 [Auditing][1]

One of the auditors of your firm, O'Brien, Sherrill, and Sherrill, CPAs, was negligent in planning the audit of a client, Dingell, Inc., a publically traded brokerage company, and did not follow Generally Accepted Auditing Standards (GAAS). Unfortunately, an employee of Dingell had engaged in a massive embezzlement scheme that would have been uncovered if the audit had been accomplished in conformance with GAAS. Many customers and shareholders of Dingell suffered large losses resulting from the embezzlement.

Hugh Brogan, partner-in-charge of your firm, has asked you to write a report discussing the different theories of liability available to the customers and stockholders of Dingell under common law as well as what liability your firm may have under the Securities Exchange Act of 1934.

Write the report requested by Mr. Brogan.

## Exercise 11–4 [Financial]

Write a report analyzing the most recent financial aspects of a publicly traded company of your choice. Include an analysis of (1) liquidity, (2) profitability, (3) productivity, and (4) debt management. If your analysis uncovers any problems, include recommendations on how they may be overcome.

Assume you are preparing the report for Cindy Baer, the president of the company you are analyzing. Ms. Baer is knowledgeable about business and her company's industry, but she does not have a strong background in accounting.

## Exercise 11–5 [Systems]

The company you work for, Chung Industries, intends to upgrade its database management system (DBMS). Your boss, Susan Chung, has asked you to research and write a report on how businesses use DBMSs. As part of your report, you should be sure to cover DBMSs for use on microcomputers versus those designed for use on mainframes.

## Exercise 11–6 [Auditing]

As a staff member of Norton, Price, and Cummings, CPAs, you have been asked to prepare a report on "Materiality" that will be circulated to all staff as part of the firm's continuing education program. It has been suggested that the report should cover the definition of materiality, why the concept is important to auditing, and how to measure it among other aspects of materiality you may find important.

Write the report as requested.

## Exercise 11–7 [Tax]

You are on the financial staff of Governor James Cash, who is governor of a large state. He has been a prominent supporter of the flat tax idea for many years. Now, as governor, he is considering pushing for the adoption of a flat tax to replace the current progressive state income tax. He has asked you to prepare a report for him covering the pros and cons of a flat tax and how, if he decides to pursue the idea, he should respond to critics.

Write the report for Governor Cash.

## Exercise 11–8 [Systems]

You are an accounting information systems specialist working for Great Lakes Cargo, Inc. The company's president, LaToya Evans, has asked for your help. Recently she read a news story about the business reporting language XBRL, which, she learned, has greatly changed the way financial data is communicated. She has asked you to research XBRL and write a short report to distribute to the company's executive committee. The committee will need sufficient information about XBRL to make an informed decision about the potential use for Great Lakes.

Write the report for the committee. The transmittal document should be addressed to Ms. Evans. Remember that neither she nor the other committee members have specialized knowledge about accounting information systems.

## Exercise 11–9  [General]

You are employed by a large CPA firm that publishes reports on accounting, auditing, and policy issues. The firm distributes these reports to its clients, employees, and the public at large. Your boss, who is in charge of producing these reports, has asked you to write a report covering the benefits and costs of the Sarbanes-Oxley Act (SOX) from both a compliance and public policy prospective.

Write the report for your boss. You are aware that much has already been published about the costs and benefits of SOX, which you will have to research. Remember the diverse backgrounds of your audience when writing.

## Exercise 11–10  [General]

As a staff member of Swobe, Deal, and Grace, CPAs, you have been asked to prepare a report on the *FASB Accounting Standards Codification*™ that will be circulated to all staff as part of the firm's continuing education program. It has been suggested that the report should cover why and how the Codification has come about and how and when to use it. You may also include other aspects of the topic you believe to be important.

Write the report as requested.

---

# NOTE

1. Adapted from Arens, Alvin A., Rendal J. Elder, and Mark S. Beasley, *Auditing and Assurance Services: An Integrated Approach*, 13th ed. (Upper Saddle River, NJ: Prentice Hall, 2010), 138.

# CHAPTER

# Writing Essay Exams: Academic Courses and Professional Certification Exams

This chapter discusses strategies you can use to answer essay exams successfully. Because you may encounter essay or discussion questions in accounting courses or on professional certification exams, this chapter suggests ways to prepare for and answer those questions.

## ESSAY EXAMS

Essay or discussion questions that appear on exams may cause you some anxiety, but they give you a chance to practice for the writing demands that you may face later in your career. You can learn how to study for an essay exam and strategies for writing your answer and managing the pressure. You can also learn how to write an answer so that you receive full credit for what you know.

### Preparation

Although much of your studying for an objective examination will also help prepare you for essay questions, you need to do a different kind of studying as well. Remember that a discussion or essay question requires that you show a mastery of ideas. You may be asked to explain a concept, compare or contrast two methods of doing something, evaluate alternative treatments for a given situation, or justify a recommendation. Therefore, when you are reviewing your class notes and assigned reading material, you should note concepts and explanations that would lend themselves to this type of question.

One good way to prepare is to outline any notes you have, especially lecture notes. It's also a good idea to highlight and then outline key ideas and explanations from assigned readings. When your notes and outlines are ready, review them and try to guess questions that might appear on the exam, paying particular attention to concepts stressed in a lecture or important discussions in the text. Then make outlines of the information you would include in your answers to those questions. With any luck, you will predict at least a few of the questions that appear on the exam.

It's also helpful to study in a small group of students, after all group members have prepared their notes and outlines. This group can brainstorm possible questions and answers and check that everyone in the group understands the material that will be covered on the exam.

## Taking the Exam

Actually writing the answer to an essay or discussion question is easier if you have a strategy for using your time and composing your answer. For some exams you may handwrite your answers, or you may answer the exam on a computer. This strategy works for either situation.

### Budget Your Time

Managing your time well is a crucial part of your strategy. You may not have as much time as you would like to plan in detail, revise extensively, and then copy your answer over to create a perfect paper. Make the time you have work to your advantage by following the three steps of the writing process: planning, writing, and revising.

First, take a few minutes to read the question carefully to be sure you know what is being asked. Underline key phrases in the question so that your answer won't overlook something important. Then jot down the main ideas you want to include in the answer. Put numbers by these ideas or draw arrows to arrange them in the most effective order. If you have 30 minutes to answer a question, planning your answer, the first step in the writing process, should take about 5 minutes.

The next step, writing your answer, should take most of the remaining time. If you're writing by hand, write as legibly as possible, and write on every other line to allow room for editing. Whether you write by hand or on a computer, write as well as you can, but don't spend much time looking for the perfect word or phrase if it doesn't come quickly. The most important objective is to get the ideas down on paper to get credit for what you know.

Finally, allow at least five minutes to edit your answer. When you edit, check that all words are correctly spelled and that sentences are grammatically correct and clearly constructed. For handwritten essays, it's acceptable to neatly cross out words and write your revisions in the line above as long as the essay remains legible.

Time is a big factor in answering essay and discussion questions, so use it wisely. Budget your time so that you can plan, write, and then revise.

*Organize Your Answer*

The goals for organizing your answer are to help the instructor read it easily and to receive full credit for what you know. Thus, you should apply one of the primary recommendations emphasized throughout this book: Use summary sentences so that your main ideas stand out. In an essay or discussion question, the key is to begin the answer with a thesis statement and to use topic sentences at the beginning of each paragraph.

The thesis statement should echo the question and summarize the main ideas of your answer. Suppose you find this essay question on an exam:

Explain the matching concept in accounting.

Your answer to this question might begin this way:

The matching concept is used to determine what expense amounts should appear in the income statement for a particular period.

For short discussion questions, your answer might be only one paragraph long. In this case, the thesis statement for the answer would also function as the topic sentence for the paragraph. For more extensive questions, organize your answer into several paragraphs, each discussing one aspect of your answer. Each paragraph will have a topic sentence that provides a transition from the previous paragraph, where needed, and that summarizes the main idea to be discussed in the new paragraph. Suppose you're asked this question on an exam:

Discuss how the definition of an asset changed after the Accounting Principles Board was replaced by the Financial Accounting Standards Board.

Your answer might be organized like this:

### Thesis (first paragraph of your answer):

When the Financial Accounting Standards Board replaced the Accounting Principles Board, it switched the focus of income determination from the Expense/Revenue View to the Asset/Liability View.

### Topic sentence for paragraph 2:

Under the Expense/Revenue View previously taken by the Accounting Principles Board, assets were merely debit balances left over after deciding the proper amount of expenses to match with revenues in the income statement.

### Topic sentence for paragraph 3:

Under the Asset/Liability View favored by the Financial Accounting Standards Board, net income is determined by directly measuring changes in the value of net assets adjusted for changes resulting from owners' equity transactions.

One final reminder about organization: When deciding how many paragraphs to use for your answer, remember that readers usually find shorter paragraphs easier to read, as long as you provide adequate transitions so that they can follow your train of thought.

For a further discussion of organization, review Chapter 3.

*Use Document Design*

Sometimes the best way to include several points in your answer in a minimum amount of time is to use the document design principles explained in Chapter 6, especially set-off lists and headings. The sample question and answer adapted from a CPA exam and given in Figure 12–1 show how to use a list to organize the answer to a short question. For a longer essay especially, headings may be a good way to divide your answer into its main components.

## Qualities of a Good Essay

The discussion so far has already suggested several qualities of an effective answer to an essay or discussion question. Here is a summary of those qualities, plus a few additional pointers:

- When you handwrite an exam essay, your handwriting should be legible and your pages neat and easy to read. Corrections, additions, and deletions should be made as neatly as possible.
- Main ideas should be easy to identify; the flow of thought should be easy for the grader to follow.
- Answer the question directly and completely. Supply adequate details and examples to support your assertions.
- Sentences should be concise, clear, and readable. Grammatical and mechanical errors should not distract the reader.

These qualities of a good essay and the strategy you use to prepare for and write an academic essay exam also apply to professional examinations, with a few modifications.

## PROFESSIONAL CERTIFICATION EXAMS

Some certification exams require candidates to write answers to essay or short answer questions. The professional associations sponsoring these exams recognize that it isn't enough for professional accountants to be able to "crunch numbers." They must be able to communicate their findings to others as well.

Since 1994, the writing skills of candidates for professional CPA certification have been explicitly evaluated. The CPA exam is given in computerized form consisting of multiple choice questions and

**FIGURE 12–1**[1]   Sample Question and Answer Adapted from a CPA Exam

**Number 4 (Estimated time — 25 to 35 minutes)**

North, CPA, is planning an audit of General Co.'s financial statements. To determine the nature, timing, and extent of the auditing procedures, North is considering General's internal audit function, which is staffed by Tyler.

**Required:**

    **a.** In what ways may Tyler's work be relevant to North, the independent auditor?

    **b.** What factors should North consider and what inquiries should North make when deciding whether to use Tyler's work?

**Answer 4 (10 Points)**

    **a.** Tyler's work may be relevant to North in three ways:

- obtaining a sufficient understanding of the design of General's internal control structure policies and procedures
- determining whether they have been placed in operation
- assessing risk

Because an objective of most internal audit functions is to review, assess, and monitor internal control policies and procedures, the procedures performed by Tyler in this area may provide useful information to North.

Tyler's work may also provide direct evidence about material misstatements in assertions about specific account balances or classes of transactions. Therefore, Tyler's work may be relevant to North for planning substantive procedures. Consequently, North may be able to change the nature, timing, or extent of certain procedures.

North may request direct assistance from Tyler. This direct assistance relates to work North specifically requests Tyler to perform to complete some aspect of North's work.

    **b.** If North concludes that Tyler's work is relevant to North's audit of General's financial statements, North should consider whether it would be efficient to consider how Tyler's work might affect the nature, timing, and extent of North's audit procedures. If so, North should assess Tyler's competence and objectivity in light of the intended effect of Tyler's work on North's audit.

North ordinarily should inquire about Tyler's organizational status within General and about Tyler's application of the professional internal auditing standards developed by the Institute of Internal Auditors and the General Accounting Office. North also should ask about Tyler's internal audit plan, including the nature, timing, and extent of the audit work performed. In addition, North should inquire about Tyler's access to General's records and whether there are any limitations on the scope of Tyler's activities.

condensed case studies called "simulations." Each simulation requires the candidate to read the case and then write a memo, letter, or other document as directed. Responses are then evaluated based on the following criteria:[1]

- ***Organization:***   Structure, order of ideas, and connecting ideas, including using an overview or thesis statement, unified paragraphs, and transitions and connectives
- ***Development:***  The use of supporting evidence and information to clarify thoughts, including using details, definitions, examples, and rephrasing
- ***Expression:***  The use of standard English including grammar, punctuation, word usage, capitalization, and spelling

The quality of the writing on any professional exam affects whether candidates receive credit for what they know. You are more likely to receive full credit for the content of your answer if the grader has an easy time reading and understanding what you've written.

Even when an answer is not evaluated explicitly for writing skills, how well it is written can influence the score. Exam graders have a lot of work to do in a short amount of time. Their job is to determine whether the candidates know the answers to the questions asked. Thus, graders appreciate essays that enable them to spot main ideas quickly and easily. They also appreciate sentences that are clear and readable.

Like business document readers, exam graders want essays to be coherent (main ideas easy to identify, flow of thought easy to follow), concise (no wasted words), and clear (no guesswork about meaning, no distractions caused by nonstandard English). Thus, the writing skills emphasized in this book apply to professional exams as well as to more common forms of business writing.

## Preparing For and Taking the Exam

Preparing for professional examinations is much more involved than studying for an exam in a course. You will study many long hours, perhaps with the help of an exam review text or course. However, the types of questions you are asked may resemble those in your course exams, perhaps to explain a concept, describe a process, or analyze a situation.

### Managing Your Time

The pressure caused by the time constraints in a professional examination may be even greater than the stress you feel during a course exam because your ability to be a certified accounting professional depends on how well you do. However, the strategies for managing this stress remain the same regardless of the type of exam you're taking. The keys are to budget your time so that you can plan your answer, draft the essay, and edit what you've written.

*Use the Question to Organize Your Essay*

As with the essay and discussion questions you write for your accounting courses, you can help exam graders identify your main ideas by writing in short paragraphs with strong topic sentences. The question itself can suggest the wording of the topic sentences. Sample questions and answers from past exams show how this strategy works. Figures 12–1 and 12–2 contain adapted CPA exam questions and unofficial answers suggested by the AICPA.[2]

Part a of an auditing question (refer to Figure 12-1) states this requirement:

> In what ways may Tyler's work be relevant to North, the independent auditor?

The answer begins with a variation of the question:

> Tyler's work may be relevant to North in obtaining . . . .

The answer then continues with a discussion of several specific ways Tyler's work may be relevant to North. Notice how the discussion is divided into short paragraphs, each beginning with a strong topic sentence.

Another question adapted from a past CPA exam is shown in Figure 12–2. For this question, the requirements specify the organization of the answer:

> In separate paragraphs, determine whether Suburban's positions are correct, and state the reasons for your conclusions.

---

**FIGURE 12–2**[2]    Sample Question and Answer Adapted from a CPA Exam

---

**Number 5 (Estimated time — 15 to 25 minutes)**

Suburban Properties, Inc. owns and manages several shopping centers. On May 4, 2011, Suburban received from Bridge Hardware, Inc., one of its tenants, a signed letter proposing that the existing lease between Suburban and Bridge be modified to provide that certain utility costs be equally shared by Bridge and Suburban, effective June 1, 2011. Under the terms of the original lease, Bridge was obligated to pay all utility costs. On May 5, 2011, Suburban sent Bridge a signed letter agreeing to share the utility costs as proposed. Suburban later changed its opinion and refused to share in the utility costs.

On June 4, 2011, Suburban received from Dart Associates, Inc. a signed offer to purchase one of the shopping centers owned by Suburban. The offer provided as follows: a price of $9,250,000; it would not be withdrawn before July 1, 2011; and an acceptance must be received by Dart to be effective. On June 9, 2011, Suburban mailed Dart a signed acceptance.

**FIGURE 12–2** (*Continued*)

On June 10, before Dart had received Suburban's acceptance, Dart telephoned Suburban and withdrew its offer. Suburban's acceptance was received by Dart on June 12, 2011.

On June 22, 2011, one of Suburban's shopping centers was damaged by a fire, which started when the center was struck by lightning. As a result of the fire, one of the tenants in the shopping center, World Popcorn Corp., was forced to close its business and will be unable to reopen until the damage is repaired. World sued Suburban, claiming that Suburban is liable for World's losses resulting from the fire. The lease between Suburban and World is silent in this regard.

Suburban has taken the following positions:

- Suburban's May 5, 2011, agreement to share equally the utility costs with Bridge is not binding on Suburban.
- Dart could not properly revoke its June 4 offer and must purchase the shopping center.
- Suburban is not liable to World for World's losses resulting from the fire.

**Required:**

In separate paragraphs, determine whether Suburban's positions are correct, and state the reasons for your conclusions.

**Answer 5 (10 Points)**

Suburban is correct concerning the agreement to share utility costs with Bridge. A modification of a contract requires consideration to be binding on the parties. Suburban is not bound by the lease modification because Suburban did not receive any consideration in exchange for its agreement to share the cost of utilities with Bridge.

Suburban is not correct with regard to the Dart offer. An offer can be revoked at any time prior to acceptance. This is true despite the fact that the offer provides that it will not be withdrawn prior to a stated time. If no consideration is given in exchange for this promise not to withdraw the offer, the promise is not binding on the offerer. The offer provided that Suburban's acceptance would not be effective until received. Dart's June 10 revocation terminated Dart's offer. Thus, Suburban's June 9 acceptance was not effective.

Suburban is correct with regard to World's claim. The general rule is that destruction of, or damage to, the subject matter of a contract without the fault of either party terminates the contract. In this case, Suburban is not liable to World because Suburban is discharged from its contractual duties as a result of the fire, which made performance by it under the lease objectively impossible.

Notice how each paragraph of the answer begins with a topic sentence that summarizes the main idea of the paragraph.

*Use Formatting Techniques to Make Your Essays Easy to Read*
Good document design makes it easier for graders to read your essays and give you full credit for them. Although you are obviously limited to what you can accomplish quickly, formatting techniques such as bullets and set-off lists may make it easier for graders to spot main ideas and follow your train of thought.

## Qualities of a Good Answer

The AICPA has defined the effective writing qualities you should strive for in the essays you write. These guidelines apply not only to the CPA exam, but also to other professional certification exams because these qualities apply to any well-written essay. According to the AICPA, writing is graded on the CPA exam on the basis of organization, development, and expression, as follows:[3]

ORGANIZATION: the document's structure, ordering of ideas, and linking of one idea to another

- Overview/thesis statement
- Unified paragraphs (topic and supporting sentences)
- Transitions and connectives

DEVELOPMENT: the document's supporting evidence/information to clarify thoughts

- Details
- Definitions
- Examples
- Rephrasing

EXPRESSION: the document's use of conventional standards of business English

- Grammar (sentence construction, subject/verb agreement, pronouns, modifiers)
- Punctuation (final, comma)
- Word usage (incorrect, imprecise language)
- Capitalization
- Spelling

As you probably realize, the AICPA's criteria are the qualities of effective writing stressed throughout this book.

When you are studying for a professional certification exam, you may find it helpful to review the chapters of this book that discuss these qualities of effective writing. The following chapters will probably be the most useful to you:

- **Chapter 2:** Writing appropriately for the reader and responding to the requirements of the questions

# EXERCISES

## Exercise 12–1 [Managerial]

You are a staff accountant for CBS Manufacturing, Inc., a large electronics manufacturing company. CBS has four sales divisions, three manufacturing plants, and a home office in Dearborn, Michigan, which houses all the administrative offices. Management is considering employing responsibility accounting methods for the first time. You have been asked to answer the following questions in writing:

- What is responsibility accounting?
- How might CBS Manufacturing employ responsibility accounting for control and management evaluation purposes?
- Assuming responsibility accounting techniques are used, are there any precautions that should be taken to ensure that the techniques are used properly? If so, what are they?

Write an essay containing the answers to these questions. You should plan, write, and revise your answer in about 30 minutes.

## Exercise 12–2[4] [Auditing]

Questions are often raised "regarding the responsibility of the independent auditor for the discovery of fraud (including misappropriation of assets and fraudulent financial reporting) and concerning the proper course of conduct of the independent auditor when his or her audit discloses specific circumstances that arouse suspicion as to the existence of fraud."

Write an essay covering the following issues:

- What are (1) the function and (2) the responsibilities of the independent auditor in the audit of financial statements? Discuss fully, but in this part do not include fraud in the discussion.
- What are the responsibilities of the independent auditor for the detection of fraud? Discuss fully.
- What is the independent auditor's proper course of conduct when the audit discloses specific circumstances that arouse suspicion as to the existence of fraud?

## Exercise 12–3 [Auditing]

In 2007, the International Auditing and Assurance Standards Board (IAASB) was actively involved in recasting old standards and casting new standards in a form that is intended to be clearer, basing standards on objectives rather than procedures and using the word "shall" to indicate requirements that must be followed. Other improvements are intended to make standards easier to read and understand.[5] Write an essay discussing the relationship between the IAASB and the Auditing Standards Board (ASB) in the United States and how this effort of the IAASB may affect the output of the ASB. Your essay should be long enough to completely cover the important issues involved.

## Exercise 12–4[6] [Systems]

One morning, the computers at U.S. Leasing Company began acting sluggishly. Computer operators were relieved when a software troubleshooter from IBM called several hours later. They were more than happy to help the troubleshooter correct the problem they were having. The troubleshooter asked for a phone number for the computers as well as a log-on number and password.

The next morning, the computers were worse. A call to IBM confirmed U.S. Leasing's suspicion: Someone had impersonated an IBM repairman to gain unauthorized access to the system and destroy the database. U.S. Leasing was also concerned that the intruder had devised a program that would let him get back into the system even after all the passwords were changed.

Write an essay discussing what techniques the imposter might have employed to breach U.S. Leasing's internal security and how U.S. Leasing might avoid these types of incidents in the future.

## Exercise 12–5 [Tax]

Write an essay discussing the important tax and legal advantages and disadvantages in organizing a business as either a partnership, an S Corporation, or a Limited Liability Company.

---

# NOTES

1. "Written Communication." www.cpa-exam.org/cpa/written_communic.html (26 June 2004).
2. Adapted from American Institute of Certified Public Accountants, *Uniform CPA Examination: May 1994 Questions and Unofficial Answers* (New York: American Institute of Certified Public Accountants, 1994), 15, 34, 69, 72, 75, 82. These questions and answers are adapted from old CPA exams when the AICPA published both questions and unofficial answers subsequent to giving each exam. The AICPA no longer does this. However, both the subject matter of these questions and the answers are still relevant.

3. American Institute of Certified Public Accountants, "Written Communication." 2007. www.cpa-exam.org/cpa/written_communic.html (14 April 2010).

4. This exercise has been borrowed with permission from Alvin A. Arens, Randal J. Elder, and Mark S. Beasley, *Auditing and Assurance Services: An Integrated Approach*, 13th ed. (Upper Saddle River, NJ: Prentice Hall, 2010), 167.

5. Glenn Cheney, "International auditing standards may get clearer," www.accountingtoday.com/ato_issues/2007_1/22985-1.html (9 December 2010).

6. This exercise has been adapted with permission from Marshall B. Romney and Paul John Steinbart, *Accounting Information Systems*, 11th ed. (Upper Saddle River, NJ: Pearson Prentice Hall, 2009), 178.

# CHAPTER 13

# Writing for Employment: Résumés and Letters

Finding a job after graduation is a concern for most accounting students. Your communication skills can be your greatest asset in finding that job. A study discussed in Chapter 1 pointed out that an applicant's communication skills may be the *single most important factor* in employers' hiring decisions. This chapter focuses on several important skills you need to get a good job: researching a targeted company, preparing a résumé and letter of application, and writing a thank-you letter to follow an interview.

## STARTING THE JOB SEARCH: RESEARCHING POSSIBLE EMPLOYERS

The way you begin your job search depends to some extent on where you are when you begin. If you are still a student in a large university, you will probably work with your school's job placement office, its faculty, and the recruiters who visit your campus. If you are a student in a small school, opportunities for on-campus interviews may be more limited, and you may find it helpful to work with the accounting faculty to identify potential employers. If you have already graduated, then you may be on your own in locating potential jobs and establishing initial contacts with employers although the placement office of the school from which you graduated may still work with you.

Regardless of how you begin your job search, you need to write certain documents to secure the job, including a letter of application, a résumé, and a thank-you letter after you have had an interview. For all these documents, knowledge of the targeted employer is important because you will want to tailor what you write to the potential employer's needs. You will also want to show the people who read these documents that you are familiar with the company and that you did the preparation necessary to make a good impression. (By now, you probably recognize the strategy that underlies this preparation: analyze your reader's interests and needs.)

After you decide to apply for a job at a particular company or organization, you need to find as much information as possible about both the organization as a whole and the particular job for which you are applying.

If you are applying for a specific job opening, you will probably have general information about the position in a job announcement. Read the announcement carefully so that you learn as much as possible about the position's requirements and the credentials the employer is looking for. This information can guide you when you prepare your résumé and application letter.

You also need general information about the organization that is hiring. You can begin your research by studying the organization's Web page. You can also search the Internet for articles and news items in the financial press, and you can talk with business faculty about the organization. Your school's job placement office may also have an information file on the company. Perhaps you will also be fortunate enough to meet recruiters from the organization on campus at accounting club meetings or job fairs. If you have this opportunity, listen carefully to what the recruiters say about their organization and ask appropriate questions. Show with polite, attentive listening that you are interested in what the recruiters have to say, and remember the names of the people you meet!

All this information about the organization or company, the names of individuals you have met, and the requirements for particular job openings will be important as you write your letter of application and edit your résumé.

## PREPARING A RÉSUMÉ

Preparing a résumé may be one of the most important steps you take in finding a good job. A tongue-in-cheek saying actually has some truth when applied to résumés: "An ounce of image is worth a pound of performance." Of course, your performance in school and in previous jobs is essential; but if the résumé doesn't project a professional, competent image, your performance won't be considered seriously. So take the time and the care necessary to do a good job on your résumé.

Figure 13–1 illustrates an effective résumé, which you may want to use as a model for preparing your own. This example is not the only way to prepare a good résumé, however, and you may find other models in business communication texts or in materials supplied by your school's job placement office. We will consider the résumé in Figure 13–1 as a generic model that you can adapt to your own situation.

**FIGURE 13–1**    Sample Résumé

**Shane W. Brown**

| | |
|---|---|
| 1324 Horsetooth Road | Phone: (970) 435-1234 |
| Fort Collins, Colorado 80125 | e-mail: sbrown@csu.edu |

**CAREER OBJECTIVE**    An accounting position that will allow me to build on my academic and employment background and provide opportunities for professional growth and development. Willing to travel.

**SUMMARY OF QUALIFICATIONS**    Degree in accounting; honor student; experience with corporate staff; experienced in customer service.

**EDUCATION**    Bachelor of Business Administration, University of Georgia, June 2011.
Major: Accounting
GPA: 3.55/4.0

**WORK EXPERIENCE**

June 2010–
September 2010    **Jaymart, Inc.; Executive Offices,** Norcross, Ga.
*Accounting Internship*
- Assisted in the preparation of year-end audit work papers.
- Worked on depreciation schedules; updated property, plant, and equipment accounts.
- Participated in the preparation of the 2010 corporate tax return work papers, and set up schedules for the 2011 corporate return.
- Prepared 2011 income tax projections for individual corporate officers.

March 2009–
June 2010    **University of Georgia Language Laboratories,** Athens, Ga.
*Laboratory Assistant*
- Supervised foreign language students using the laboratory.

June 2008–
September 2008    **AT&T Information Systems,** Atlanta, Ga.
*Support Services*
- Assisted AT&T employees with their mailroom needs.

June 2007–
September 2007    **Food Giant,** Atlanta, Ga.
*Courtesy Clerk, Produce Department*
- Promoted to Produce Department Manager in July 2007. Assisted customers.

**HONORS AND ACTIVITIES**    Association of Students of Accounting; Beta Alpha Psi Initiate (Accounting Fraternity); University Honors Program, Recipient of Junior Division Honors; Program Certificate; Beta Gamma Sigma (Business Honor Society); Dean's List (seven of eleven quarters); Phi Eta Sigma; Tau Epsilon Phi (Social Fraternity); Finance Club; College Republicans; Intramural Softball, Volleyball.

**INTERESTS**    Racquetball, current events, travel, music.

## Format

First of all, look at the document design of the résumé in Figure 13–1. Notice the placement of text on the page and the pleasing use of white space, headings, fonts, and bullets. The résumé is arranged so that it has an attractive, professional appearance; it is also easy to read because it's not crowded, and important information is easy to find. You'll see how these design techniques can be used with the various parts of a résumé.

### Name and Address

Center your name in bold print at the top of the page. On the next line, put your address at the left margin and your phone number (including your area code) at the right margin, as shown in Figure 13–1. Place your e-mail address below your phone number. Place a horizontal line under this portion to separate your identifying data from your qualifications.

### Career Objective

Be as specific as possible about the kind of job you're looking for so the employer can easily determine whether your goals match any available openings. You might indicate an accounting specialty such as tax, auditing, or systems, for example. At the same time, you don't want to close any doors you will later wish you had left open, so consider describing your objective in a way that will allow for all reasonable possibilities of employment for which you're qualified. As an alternative, you might edit your résumé so that your objective fits specific openings for which you're applying.

### Summary of Qualifications

Employers that receive a large number of résumés (and that covers just about everyone) do not have time to study the detailed information the résumés contain. Therefore, it's important to provide a "snapshot" of your qualifications that will immediately catch the employer's eye. Notice Shane Brown's Summary of Qualifications section in Figure 13–1. In one quick phrase he sums up why the employer should pick him for the job.

### Education

Beginning with your most recent degree or school, provide information in reverse chronological order about your education to show your qualifications for employment. You need to include the following information:

- Degree(s) you have completed or are working on
- Complete name of the school granting this degree
- Date of the degree, or expected graduation date

- Your major and, if applicable to the job, your minor
- Grade point average, if it is above 3.0 on a 4.0 scale (Figure your GPA several ways to try to reach at least a 3.0—for example, cumulative GPA, GPA in your major coursework, GPA in upper level courses, and so on—labeling it accordingly.)
- Approximate percentage of your college expenses you financed yourself if this amount is significant

If you have attended several colleges or universities, include information about all of them, especially if you received a degree. If you attended schools without completing a degree, give the dates of your attendance.

You don't need to include information about your high school education, unless that information is relevant to a potential employer. If you're applying for summer employment, but still have some time before you graduate from college, then you might list your high school and date of graduation.

### Work Experience

Again in reverse chronological order, provide information about the jobs you have held, both full- and part-time. You can even list volunteer work if it's relevant to the job for which you're applying. For each job you list, provide the following information:

- Dates of employment (You may decide to put the dates in the left margin, as in the sample résumé.)
- Name and location of the organization for which you worked
- Your position
- A description of your responsibilities, with emphasis on the ones that show you are qualified for the job you are now seeking (Note any promotions or honors you received. Whenever possible, describe your responsibilities using active voice verbs such as *assisted, completed, prepared,* and *supervised.*)

### Honors and Activities

List the organizations you belonged to, the honors you received, and any other activities that show you to be a well-rounded, active person. List these activities from most important to least important, *from the potential employer's point of view.* If you held an office in an organization or had significant responsibilities, add this information as well. If an organization or honor is not self-explanatory, give a brief explanation of its significance. You might explain the importance of honorary societies, for example, as shown in the sample memo in Figure 13–1.

### Interests

Information about your hobbies and interests is optional on a résumé. The advantage of including this information is that it can show that you are a well-rounded person with interests that might help you relate to other people, such as your co-workers and clients.

### References

Choosing whether to list your references on your résumé is sometimes a difficult decision. If you provide the names, addresses, and phone numbers of your references, the employer can contact them easily. However, you run the risk that an employer will call your reference at an inconvenient time, or that the reference will not immediately recall detailed information about you. As a general rule, do not include references unless they are specifically requested. However, you will normally be asked for references when you fill out a formal job application, so it's important to have them ready.

If you don't include references on your résumé, indicate on your résumé that references are available on request. The best solution, if you are enrolled or recently graduated from a college or university, is to have letters on file with your school's job placement office. Then your résumé can have a line such as this one:

References available upon request from:

Placement Office
University of Manhattan
Manhattan, Georgia 30678

One final word about references: Never list people as references without first asking their permission. Ask people to be references who are likely to remember you well and have favorable things to say about you. Former instructors and employers are good candidates.

## What *Not* to Put on a Résumé

Remember that there are laws against hiring discrimination on the basis of age, sex, race, religion, marital status, or national origin, so do not put information of this nature on a résumé. Also, when preparing résumés try to avoid phrases such as the following:

- Gets along well with coworkers
- Pleasant disposition
- Always eager to please

These phrases make you sound as if you were applying to be a pet rather than an employee. "Fluff" phrases like these are guaranteed to send your résumé straight to the bottom of the pile.

Generally, employers hiring for accounting positions are interested in two things: what you know and what you can do. Therefore, your résumé should specifically state what you know and what you can do.

# WRITING A LETTER OF APPLICATION

Often you will send your résumé to a potential employer with a formal letter of application, or you will write to follow up some earlier communication. Like the résumé, the letter must be professional and well researched.

Your letter should follow the general advice for letters discussed in Chapter 9, including these guidelines:

- Address the reader by name. Get the appropriate name over the telephone or by other means.
- Give your letter an attractive, professional appearance. Use good stationery and a high-quality printer. The letter and résumé should be printed on matching paper and both should match the envelope.
- Write in short, concise paragraphs and clear sentences. A courteous, conversational tone is best.
- The spelling, grammar, and mechanics of your letter should be perfect.

The content of your letter will depend on your particular situation. If you have already discussed the job or possible employment with an employee of the company, you should refer to this person by name and say exactly why you're sending the résumé. You might write an opening such as this one:

> Sara Evans suggested that I write you about a possible opening in your auditing department. I had the pleasure of talking with Ms. Evans at a meeting of our Accounting Club here at the University of Central California.
>
> As you will see in my enclosed résumé, . . .

For a formal letter of application, you might begin with a sentence such as this:

> I would like to apply for the position of staff accountant that you advertised in the June 25, 2011, issue of the *Denver Press Register*. My résumé is enclosed.

After the introduction to your letter, you need to show the reader two things: that you are familiar with the organization doing the hiring and that you have the credentials the organization is seeking. Thus, you can briefly refer to what you've learned about the company from your research and highlight the information on your résumé that shows you to be especially interested in, and qualified for, the position. In other words, you use the letter of application—from one to three short paragraphs—to sell yourself as the best person for the job. The following paragraphs show examples from two different letters:

> As you will see on my enclosed résumé, I will graduate from the University of Northern Idaho in June with a Master of Accounting

degree and a specialty in tax, so my training should qualify me for an entry-level position in your tax department. In addition, I have worked as a tax assistant with the Smith Company during the past two summers.

\* \* \*

While at the University of Tempe, I have worked an average of twenty hours a week to pay approximately half my college and living expenses. At the same time I have maintained a cumulative GPA of 3.3 and have been active in a number of campus organizations. I believe this record shows that I am a conscientious worker with an ability to organize my time and achieve goals in a deadline-intensive environment.

The final paragraph should include a courteous closing and suggest a response from the reader or follow-up action you will take. You might suggest that you will call in a week to see if the employer needs additional information. At the least, express enthusiasm for the position and a hope that you will hear from the employer soon:

I hope that you will find my education and experience suitable for this position and that we can set up an interview soon to discuss the position further. I look forward to hearing from you.

Figure 13–2 shows a letter of application.

Mail your letter of application and résumé in a flat business envelope so that you won't have to fold your documents.

## WRITING A THANK-YOU LETTER

With an impressive résumé and application letter, good credentials to support them, and a little luck, you will probably have one or more interviews for jobs. After the interviews, you need to write letters to the people who met with you to thank them for their hospitality and to show enthusiasm for what you learned about the organization and the position for which you're applying.

This letter need not be long; two or three short paragraphs are usually long enough. Again, you need to address your readers by name and refer specifically to your meeting and to one or two of the topics you discussed. If you met any of the firm's other employees, you should express pleasure at having had that opportunity. End your letter with a courteous closing and express the hope that you will hear from your reader soon.

This letter, like the application letter, should follow the guidelines for letters covered in Chapter 9. A sample thank-you letter is shown in Figure 13–3.

**FIGURE 13–2**    Letter of Application

2134 Roxboro Road
Atlanta, GA 30378
January 15, 2011

Ann Bradbury, Partner
Bradbury, Ellis, and Gomez, CPAs
33 Hightower Building
Atlanta, GA 30391

Dear Ms. Bradbury:

It was a pleasure meeting you and George Ellis last week at the
Accounting Club meeting here at Fulton University. As you suggested, I am sending you my résumé because you anticipate having
an opening soon for which I would be qualified.

As my résumé shows, I will graduate from Fulton in May with an
MACC degree and a specialty in auditing. As an intern with Brown and
Hill, CPAs, I participated in several audits in the north Georgia area. I
hope you will find that my education and experience make me a good
candidate for an auditing position with Bradbury, Ellis, and Gomez.

I would very much appreciate the opportunity to talk with you further
about possible future employment. I look forward to hearing from you.

Sincerely,

*Carla Brown*

Carla Brown
Enclosure

## ELECTRONIC SUBMISSIONS

For some jobs, you may decide to submit your résumé and application letter electronically. Some job announcements request an electronic submission, or you may find it an advantage to submit your
materials quickly. In situations such as these, you can attach your
résumé to an e-mail. The e-mail itself will be your formal letter of
application, with your résumé as an attachment. Select the "rich text"
option for your e-mail in order to preserve the formatting of your
application letter.

A word of caution about e-mail submissions, including the e-mail
itself: Take the same care you would for any professional document,
including careful editing and proofreading. Remember that this submission is your first chance to make a good impression on your
prospective employer.

**FIGURE 13–3**    Thank-You Letter

2134 Roxboro Road
Atlanta, GA 30378
April 23, 2011

Ann Bradbury, Partner
Bradbury, Ellis, and Gomez, CPAs
33 Hightower Building
Atlanta, GA 30391

Dear Ms. Bradbury:

Thank you very much for meeting with me last week to discuss the possibility of my working for Bradbury, Ellis, and Gomez after my graduation next month. I enjoyed the opportunity to visit your office and meet the other members of your auditing staff. The lunch with June Oliver and Richard Wang was particularly pleasant and informative because they were able to share their experiences as first-year auditors.

I would very much welcome the opportunity to work as an auditor with your firm, so I hope that you will decide my qualifications meet your needs. Please let me know if I can provide any additional information.

Thank you once again for your hospitality. I look forward to hearing from you.

Sincerely,

*Carla Brown*

Carla Brown

Finally, mention in your e-mail that you will send a hard copy of your letter and résumé by regular mail. The prospective employer will thus see your materials twice.

## EXERCISES

### Exercise 13–1 [General]

Imagine that you are an employer who received the résumé shown in Figure 13–4. How would you react to the résumé? Would you be likely to give the applicant an interview? Why or why not?

Examine the résumé closely, noting the applicant's accomplishments and experience. Does this person have credentials that might make him a good employee?

**FIGURE 13–4**   Résumé to Accompany Exercise 13–1

William H. Bonney

| PRESENT ADDRESS | PERMANENT ADDRESS |
|---|---|
| 745 Main St. | 1634 Scaffold Lane |
| Athens, GA 30600 | Highnoon, Ga 31200 |

EDUCATION

| | GRAD. DATE | DEGREE MAJ. GPA | CUM GPA |
|---|---|---|---|
| University of Georgia | 6/10 | 3.4 | 3.5 |
| Oconee Springs High School | 6/06 | | 3.9 |

MAJOR COURSES
Principles of Accounting I and II; Financial Accounting I, II, III; Systems I.

WORK EXPERIENCE

| | TITLE | FROM | TO |
|---|---|---|---|
| Auto Stores, Inc. Clarkstown, Ga. | Cashier | 7/09 | 9/09 |
| Hamilton's Coldwater, Ga. | Cashier | 5/09 | 9/09 |
| Tulips Discount Stores Roosevelt, Ga. | Clerk | 6/08 | 9/08 |
| Sam's Market Athens, Ga. | Salesperson | 11/07 | 1/08 |
| Esops, Inc. Athens, Ga. | Office/Customer svc. | 6/07 | 10/07 |
| Telemarketing, Inc. Athens, Ga. | Telemarketer | 7/09 | Present |

HONORS AND ACTIVITIES
Honors Program
Dean's List
Golden Key
Outstanding College Students of America
Phi Chi Theta Business Fraternity
Association of Students in Accounting
James E. Cassidy Scholarship

PERSONAL
Date of Birth - October 20, 1991; excellent health; prefer to work in the north Atlanta area.

Rewrite this résumé so that the applicant's credentials show to good advantage. You may have to make up some details so that the résumé is complete.

### Exercise 13–2 [General]

Visit your school's placement office to find out about jobs for which you will soon be qualified. If you're close to graduation, consider positions that require a degree. If you still have a year or more before you complete your degree, identify internship positions.

Draft a résumé suitable for submission for a position that interests you.

### Exercise 13–3 [General]

Exchange the résumé you wrote for Exercise 13–2 with one or more of your classmates. Critique the résumés, checking for effective organization, wording, and page design. Proofread each other's résumés to be sure there are no mechanical or typographical errors. After you receive suggestions from your classmates, revise your résumé accordingly.

### Exercise 13–4 [General]

Imagine that you find the following job announcement at your school's placement office. Prepare an application letter for this position to accompany your résumé.

> ACCOUNTANT Entry-level staff accountant for a midsize business services firm. Degree required. Send résumé to Hugh Lee, Director of Human Resources, North Carolina Systems Consultants, Durham, NC 60314. An equal opportunity/affirmative action employer.

### Exercise 13–5 [General]

The application letter you prepared for Exercise 13–4 was so effective and your résumé looked so impressive that you had an office interview with North Carolina Systems Consultants. At the interview, you met the company's president, George Owen, and several other accountants in the accounting department. You had lunch after the interview with Mary Wilson, a senior accountant in the firm, as well as the controller, Robert Wages. You learned that the company has been in business for six years, but that it is now expanding into a larger market and adding additional services for its customers.

Write a thank-you letter to follow up on your interview.

# CHAPTER

# Writing for Publication

# 14

As a practicing accountant or business services professional, you may decide at some point in your career to write an article for publication. This might be a short article for a newsletter, perhaps published by the organization you work for, or it might be a longer article for a professional journal, such as the *Journal of Accountancy* or *The CPA Journal*. Most of the techniques discussed in this book apply to writing for publication, but we consider some additional pointers in this chapter.

## PLANNING YOUR ARTICLE

To plan your article, start by considering the publication that you want to write for and the topic you want to write about. Most likely, you'll be writing about your experience in practice, such as a better way to approach an accounting procedure or solve an accounting problem. You may also write a position paper to express your opinion on some controversial accounting or business issue currently under discussion in the profession.

Whatever the topic you've chosen, target your writing to the editorial practices and readers of the publication to which you're submitting the article. One of the best ways to have an article published is to write on a subject that is interesting and relevant to a wide range of the publication's readers.

Consider the type of writing typically published by the targeted publication. Do the editors prefer articles on scholarly research? *The Accounting Review* is an example of this kind of publication. Other journals prefer practical articles about the practice of accounting. *Journal of Accountancy* publishes practical articles on public accounting, and about practical concerns shared by accountants. Journals and newsletters published on the state or local levels might publish articles of general interest to accounting professionals, but they also include articles of local interest.

Here are other questions to consider about the publication in which you hope to publish your writing:

- Who are the readers of the publication? What are their interests and concerns? How much technical expertise on your topic are they likely to have?
- What format, organization, and length do the publication's editors prefer? You can learn this either from an editorial policy statement or by studying articles already published.
- What style of documentation does the publication use?
- What writing style do the editors prefer? Articles in professional accounting journals may be written either in a serious, scholarly style or in a light, conversational one. All publications, however, prefer prose that is clear, readable, and concise, with little, if any, accounting jargon.

# RESEARCH

After you've chosen a topic and publication to target, find out what else has been written on the topic lately, especially if you are hoping to publish the article in a national or regional journal. You can search the Internet or visit a good library to find this information. This research will help in several ways:

- You'll find out what has been published recently on the topic so your article will not repeat what has already been done.
- You'll find out what issues or approaches are of current interest in the profession.
- You may find references that you can use in your article to support your position. Alternatively, you may find positions taken by other people that you want to refute.

In addition to this background research to find out what has already been published on the topic, you may need to do some original research to back up your writing with sound observations and reasoning, and perhaps with authoritative accounting pronouncements as well. You may find it helpful to review Chapter 8 of this handbook, which discusses accounting research in more detail.

# DRAFTING AND REVIEWING THE ARTICLE

After you have planned the article and done any necessary research, you're ready to begin writing. Draft and revise your article according to the guidelines discussed throughout this book. When you feel reasonably satisfied with the article, ask colleagues to critique it. People who have successfully published may be particularly helpful.

For the final manuscript you will submit for publication, pay particular attention to a professional presentation, including an accurate and complete documentation of any sources you have used, prepared according to the guidelines of the journal to which you're sending the article. Professional appearance of the document pages is also important, and grammar and mechanics should be flawless.

## SUBMITTING THE ARTICLE

When you're finally ready to submit your article to the targeted publication, send it along with a cover letter addressed to the editor by name. This letter should be concise and courteous and should mention the title of your article. Explain briefly why you think the article would interest the publication's readers.

Be sure you have complied with the publication's submission requirements; for example, the publication may require that you write the article in Microsoft Word and submit it electronically or on disk. A publication may also require that you submit multiple hard copies of the article. Whatever the submission requirements are, follow them precisely.

After all this preparation, your article should have a good chance of acceptance for publication. However, be prepared for the possibility that your article will be rejected by the first publication to which you send it. If your article is rejected, turn it around and send it somewhere else. Be sure to revise it to suit the readers and editorial policies of the new journal: type of articles published, interests and needs of the readers, length and style of writing, and style of documentation.

Writing for publication can be a rewarding component of your professional accounting career, but like all the writing discussed in this book, it requires planning and attention to detail, including a concern for the readers.

## EXERCISES

### Exercise 14–1 [General]

Obtain a recent issue of several professional business publications. For each of these publications, answer the following questions:

1. What type of writing do these publications publish? Possibilities include academic research, practical accounting applications for public or managerial accountants, articles of organizational or local interest, or articles addressed to some special-interest group.
2. Who writes the articles for these publications? They may be written by members of a sponsoring organization, professional writers, professors, or other accounting professionals.
3. Analyze the specific articles published. Are they all the same length, format, and style? Some publications may publish a variety of articles, such as short notes and longer essays and articles.

4. What are the standard editorial practices, such as article length and style of documentation?

## Exercise 14–2 [General]

Identify a topic that has recently been in the financial news, such as a news item from *The Wall Street Journal*. Select one of the periodicals you identified in Exercise 14–1. Summarize the news item in a way that would be relevant to the readers of that periodical. Remember to document your sources properly and prepare your article according to the submission requirements for the targeted journal.

## Exercise 14–3 [Tax]

Identify a tax article that has appeared in *Journal of Taxation*. Summarize the article in a style that would be appropriate for the readers of *The Wall Street Journal*. Remember to document your sources properly and prepare your article according to the submission requirements for *The Wall Street Journal*.

## Exercise 14–4 [Financial]

Identify a recent FASB Accounting Standards Update (ASU). Summarize the Statement in a style that would be appropriate for the readers of *The Wall Street Journal*. Remember to document your sources properly and prepare your article according to the submission requirements for *The Wall Street Journal*.

## Exercise 14–5 [Financial]

Identify a recent FASB Accounting Standards Update (ASU). Summarize the Statement in a style that would be appropriate for the readers of the U.S. edition of *The Economist*. Remember to document your sources properly and prepare your article according to the submission requirements for *The Economist*.

## Exercise 14–6 [Auditing]

Prepare an article for *Bloomberg Businessweek* on the role of auditing in helping to protect investors. In your article, explain how an audit is undertaken, the reliance on internal controls put in place by management, and the responsibility of management for the financial statements.

Remember to document your sources properly and prepare your article according to the submission requirements for *Bloomberg Businessweek*.

# CHAPTER

# Oral Communication:
# Listening and Speaking

Communication, as we all know, is a multifaceted process. It includes verbal skills such as reading, writing, listening, and speaking, as well as various forms of nonverbal communication: gestures, facial expressions, and other forms of body language. Moreover, all of these components of communication are interactive, making communication a complex process indeed.

So far in this text we've focused primarily on the writing skills you'll need as a professional accountant. This final chapter will examine two important oral communication skills, listening and oral presentations, both of which will play an important part in your professional success.

## LISTENING SKILLS

Chapter 1 pointed out that listening skills are an important part of effective communication. What you hear from other people often provides much of the information you need to perform your job well. When you listen carefully, you'll find out what other people may know about the situation you're involved in, what their expectations are, what their attitudes are, and ideas they have about the work in progress.

In addition, the willingness and ability to listen carefully to what others say contribute to good relationships between you and your colleagues. In fact, listening attentively to what other people are saying might even be considered an ethical issue because it involves respect for others. Unfortunately, we often fail to take the care we should to learn listening skills and to practice them consistently. Here are some guidelines to keep in mind as you learn to be a good listener. Some of these skills apply to one-on-one or small group communication, and some apply to listening in a larger group setting, such as a meeting. Many of the guidelines apply to all situations in which good listening is important.

239

## For Conversations with Another Person or in a Small Group

- Focus your attention on what the speaker is saying and don't let your mind wander to other topics. In particular, don't rehearse your own response to what is being said while the speaker is still talking.
- Don't interrupt the speaker. If you must interrupt for clarification, wait for a pause and then apologize: "I'm sorry to interrupt, but I want to be sure I understand this point before we move on. Did you mean . . . ?"
- Look at the speaker, maintaining good eye contact. Your face should express sincere interest and, where appropriate, empathy with what the speaker is saying.
- Avoid distracting gestures or movements, such as playing with a pen. *Leave your cell phone or other electronic equipment turned off and put away!*
- When the speaker has finished talking, ask questions for clarification or for additional information, if needed.
- When the situation requires that you understand and remember precise, accurate information, summarize what the speaker has said and ask whether you've understood correctly.
- For some more formal situations, such as an interview, prepare topics for discussion or questions in advance. Anticipate what questions you'll be asked and have answers in mind. Think also about the questions you'll want to ask. Take your notes with you to consult as the discussion progresses. Leave space in your notes to record important information.

## For Large Group Discussions, Lectures, and Meetings

- Depending on the situation, take notes so you won't forget important information. This advice applies especially to an interview, meeting, or lecture.
- In a meeting or large group discussion, as with a smaller group, listen attentively. Maintain steady eye contact with the speaker. Sit quietly and avoid distracting others. Leave electronic equipment turned off and out of sight.
- Don't become involved in side conversations during a meeting, for example with the person sitting next to you even if the side conversation relates to the topic of the meeting. These side conversations are distracting to others, including the speaker.

When you master listening skills such as these, you'll have much better information to use as the basis of further work. You'll also have contributed to a respectful, professional environment and better relationship with your colleagues.

## ORAL PRESENTATIONS

Speaking before a group, like writing, is often an important part of an accountant's professional responsibilities, yet public speaking creates anxiety for many people. If you learn a few strategies for public speaking, however, and practice as often as possible, your fear of these situations will diminish. With guidance and practice comes mastery, and with mastery comes control.

In the remainder of this chapter, you'll see that effective oral presentations, like writing, result from a process: preparation, practice, and delivery. This chapter shows you how to prepare for speaking before a group. We begin by discussing the first step in any important communication: analyzing the purpose of the presentation and the needs and interests of the audience.

## Planning the Presentation: Analyzing Purpose and Audience

The first step in planning your presentation is to analyze its purpose. Perhaps you need to inform the listeners about the progress you've made on a project, or to propose that the decision makers in the group approve a new project. You may be convincing senior management to invest in a new computer system or explaining to co-workers how to implement the system already adopted. Remember that no matter what the primary purpose of your presentation is, it has an important secondary purpose as well: your desire to impress your listeners as a competent professional.

As you analyze the presentation's purpose, think also about the audience. To how many people will you be speaking? Will they be a fairly homogeneous group, or will you be speaking to people with different degrees of knowledge about your topic and different interests? An important consideration about the audience is which decision makers will be present. In planning your presentation, the needs and interests of these decision makers should be a primary concern.

Critical thinking techniques apply just as much to an oral presentation as they do to a written document. Think in advance about the questions the audience will have about the topic, whether or not there will be a formal question-and-answer session as part of the presentation. By anticipating listeners' questions, you can explain your ideas in a convincing way. Anticipating listeners' questions and having the information ready to answer them also shows the audience that you are thoroughly prepared, credible, and professional.

Throughout the planning and preparation of the speech, always think about the audience: what they know about your topic, what they need to know, what their concerns and interests are, and what their attitudes may be toward your point of view and the information you'll present.

## Other Things to Consider

In addition to analyzing your purpose and audience, you need to determine how much time you'll have for the presentation. Find out also how you will be speaking to your audience: formally from a podium or, perhaps, informally from your seat in a conference setting.

Yet another consideration is whether to illustrate your speech with visual aids, such as charts or other graphic material. If you decide to use visual aids, consider the room where the presentation will be made. Will the space and facilities allow you to use the visual aids you prefer? A later section of this chapter discusses how to prepare effective visual aids. For now, the important point to remember is that you need to start planning visual aids early.

Finally, budget your time so you can complete the work needed to gather information, compose the speech, make notes, prepare visual aids, and practice the presentation. All these steps take time, particularly if your topic requires much underlying research.

The key to handling all these tasks is to make a schedule with dates for completing each step. It's important to plan your work and budget your time.

## Gathering Information

The next step in preparing the presentation is to gather the necessary information. Be thorough in your research so that you can answer any questions the audience may raise. When you are thoroughly prepared, you'll seem competent and professional, and your presentation will have an excellent chance of success.

Before you begin the research for your presentation, you may want to review Chapter 2, which discusses how to generate ideas, and Chapter 8, which covers accounting research.

## Composing the Speech

After you've gathered the information you need, organize the material into an outline. Keeping in mind the purpose of the speech and the interests of your audience, identify the main points you want to make. *Your speech should contain no more than three to five main points.* These main points, with an introduction and conclusion, are the outline of your presentation. Let's look now at how to fill in that outline.

### Introduction

The introduction should do two things: get the listeners' attention and preview the main points you will cover.

When you plan the opening sentences of the presentation, consider the listeners' point of view. Why should they listen to what you have to say? Will your speech be meaningful to them, perhaps helping them solve a problem or accomplish a goal? What do you and your listeners have in common that would make them interested in your presentation? What makes your topic particularly timely and relevant to your listeners? Why are you qualified to speak on this topic? Questions such as these can help you compose the opening sentences of your presentation to get your audience's attention. Here are a few additional suggestions:

- Begin with an interesting story or example to introduce your topic.
- Cite a startling statistic.
- Ask a rhetorical question—one that you don't expect your audience to answer, but that will start them thinking about the topic.

After your opening sentences, provide a brief preview of what the speech will cover. If you tell the audience what the main points will be, you'll help them remember what's important as you progress through your presentation.

### Body of the Presentation

In the body of the presentation, you present again your main points and develop them in detail. Be specific and concrete: Use facts, examples, and, where appropriate, statistics.

As you move from one main point to the next, you can help your listeners remember main ideas with two techniques: internal summaries of what you've already said and clear transitions that lead into the next main topic. For example, you might say something like this:

> So one advantage of this new software is that it would reduce the time needed to process customer accounts. [This is an internal summary. We know it's a summary because of the word *so*.] The second advantage is that the software would provide us with better records for our sales managers. [This sentence provides a transition into the next major section of the speech and identifies the second main point for the listeners.]

By providing internal summaries and obvious transitions, you can help your listeners remember main ideas as you give your presentation.

### Conclusion

The last part of the formal presentation is the conclusion. Once again, you will help the listeners if you summarize the main ideas you want them to remember. Your presentation will be most effective, however, if you end with a forceful closing. Here are some suggestions:

- Ask your audience to do something. This call to action may be low key— a request that they consider your recommendation, for example. However, you may want to be more forceful, and sometimes even dramatic, if you think the topic warrants this approach and if this tone is suitable for your audience.
- Refer again to the opening sentences of your presentation. If you used a story, example, or statistic, suggest how the ideas expressed in your speech relate to these concepts.

- Remind your audience of the benefits they will receive if they follow your recommendations.

For additional help in composing your speech, review Chapter 3, which covers the principles of coherent organization.

## MAKING NOTES

After you have gathered your material and completed the outline, you are ready to put your notes in final form—the form from which you will actually speak. Notice that this section is not called "Writing Your Speech," and for a very good reason. Most experienced speakers find it unnecessary to write down every word they want to say. In fact, having a word-for-word manuscript of your speech could lead you to make two mistakes in your presentation: reading the speech or trying to memorize it (more about these pitfalls later).

The most helpful way to prepare notes is in outline form. You should already have this outline because you prepared it as you gathered information and organized your materials. Your job now is to put this outline into notes you can use as you speak. Here are a few pointers:

- Transfer the outline to note cards or standard-size paper. Write large enough that you can see at a glance what you've written.
- Include main points as well as supporting details and examples.
- Write out the opening sentences and the conclusion. (This is the exception to the advice not to write out the speech word for word.)
- Indicate in your notes where you will use your visual aids.
- As you review your notes, highlight or underline key phrases in a contrasting color of ink. When you make the presentation, these underlined phrases will remind you of the points you want to make.
- Number the notecards or pages and clip them together.

When we discuss practicing and delivering your presentation, you'll see how notes prepared in this way will help you make a smooth presentation.

## PREPARING VISUAL AIDS

To appreciate how visual aids can contribute to an effective presentation, consider your audience's point of view. When people read, they have a number of visual cues to help them identify and remember main ideas. They have titles and headings, paragraph breaks to signal a shift in topic, and often graphic illustrations. If they need to review something that has already been covered, they have only to turn back the page to see that material again.

Those listening to an oral presentation have none of these visual cues to help them follow the flow of thought, unless the speaker provides them with visual aids. A major advantage of visual aids is that they help listeners identify and remember main ideas. They offer another advantage as well: Well-constructed, attractive visual aids make the presentation more interesting.

In summary, visual aids appeal to the audience by making the presentation easier to follow and more interesting. But what are the best kinds of aids to use?

To some extent, your choices depend on where you'll be speaking. If you are making a classroom presentation, for example, you can prepare handouts, write on the board, prepare posters and charts, or use an overhead projector. You may also have access to a CD or DVD player or projection equipment that can be run by a computer, such as a digital presenter. If you have access to computer projection equipment, you may consider using slides produced on the computer using PowerPoint.

You may decide to use more than one kind of visual aid. For example, handouts give your listeners something to take with them to reinforce what you've said, especially when you want to give them lengthy or detailed information. However, you don't want them reading the handout instead of listening, so illustrate your presentation with posters, charts, overhead transparencies, or PowerPoint slides, and distribute the handouts after the presentation.

Let's look more closely at guidelines for preparing visual aids such as overhead transparencies and PowerPoint slides:

- Be selective in planning your aids, and limit the amount of information you present visually to key ideas. If your audience is kept constantly reading material presented visually, they may not listen to what you're saying.
- Keep your aids simple. Use keywords and phrases rather than sentences, and limit each aid to about five or six lines.
- Be sure the writing is legible and large enough to be read from the back of the room. It's much better to prepare the aid using a software package, but if you must write by hand, write clearly in a dark or bright color so that the writing is easy to see.
- If possible, use bright colors to make your aids more attractive. (Avoid yellow, which is often hard to see from a distance.)
- Make your aids neat and professional looking. A computer with a graphics package will help you achieve a professional appearance. You might even consider having the aids professionally prepared.

You can include any information on your visual aid that will help your listeners understand and remember your message, but visual aids are particularly helpful in identifying your main points, summarizing your recommendations or conclusions, or providing a vivid illustration. You can also summarize statistical information in a table or graph. Yet another technique is to reproduce cartoons to amuse your listeners as you illustrate a point.

After you have prepared your visual aids and notes, you are ready for the next important step in the preparation of the oral presentation: practice.

## PRACTICING THE PRESENTATION

Practicing the presentation is essential for several reasons. For one thing, the more often you review the speech, the more familiar you become with it, so that when you speak before an audience you will appear knowledgeable and convincing. You'll also feel more confident that you have mastered the ideas you want to present. When you practice, especially before other people, you also identify in advance any potential problems that could occur, such as a presentation that is too long or too short for the allotted time.

Here are some strategies that will make your practice time most useful:

- Practice the speech out loud. Pay attention to your voice, posture, and gestures.
- Time the presentation to make sure it is the appropriate length.
- Practice using the visual aids, including any equipment you will be using, such as equipment for a PowerPoint presentation.
- If possible, practice in the actual room you'll be using for the presentation.
- Practice before a live audience, such as friends, family, or co-workers. Ask them to be critical of the content and delivery of the speech.
- If you have access to video recording equipment, ask someone to record the presentation so that you can identify and correct any problems.

In addition, avoid this common pitfall:

***Never read or try to memorize your speech!***

The only exception to this guideline is that you may find it helpful to memorize your opening and closing sentences.

## CHECKING THE ARRANGEMENTS

For some oral presentations, preparations include arranging for a room and equipment. Even if someone else is responsible for these duties, it may be a good idea to check them yourself. Be sure that the room will be unlocked in time for the early arrivals at the presentation and that the equipment will be delivered and set up in working order.

Check again on these arrangements a short time before the presentation begins. If an unforeseen problem arises, such as malfunctioning equipment, you'll have time to correct it.

## APPEARANCE AND DRESS

A final consideration in the preparation for your presentation is appearance and dress. As in any professional situation, your grooming should be impeccable. The clothing you wear will depend to some extent on the situation, but professional styles and colors are almost always preferable. If you are in doubt, it's better to err on the conservative side.

In summary, thorough preparation for the presentation—your appearance, the arrangements, your visual aids, and the speech itself—will ensure good results when you speak before a group.

# MAKING THE PRESENTATION: POISE AND CONFIDENCE

Earlier, we discussed the steps of preparing an oral presentation before you actually give it: planning, composing, and practice. Now we'll look at the qualities of effective delivery and strategies to help you become an accomplished public speaker.

The effect you should create on your audience is one of poise and confidence. With adequate practice and preparation, you are well on your way to reaching this goal. Let's look at techniques of actual delivery that contribute to an effective presentation.

### Eye Contact

One of the secrets of public speaking is eye contact between the speaker and the audience. When you look your listeners in the eye, you involve them in the topic and help ensure that they listen carefully.

Establish eye contact when you first stand before the audience: stand straight, smile, and look around the room. Look directly at various people at different locations. This initial eye contact should last for a few seconds.

As you begin the presentation and progress through it, continue to maintain this eye contact. Hold the eye contact with each person for several seconds, perhaps the length of a complete phrase. Shift the contact from one side of the room to the other, front to back, and at various points in the middle. If your audience is small, you may be able to make eye contact with everyone in the room several times.

Regardless of the size of your audience, however, it's essential to establish eye contact with one important group of listeners: the decision makers. They will be judging the ideas you present and your effectiveness as a speaker. Good eye contact will help you keep their attention. You'll also seem confident and in control of the situation.

You may also find it helpful to look frequently at the listeners who seem most interested and supportive of what you are saying. You can recognize this group by their expressions of interest and attention, or perhaps even nods and smiles. Their enthusiasm can give you extra energy and confidence.

Here's a final word about eye contact and the use of visual aids, including PowerPoint. When you refer to your aids, don't turn your back on the audience except briefly if you need to locate and point to something specific. Maintain eye contact as you refer to the aid so that your audience will listen to your explanation.

When you think about the importance of maintaining good eye contact with the audience, it's obvious why you shouldn't read your speech and why you should be so familiar with your notes that you only glance at them from time to time.

### Body Movement and Gestures

Poised, natural use of your body and gestures also contributes to an effective presentation. Stand still, with good posture, and look directly at the listeners. Don't move about, except to use your visual aids (for example, to point to something on a chart or to change a transparency on an overhead projector).

Natural, expressive use of your hands is an effective way to emphasize ideas and feelings. For this reason, it's better to place your notes on a table or lectern so that your hands are free for gestures.

### Voice

Three elements of your voice contribute to a presentation's effectiveness: pitch, volume, and speed. *Pitch* is the high or low tone used for speaking. Most people's natural pitch is fine and requires no modification for public speaking. A few people need to pitch their voices a little lower than normal, especially if they are nervous when they speak.

*Volume* and *speed* may require more attention. The key to speaking at the correct volume is to speak loudly enough so that people in the back of the room can hear you. Be consistent; for example, don't let your voice drop at the ends of sentences or your audience will miss the last words or will have to strain to hear you.

When you practice the presentation, pay particular attention to the speed at which you are speaking. You should speak slowly enough to enunciate each word clearly. Some speakers have a tendency to speak more rapidly when they are nervous. If you fall into this category, make a conscious effort to slow down.

### Managing Stage Fright

Now that we've introduced the topic of nervousness, let's think for a minute about how to manage what for many speakers is the worst part of public speaking: stage fright. Notice that the heading for this section is "*Managing* Stage Fright," not "*Eliminating* Stage Fright." Even the most experienced, effective speakers may have some stage fright; furthermore, they use this emotional energy to help them make a more effective presentation. The emotion, if kept in control, can give you the extra charge to make an energetic, enthusiastic, and convincing presentation.

Of course, too much stage fright is counterproductive. Let's look at some strategies you can use to manage stage fright before and during your presentation.

### *Prepare Well in Advance*

One advantage of thorough preparation and practice is that they help prevent stage fright. When you know you thoroughly understand the topic, and when you have thought in advance about the questions and interests of the listeners, you will *feel* prepared and, thus, competent. A feeling of competence, in turn, gives you confidence in your ability to do a good job.

Actual practice, especially before a live audience, will also increase your confidence.

### *Just Before You Speak*

Two tricks may be helpful in the last few minutes before you are scheduled to speak. The first is to use this time to go over your notes one last time to be sure your main points, as well as your opening and closing sentences, are fresh in your mind. The second trick is this:

### Don't think about how you're feeling!

If you think about being nervous, you'll only increase the feeling. Instead, think about something pleasant that is completely unrelated to your presentation. Perhaps you can think about something nice you will do later in the day.

### *During the Presentation*

Most speakers find that their stage fright goes away after the first few minutes of their presentation. When you are speaking, look directly at your listeners with poise and confidence: They'll probably reflect these positive feelings back to you. Notice which of your listeners are most interested and receptive to what you're saying, and make frequent eye contact with these people. Their enthusiasm will add to your feelings of confidence and ensure that your presentation is effective.

## SPECIAL CONSIDERATIONS IN PRESENTATIONS OF FINANCIAL INFORMATION

The standard techniques for presentations given in this chapter apply to accounting presentations, of course, but you should bear in mind a number of special considerations when you are presenting financial information. Most of the time, presentations of financial information contain numbers, tabular data, and charts that will be shown on slides or overhead transparencies. The following points apply in this type of presentation:

- Make sure your numbers are consistent. For example, if "Sales are expected to reach $7.25 million in 2012" appears on one slide, make sure your other slides don't contain some other number. It's easier to make this kind of error than you might think. When a presentation is developed, it tends to be revised several times before a final version is produced. When numbers are changed during the revisions, it's sometimes difficult to find all the places in the presentation where they appear. As a result, conflicting numbers end up in the final presentation.

- Make sure your numbers "add up." For example, if your presentation includes a statement such as "Sales are expected to grow 20 percent from their 2010 level of $7 million, reaching $8.4 million in 2011," make sure that $7,000,000 × 1.20 does in fact equal $8,400,000 (which it does in this case).

- Make sure the audience can read the charts or slides in your presentation. This applies to the size of the charts or slides as well as their design. Many audience members would have difficulty making out the slide in Figure 15–1. Although the slide illustrates where the company's funds came from and where they went, the labels on the pie slices are too small to read. Also, there is too much information on the slide to take in at once. In this case, the presenter should separate the charts into two slides and increase the font size in the labels.

- Use computer-assisted presentations wherever possible. Presentations developed in graphics programs such as Microsoft PowerPoint look very professional, and they may well make the difference between your recommendations being accepted or rejected. An example of a financial presentation created in Microsoft PowerPoint is shown in Figure 15–2.

**FIGURE 15–1**    Example of a Poor Slide

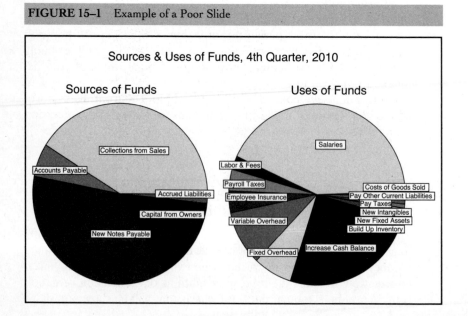

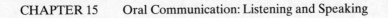

**FIGURE 15–2**    A Financial Presentation Created in MicroSoft PowerPoint
(*Continued*)

**FIGURE 15–2** *(Continued)*

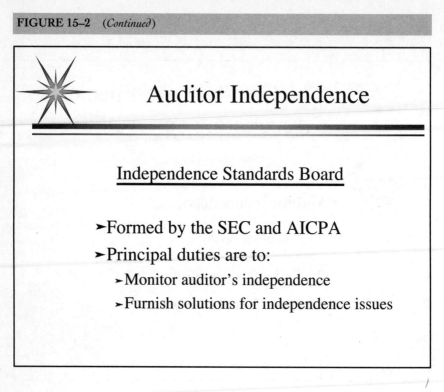

# Auditor Independence

### Independence Standards Board

➤Formed by the SEC and AICPA
➤Principal duties are to:
   ➤Monitor auditor's independence
   ➤Furnish solutions for independence issues

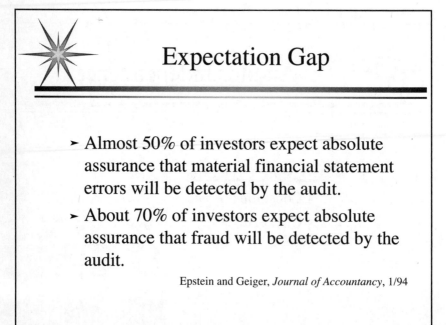

# Expectation Gap

➤ Almost 50% of investors expect absolute assurance that material financial statement errors will be detected by the audit.

➤ About 70% of investors expect absolute assurance that fraud will be detected by the audit.

Epstein and Geiger, *Journal of Accountancy*, 1/94

**FIGURE 15–2**    *(Continued)*

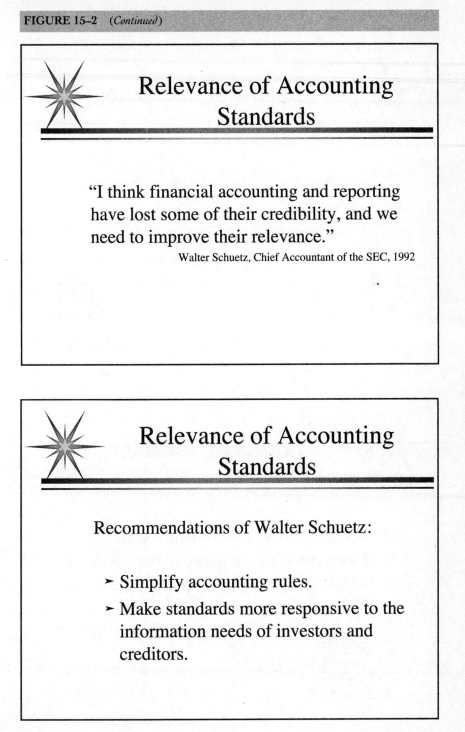

Relevance of Accounting Standards

"I think financial accounting and reporting have lost some of their credibility, and we need to improve their relevance."

Walter Schuetz, Chief Accountant of the SEC, 1992

Relevance of Accounting Standards

Recommendations of Walter Schuetz:

➤ Simplify accounting rules.

➤ Make standards more responsive to the information needs of investors and creditors.

**FIGURE 15–2** *(Continued)*

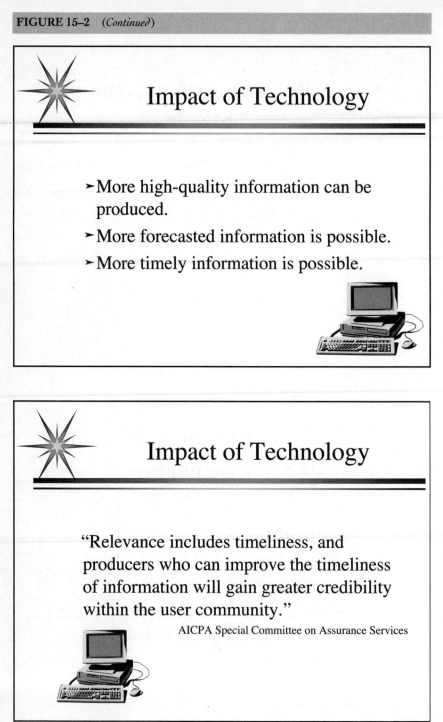

## Impact of Technology

➤ More high-quality information can be produced.
➤ More forecasted information is possible.
➤ More timely information is possible.

## Impact of Technology

"Relevance includes timeliness, and producers who can improve the timeliness of information will gain greater credibility within the user community."

AICPA Special Committee on Assurance Services

**FIGURE 15–2**    *(Continued)*

# Impact of Technology

➤ Users are demanding:

➤ Nonfinancial data

➤ Forward-looking data

➤ Relevant valuation of assets and liabilities

Although the presentation is reproduced here in black-and-white, you can imagine how the addition of color (accomplished automatically in PowerPoint) would bring the presentation to life.

## A FINAL WORD

Public speaking may always fill you with some apprehension. With practice and the mastery of technique, however, you will become much more sure of yourself and your ability to be an effective oral communicator. For that reason, it's a good idea to take advantage of every opportunity to practice your public speaking. The payoff will be greater professional success.

## EXERCISES

### Exercise 15–1  [General]

Select one of your classmates as a partner for this exercise. Imagine that you have been asked to introduce your classmate before a professional meeting of your peers. Interview your classmate, taking notes as you ask questions. Review your notes for accuracy and organize them into an outline that you can use for a two- or three-minute introduction.

(Hint: Analyze the interests of your audience as the basis for the questions you ask in your interview.)

After you have completed one interview, you and your partner can switch roles so that you are interviewed for an introduction your partner will make.

## Exercise 15–2 [General]

Select one of the following topics and prepare a five-minute presentation to give to your class:

- Career opportunities in accounting
- The Association of Certified Fraud Examiners.
- The International Accounting Standards Board
- The *FASB Accounting Standards Codification*™
- 2011 changes to the content and format of the CPA exam.

## Exercise 15–3 [General]

The more opportunities you have to speak before a group of people, the more confident you'll be of your abilities. With your instructor's approval, make these informal oral presentations:

- Introduce the classmate you interviewed for Exercise 15–1.
- Explain to the class how to work an accounting problem that was assigned for homework.

## Exercise 15–4 [Tax]

Prepare an oral presentation on itemized deductions that may be taken by an individual for tax purposes. Assume the audience for the oral presentation is a group of young people just beginning their careers. Prepare any visual aids needed for an effective oral presentation. Your presentation should be about 15 minutes long.

## Exercise 15–5 [Systems]

Prepare an oral presentation on the extensible business reporting language, XBRL. In your presentation, discuss what XBRL is, how it is used, and its advantages. Assume the audience for the oral presentation is a group of young people just beginning their financial data management studies in school. Prepare any visual aids needed for an effective oral presentation. Your presentation should be about 20 minutes long.

## Exercise 15–6 [General]

Have someone make a video recording of a presentation you make before your class. Review the video recording to identify what you did well and what areas you need to improve.

### Exercise 15–7  [Tax]

Prepare an oral presentation for class from a recent article in *Journal of Taxation*. Remember to adapt your information and presentation to the needs and interests of your classmates. Your presentation should last about 10 minutes.

### Exercise 15–8  [Financial]

Prepare an oral presentation for class of a recent FASB Accounting Standards Update (ASU). Remember to adapt your information and presentation to the needs and interests of your classmates.

### Exercise 15–9  [Auditing]

Prepare an oral presentation for class on the Public Company Accounting Oversight Board (PCAOB) and why it was formed. Remember to adapt your information and presentation to the needs and interests of your classmates. Prepare any visual aids you think may be helpful to your audience.

### Exercise 15–10  [Auditing]

In early 2007, the AICPA formed the Center for Audit Quality (CAQ). Prepare an oral presentation for class thoroughly explaining the purpose and structure of the CAQ and why the AICPA probably felt a need for such a group.

# Index